Terence Penelhum graduated from Edinburgh
and Oxford and since 1953 has taught in
North American universities. In 1963 he was
appointed to the University of Calgary, where he
is now Professor of Philosophy and Religious
Studies. He is co-editor of the *Canadian Journal
of Philosophy*, and his published writings
include *Survival and Disembodied Existence*
(1970), *Religion and Rationality* (1971) and
Problems of Religious Knowledge (1972).

P £ 6·95

D0874053

Philosophers in Perspective

There is an abundance now of books of 'readings' from the major philosophers, in which the selections are so often too brief and snippety to be of any great value to the student. There are also many collections of essays and articles about the major philosophers on the market. These too are unsatisfactory from the student's point of view in that they suffer severely from the defect of discontinuity and are unable to trace the scope and articulation of a man's work, as each contributor writes from the standpoint of his own interpretation.

There is a great need for books that are devoted to a single philosopher and that are written by a single author who is allowed the room to develop both his exposition and his examination of his subject in sufficient detail. *Philosophers in Perspective* satisfies this demand and makes available to students studies of all the major philosophers, and some of the undeservedly minor ones as well, which will afford them for the first time the opportunity of understanding the philosopher, of coming to grips with his thought, and of seeing him in his place in the development of philosophy, or of his special area of it.

Each book in the series fits into this framework, but the authors are given the freedom to adapt it to their own requirements. Main emphasis will be placed on exposition and examination of the philosopher's thought, but enough will be written about the influences on him and about his own influence on subsequent thought, to show where he stands in the perspective of his subject. Wherever relevant, particular emphasis will be placed on the philosopher's contributions to moral and political thought, which have often in the past been treated cursorily as tailpieces to his writings on metaphysics and epistemology. This aspect of the series will prove most useful to students of politics, history and sociology.

Philosophers in Perspective
General Editor: A. D. Woozley

HUME

Terence Penelhum

*Professor of Philosophy and Religious Studies,
University of Calgary*

First published 1975 by
THE MACMILLAN PRESS LTD
London and Basingstoke
Associated companies in New York Dublin
Melbourne Johannesburg and Madras

SBN 333 12008 6

Typeset in Great Britain by
PREFACE LIMITED
Salisbury, Wilts
and printed in Great Britain by
UNWIN BROTHERS LIMITED
The Gresham Press, Old Woking, Surrey
A member of the Staples Printing Group

B
1498
.P46

Contents

To Edith

Preface

Every student of philosophy reads Hume, and reads him very early. He is so widely read, and writes so much more engagingly than a commentator can pretend to do, that anyone who produces another book about him needs to justify himself. It is hardly enough justification to say that the series the book belongs to cannot leave Hume out!

I do not claim that this book offers any fundamental re-interpretations of Hume's system; nor can a work as short as this compete with substantial studies of particular themes within it, such as those by Ardal, Kydd or Mercer. I have tried instead to produce a short but reasonably comprehensive study that will assist the serious student to come to grips with the detailed arguments of Hume's major philosophical writings in a manner that does not let him lose sight of the general philosophical vision that these writings contain. I have assumed that the reader will be approaching Hume with some background in present-day philosophical debates, but also with a recognition that every thinker needs to be read in his own idiom and not someone else's. I have tried to strike a balance between exegetical detail and philosophical criticism.

These objectives are hard to attain in a small space. Inevitably much has to be left out. In deciding what to omit, I have been guided by the fact that most students of philosophy read Hume only in bits, and often in anthologies. The bits they read tend, overwhelmingly, to be taken from Book I of the *Treatise* or from the first *Enquiry*, and they are consequently much better informed about his epistemology than about his theories on the passions, morality, or religion. In the realm of Hume scholarship a good deal has been done to redress the balance, but this has not been reflected sufficiently in less specialised studies. I have therefore pruned most severely in the area that is most familiar, and the epistemology is represented here by the three relatively brief chapters on causation and induction, perception, and the self: all themes that it would have been absurd to omit. I have also felt constrained to stay in areas that Hume deals with in the *Treatise*, the *Enquiries*, and the *Dialogues*, looking elsewhere only incidentally. I have sometimes had to present interpretations without supporting them by detailed argument; I hope I have made it clear when this has happened. It is most obvious in Chapter 1, but the general discussions there could be omitted, or read last, by those already acquainted with Hume's terminology.

I would like to acknowledge help and kindness from several sources: first, from Professor C. W. Hendel – his kindly reception of a visiting graduate student at Yale I still remember gratefully, and his Hume seminar was a scholarly education; second, from my colleagues Brenda and John Baker, Brian Grant, and Robert Jewell, of Calgary, with whom I worked very enjoyably on Book II of the *Treatise*, and Páll S. Árdal, who has not only produced the leading work on that theme, but has made many helpful suggestions about my chapter here; third, to my colleagues and students at the University of Waterloo, where most of this book was written – their consideration and friendliness made our year there stimulating, yet tranquil. Special thanks are also due to Professor A. D. Woozley, the editor of this series, whose own deep understanding of Hume has saved me from many errors; I must take full credit for those misinterpretations which my obstinacy has allowed to remain.

Key to Abbreviations

References to the *Treatise of Human Nature* are given in brackets after passages cited, and consist of two numbers. The first refers to the Book and page number of the two-volume Everyman's Library edition (Dent, London, 1911) and the second to the page number of the Oxford edition edited by L. A. Selby-Bigge. Other references are abbreviated as follows:

E.U., E.M. refer to the *Enquiry Concerning the Human Understanding* and the *Enquiry Concerning the Principles of Morals*; numbers given are the page numbers in the one-volume edition, *Hume's Enquiries*, edited by L. A. Selby-Bigge (Oxford, 1902).

D.R. refers to the edition of the *Dialogues Concerning Natural Religion*, edited by Norman Kemp Smith (Nelson, Edinburgh, 1947; reprinted by Bobbs-Merrill, New York [no date]).

N.H.R. refers to the edition of the *Natural History of Religion*, edited by H. E. Root (Adam & Charles Black, London, 1957).

D.P. refers to the *Dissertation on the Passions*, as found in vol. 4 of the Green and Grose edition of Hume's *Philosophical Works* (reprinted Scientia Verlag Aalen, 1964).

1 Hume's Life and Philosophical Objectives

Hume's Life

David Hume was born in Edinburgh on 26 April 1711 (O.S.). His father was Joseph Hume, of Ninewells, near Berwick. The family belonged to the minor Border gentry and had a strong legal tradition. David was the third and last child, and his father died little more than two years after his birth. His mother did not remarry. He was probably educated by private tutors, but whatever their contribution was, he was an avid reader from his earliest years. He received the Calvinist religious upbringing of his time and place, and seems not only to have attended the regular devotions of the Kirk, but also to have been given to moral self-analysis.

Hume went up to Edinburgh University in 1722, with his brother John, who was two years his senior. At Edinburgh he received training in classical languages, mathematics, and philosophy, and undoubtedly acquired a grounding in the new Newtonian principles. Although he 'passed through the ordinary course of education with success', he did not take a degree. By the time he left, some four years later, he had lost his religious convictions and had begun to base his moral reflections on classical pagan writers rather than on Christian sources. It is noteworthy, however, that his first mentors in morality were moralists in the Stoic tradition, to which his own ethical writings are fundamentally opposed.

He attempted at first to follow the family's tradition and enter the law, but his literary and philosophical enthusiasms made the law 'nauseous' to him. In 1729 he became deeply excited by a 'new scene of thought' which he resolved to pursue to the exclusion of all

11

else. He overdid it, and his physical and mental health was impaired for five years by a breakdown which his exertions brought upon him. He describes the symptoms and course of his illness in a fascinating and important letter to an unnamed physician whom Mossner identifies as John Arbuthnot.[1] At the time of writing this letter, which may not have been sent, Hume was on his way to Bristol, where he intended to abandon philosophy for a period and enter business with a merchant. A few months of this was more than enough. For the next three years Hume was in France, where the *Treatise of Human Nature* was largely composed. He lived for a while at Rheims, but mainly at La Flèche in Anjou. The main attraction of La Flèche was its cheapness. Though he loved the intellectual stimulus of Paris, he could not afford it since he had to make do on a very modest income.

In 1737 Hume returned to London to arrange for the publication of the *Treatise*. Before publishing it he excised some anti-theological passages (apparently a prototype of his later essay 'Of Miracles'), probably in order to avoid offending Joseph Butler, whose work he admired and whose approbation he (vainly) hoped for. Books I and II appeared in 1739, and Book III in 1740. The whole work was anonymous, although the author's identity was not any real secret. Hume's estimate of the success of the *Treatise* is famous: 'It fell dead-born from the press'. This is inaccurate if it means that it went unread or unnoticed; but it is entirely just if it means that none of the notices it received showed any comprehension of its revolutionary import. The only good notice it received was one written by Hume himself: the *Abstract*. This is an anonymous pamphlet in which the supposed author summarises the main arguments of Books I and II for the benefit of readers who may have found them too abstruse. But the reviews continued to be uncomprehending and hostile. Hume was greatly wounded by this poor reception by the world of letters and returned to Ninewells, where he remained for the next eight years. During this period he published two volumes of *Essays Moral and Political* (1740–1), which had better success, and helped to encourage him to present his philosophical ideas again in a more publicly palatable form.

The *Treatise* had not been so unnoticed that it did not cause him practical trouble. In 1745 Hume suffered a further blow when he was rejected in his attempt to secure the chair of Ethics and Pneumatical (i.e. mental) Philosophy at Edinburgh. The cause of his rejection was his religious heterodoxy. One may blush for those who excluded the greatest philosopher of our language on such grounds; though of course the allegation was a true one. It prompted another anonymous pamphlet from Hume: *A Letter from a Gentleman to his Friend in Edinburgh*. In this, Hume, in the guise of a well-meaning third party, attempts to show that his principles are not religiously or morally dangerous as his opponents in this dreary academic wrangle had said. Though it is a disingenuous and self-serving performance, it contains the seeds of the kind of practical accommodation between scepticism and religion which seems to have been Hume's last word on the subject.[2]

Having failed to secure an income as a professor, Hume was constrained to accept a post as tutor to the young Marquess of Annandale. The year he spent in this post was financially helpful but otherwise disastrous, because of the mental instability of the Marquess and the venality of his agent, a Captain Vincent. Hume was abruptly dismissed by the Marquess in 1746.

Immediately thereafter he was offered a position as secretary to Lieutenant-General St Clair, a distant relative, who was about to embark on a military expedition against the French in Canada. After several months' delay because of political indecisions, the expedition was suddenly ordered to raid the coast of Brittany instead – a project which turned into a fiasco. The contacts Hume made were very valuable for him, however, because he was soon asked to accompany St Clair again, this time on a military mission to Vienna and Turin. These positions had the effect of giving Hume financial independence for the first time.

He was now to gain some of the literary reputation that had so far eluded him. In 1748 there appeared the *Philosophical Essays Concerning the Human Understanding* (later re-titled the *Enquiry Concerning the Human Understanding*) in which he tried, no longer anonymously, to present anew some of the major arguments of Book I of the *Treatise*, and *Three Essays Moral and Political*. *The Enquiry Concerning the Principles of Morals* came out in 1751: in it Hume attempted a similar domestication of the arguments of Book III of the *Treatise*. He was not pleased with the reception of these works, which was better but still tepid. He did better with the *Political Discourses* of 1752. By now he was resident in Edinburgh, where he had moved from Ninewells with his sister after his brother's marriage. He began to receive, both there and elsewhere, some of the recognition he merited, though he was always to be the target of religious hostility. In 1752 he again failed to obtain a

13

professorship, this time the chair of Logic at Glasgow. In the same year he became Keeper of the Library of the Faculty of Advocates in Edinburgh. In 1755 he attempted to publish a volume of 'Five Dissertations', two parts of which (the essays 'Of Suicide' and 'Of the Immortality of the Soul') were suppressed, after printing, as a result of pressure on the publisher from a controversialist and champion of orthodoxy, William Warburton. What finally appeared, in 1757, was *Four Dissertations*, which included the *Dissertation on the Passions*, a spiritless summary of Book II of the *Treatise*, and the much more important *Natural History of Religion*, which prompted orthodox counterblasts and is probably the most openly hostile of his writings on this theme. What most secured his reputation in his own day was his six-volume *History of England*, which brought him great renown and substantial financial returns, and has been through an astonishing number of editions, in spite of being little read today.[3]

Although surrounded by warm and admiring friends in Scotland Hume was the target of religious animosity that was always liable to disturb the tranquillity of his existence. There was a movement to have him excommunicated by the General Assembly of the Church of Scotland, but this was headed off by the Moderate party within the Church, which included many of his friends. England came to attract him less and less, because of its snobberies and the growth of anti-Scots sentiment following on the Jaobite risings. France, however, lionised him. He was invited in 1763 to be personal assistant to Lord Hertford, the new ambassador to France. No sooner did he arrive than he became a social idol, a treasured member of the *salons*, and a friend of such famous *philosophes* as Baron d'Holbach, D'Alembert, and Diderot. He became Embassy Secretary in 1765, and on Lord Hertford's departure became chargé d'affaires for a few months pending the arrival of his successor.

The occasion of his coming to France being at an end, Hume returned to England. He made the mistake of taking with him the philosopher Jean-Jacques Rousseau, who was a refugee from persecution in Switzerland, and whom he felt an obligation to assist. For Rousseau persecution had to be invented where it did not exist already, and it was not long before his paranoia led him to accuse Hume of conspiring with others to defame him. Hume was obliged to defend himself against this silly and ungrateful charge by writing an account of the episode, which was published by his friends in Paris. In 1767 he became Under-Secretary of State on Hertford's

14

recommendation; but he finally made his way back to Edinburgh in 1769, and resided there, in the New Town, for the remainder of his life.

The agreeable tenor of his last years was marred by the popular success of the hostile and obtuse criticisms of James Beattie, who attacked Hume in his *Essay on the Nature and Immutability of Truth*. Beattie is now remembered only as the person whose criticisms drew Kant's attention to the importance of what Hume had written. Hume's continuing sensitivity to attack showed itself in his publicly disowning the *Treatise* as a 'juvenile work' in order to deflect Beattie's attacks upon it, and also those of Beattie's far more serious mentor, Thomas Reid.

In 1775 Hume contracted cancer of the bowel. Realising his declining state, and expecting a 'speedy dissolution' with no afterlife to follow it, he awaited the end with quiet dignity and calm, managing even to respond with good humour to the vulgar intrusion of Boswell, who was 'disturbed' to find his host free of the forebodings he considered appropriate to an unbeliever close to death. His attitudes are admirably expressed in his valedictory *My Own Life*. He was concerned at the last to ensure the posthumous publication of the *Dialogues Concerning Natural Religion*, which had been in existence in some form for about twenty years, but which Hume had elected to withhold until after his death. He asked Adam Smith to arrange it, but Smith pusillanimously refused, and the obligation passed to Hume's nephew David, who published the work in 1779. Hume died on 25 August 1776.

Hume's Temperament and His Thought

A philosopher should be judged by his doctrines and his arguments. In Hume's case, however, it is commonly agreed that the lucidity of his detailed discussions has not prevented misunderstandings of his general objectives. In evaluating his system as a whole, it is essential to take account of some of the complexities of his temperament.

Throughout his life Hume was under attack from those who abominated his opinions and sought to match their picture of his personality to fit. With the irrelevant exception of Rousseau, real acquaintance always produced a quite opposite picture, and Hume was greatly loved by many for his kindness, good humour, wit, and moderation. Although he never married he 'took a particular pleasure in the company of modest women', and his great charm was more than a compensation for the effect of his bulk and clumsiness,

15

his accent (which the French and English alike found outlandish) and his abstracted and unnerving stare. In *My Own Life* he describes himself as 'a man of mild dispositions, of command of temper, of an open, social, and cheerful humour, capable of attachment, but little susceptible to enmity, and of great moderation in all my passions'. This picture coincides with the judgements of his friends and is confirmed by numerous personal anecdotes. It has therefore given rise to a picture of Hume as a model of the complacent jollity that is popularly supposed to accompany corpulence. This tradition, when combined with the effect of the ironic and bantering tone of a great deal of his writing, has led many readers who fully concede his importance to accuse him of frivolity.[4]

The picture requires modification in several respects. Hume was undoubtedly much wounded by the incomprehension with which his philosophical discoveries were greeted. He was also reluctant to engage in controversy even with those who took his writings with suitable seriousness; for example, Reid. His animosity towards revealed religion is undoubtedly due to his experience of the gloomy Calvinism to which he was exposed in his youth, and which he rejects with a venom which can only come from someone who has been a prey to its anxieties. He also seems to have felt the perplexities and uncertainties of philosophical reflection with great intensity. In the letter written to Arbuthnot, at the age of twenty-three, he details with remarkable objectivity the depressed state into which his studies had led him, and the psychosomatic manifestations of this state — among them the onset of a ravenous appetite which appears to have been the original cause of his obesity. The same anxious intensity surfaces at the close of Book I of the *Treatise* in a form that should give pause to those who have dismissed him as a *pococurante* in philosophy.

When these facts are taken into account, we have to recognise that Hume's benign and clubbable personality was not wholly a gift but also a conscious achievement, and that it was an achievement in the face of religious upbringing, obtuse criticism, and philosophical anxiety. The lightness with which he is apt to refer to the most profound philosophical difficulties is not a sign that they are not of real concern to him, but the contrary. It is rather a sign that in spite of the intensity with which he has attempted to face them, he considers that philosophical reflection does not have the resources to resolve them, and that they can only be alleviated by drawing upon other resources in our natures. These are the same

16

resources that enable us to maintain the tranquillity of a polite social order in the face of selfishness, partiality, and religious bigotry. They are not intellectual resources. In fact our intellectual predilections are themselves potential sources of disturbance that have to be kept under control. One mechanism for controlling them is irony and self-depreciation. Another is playing backgammon and being merry with one's friends. And another is the sublimation of our intellectual energies into those pursuits where we will not be cast into despair by exceeding our capacities.

Competing Interpretations and Their Dangers

There have been two major competing interpretations of Hume. The first, associated with Reid and Beattie in Hume's own day and with T. H. Green in the nineteenth century, represents him as first and foremost an epistemological sceptic: as the thinker who finally revealed the paralysing consequences of the form of empiricism found in Locke and Berkeley, and who therefore occupies the innermost point of the cul-de-sac from which Kant is thought to have extricated us. The second, due mainly to the work of Norman Kemp Smith, tells us that Hume is first and foremost a *naturalist*: someone whose prime concern is to show us how human nature provides us with resources, mostly non-intellectual, which enable us to interpret and respond to our experience in ways which rationalist philosophers had vainly tried to justify by argument.

These two interpretations do not seem to me to be incompatible if one treats them as statements of what Hume's claims are, rather than as competing estimates of the plausibility of these claims. The Reid—Green interpretation undoubtedly leads to an over-concentration on the first Book of the *Treatise* and on the first *Enquiry*, a concentration which Kemp Smith has done a great deal to correct. But I see no reason to deny, and every reason to assert, that the Reid—Green interpretation is fundamentally correct in what it claims to be the import of Hume's arguments in those particular portions of his work. Hume does indeed show us how the Lockean 'way of ideas' leads, if unsupplemented, to a scepticism which Locke and Berkeley had no consistent way of avoiding, and did not fully recognise;[5] and he accordingly takes philosophical scepticism far more seriously than they do. He is also clearer than they are that no help can come, in the face of this threat, from the philosophical constructions of the rationalists, which he attacks with a ruthlessness and an understanding that they cannot match. He is explicit about

17

where the help has to come from. It comes from the adaptive forces in human nature which can preserve us from the immobility into which scepticism could plunge us, and from the fantasy into which untrammelled speculation can betray us. These forces, which in the sphere of belief fulfil the very function which Reid and Moore, seeking to attack Hume, ascribe to common sense, are affective and not intellectual. They, and they alone, can generate actions. They, and they alone, can ensure that the actions they generate are governed by prudential or moral attitudes. They, and they alone, generate those interpretations of our experience which scepticism questions. That they do this is an unyieldingly ultimate fact about our natures which we cannot render more intelligible by ratiocination and for which we should be thankful. It is certainly Kemp Smith, above all, to whom we owe the proper recognition that this is what Hume says. But Hume says it precisely because he holds, as Reid and Green say he holds, that our cognitive limitations would, without this assistance, lead us to a total, Pyrrhonian scepticism.

In recent years there has been an increased recognition of Hume's greatness and importance. This has had one unfortunate consequence. Hume has sometimes been read as though he himself held the views of those who have been most influenced by him in our day – most particularly Russell. The anachronisms that result do justice to no one. However much modern Phenomenalists may owe to Hume, Hume is not one of them, since he never undertakes the task of reductive translation. However much Ethical Naturalists and Ethical Non-Naturalists may each draw sustenance from passages in his writings, Hume is not engaged in the second-order battles that they continue to fight so unflaggingly. The main result of such misreadings is to lend spurious credibility to a criticism of Hume which has to be regarded with the greatest caution, even though it is part of the conventional wisdom of analytical philosophy: the charge that Hume confuses philosophy and psychology. This charge is usually based upon an understanding of philosophy as conceptual analysis, an activity in which Hume engages often enough, but only in a manner which is ancillary to his main enterprise, which is primarily, and unconfusedly, psychological.

Philosophy and Psychology in Hume

He proclaims this almost stridently, in the Introduction to the *Treatise*: 'There is no question of importance, whose decision is not comprised in the science of man; and there is none, which can be

18

decided with any certainty, before we become acquainted with that science. In pretending, therefore, to explain the principles of human nature, we in effect propose a complete new system of the sciences, built on a foundation almost entirely new, and the only one upon which they can stand with any security.' (5/xx)

This proclamation is as ambitious as any we find in Descartes, and there is no reason to think that Hume ever retracted it, even though he expresses himself more temperately as he gets older. He never ceases to believe that only an understanding of human nature that is based upon observation of its actual workings can permit scientific progress and save us from empty controversy and stultifying scepticism. In some respects the comparison with Descartes is an apt one. Both thinkers consider that philosophy needs fundamental methodological revision before it can stand comparison with other disciplines traditionally regarded as beneath it, and both think that their new method has first to be applied to the study of the mind itself. The contrast is equally fundamental. Descartes considers that the deductive procedures of mathematics have to be applied with equal rigour in philosophy, and that without this no escape from scepticism is possible. To Hume the paradigm of procedure is the 'experimental' or observational method used with such spectacular success by Newton. Kemp Smith has made us aware that Hume was convinced through his study of Hutcheson that the observational method could be applied with equal effect to the study of human nature. A result of such study is the recognition of the limits of our capacity to know and of the limits of our capacity to doubt: it is in the latter that Hume finds the antidote to scepticism that Descartes sought elsewhere, and it is in the former that Hume finds the corrective to the 'dogmatism' to which Descartes resorted. Another result of this study is the recognition of the dominance of passion, or feeling, in the areas of moral judgement and virtuous action that rationalist philosphers have tried to assimilate to deductive reasoning.

These insights (if that is what they are) are intimately related. The limitations on our knowledge turn out to be very severe, and the limitations on our power to doubt turn out to be severe also. It is not true, as Descartes thought, that what we cannot doubt we can know, or that what we cannot know we can doubt. Most topics of human enquiry belong in the sphere where the certainties of the rationalist and the chronic doubts of the sceptic are equally beyond us. This is the sphere of matters of fact. When it concerns itself with

19

this sphere Hume talks of the intellect as the understanding, rather than the reason. The understanding cannot attain to the assurances of intuition or demonstration. It has to be content with belief. Hume has a theory of sorts about what a belief is, and a variety of explanations of how particular beliefs arise. The latter are more interesting than the former. But the accounts he gives of the origins of our beliefs in the external world, personal identity, or the regularity of nature, are not edifying ones. They depend critically upon such factors as confusion, laziness, and, above all, habit. They do not ascribe our beliefs to reasoning or argument; this is why argument cannot dislodge them. Hume derives some amusement from recognising how disconcerting it is to see that our most important beliefs are not based on reasoning. When we first see this we incline to be overwhelmed by scepticism. But the very forces that create the beliefs can be relied upon to dislodge the scepticism after a brief time. But when this happens we are apt, if we are not careful, to look with favour upon those arguments which metaphysicians have used to try to demonstrate the propositions that we all believe. Yet these arguments, even if intelligible, are attempts to extend the sphere of knowledge into the realm of natural beliefs, and they have no source of plausibility except the very beliefs that they are supposed to justify.

Belief, then, is 'more properly an act of the sensitive, than of the cogitative part of our natures' (I 179/183). It arises from non-rational causes. This means that the genesis of our beliefs is more like that of our emotions than we incline to think. Hume's claim is that the same pyschological principles (the principles of association) that govern the passions, also govern the understanding. Although he uses the word 'passion' very widely, it is incorrect to say that he thinks belief *is* a passion. (He says that a belief is an idea present to the mind under special circumstances, whereas a passion is an impression.) But belief still has an aetiology which resembles that of the passions, and it shares with them the essential *passivity* which the rationalist and the sceptic alike refuse to concede. So Hume's psychology provides an intimate link between his epistemology and his theory of the passions.

Hume also insists that investigation will reveal that it is passion that governs our conduct. That it does so sometimes we can all agree. Many bewail it. Hume insists that it is useless to bewail it, because when we look at what happens, rather than at some philosophical theory about what happens, we shall find that there is no aetiological difference between what we do when we act 'in a passion' and what we do when we act 'rationally'. In both cases a passion operates, though of course a different one. He goes further. The very moral discriminations we make *about* our actions are themselves manifestations of feeling, and not functions of reason or understanding. These psychological discoveries refute rationalistic moralists who say that our moral discriminations can be demonstrated, and answer those such as Hobbes, who insist that men are merely creatures of selfish impulse, and that moral discrimination has no real bearing on our conduct.

It is not to be denied that there are many places where Hume offers us arguments which he regards as psychological ones, but which most contemporary philosophers would not. Criticism to this effect will appear in the following pages. But it is quite false to think that Hume is confused *in general* between philosophical and psychological considerations, and if one reads him as though he is, there is a constant danger of anachronistic interpretation.

In the theory of knowledge Hume uses philosophical arguments to show that our most fundamental beliefs are not rationally grounded. From this he infers the psychological conclusion that we have not been led to hold them by rational arguments — as he puts it, they cannot be due to reason. He then proceeds to give a genetic account of how the beliefs arise, and makes the further psychological point that our commitment is too strong to be dislodged by the philosophical arguments that he has offered, or to need to be reinforced by rationalist counter-arguments (which are in any case bad ones). So men are not creatures of reason in the way they would have to be if the arguments of philosophers were to have any real effect upon them. From this psychological discovery the philosopher must draw his own conclusion about the conditions under which philosophical argument is worth engaging in. Hume's own recommendation is that philosophy should either be recognised for an enjoyable pastime, or should confine itself to the concerns of common life, where the philosopher's acumen can serve our natural human enterprises instead of placing worrisome question-marks against them. This is a complex position, which is certainly a *mixture* of philosophy and psychology, but does not confuse them with each other.

In the theory of morals Hume insists that there are no rational bases for our moral distinctions: a philosophical thesis from which he thinks it follows that rationalists are mistaken in thinking that

21

when we act upon them we are demonstrating the unique rationality of human nature. Their mistake is a psychological mistake. He thinks, on the contrary, that our moral evaluations can be subsumed under a general psychological account of the emotions, which will be found to include modes of feeling which are the actual sources of our moral attitudes. This will show our preferences to be non-rational in origin, and largely beyond the power of reasoning to change. This in turn will show the philosopher that he should not waste his time constructing *a priori* moral systems to control our allegedly bestial impulses, but should devote himself to the formulation of policies which promote the natural preferences on which the benefits of society depend. This also is a mixture of philosophy and psychology, but does not confuse them.

So the impotence of philosophical reasoning leads to the psychological discovery that our interpretations of experience, and our evaluations of it, are alike matters of feeling and not of reason. When the philosopher learns this lesson, and accepts that reason cannot replace or master our passions, he will be satisfied to let it be their slave. For they are not as ugly taskmasters as rationalists say they are; and slaves do have important work to do.

Scepticism

Hume is manifestly some sort of sceptic. What sort? If the title is taken to mean a thinker who denies we have adequate grounds for our most fundamental beliefs, then Hume does hold this, but he combines it with much more. It has been argued persuasively by Popkin that the composite Humean position that Kemp Smith calls 'naturalism' is best regarded as a form of classical scepticism.

Hume dissociates himself from the sceptical position he describes as 'Pyrrhonian' and commends a 'mitigated' scepticism supposed to be free of its defects. To understand his attitudes here it is essential to bear in mind that he is not only the intellectual inheritor of the work of Locke and Berkeley. He was influenced at least as much by the continental sceptics, especially Bayle. They in turn were adapting to the intellectual and religious problems of their age, the work of the ancient Sceptics, both those of the later Academy and those, such as Sextus Empiricus, who followed Pyrrho. Both groups were opposed to the 'Dogmatist' view that reason can attain to certain knowledge of man's place in the universe; the Academic sceptics holding that, on the contrary, nothing is certain, and the Pyrrhonians holding, with more apparent consistency, that the defects of sense-perception and philosophical argument would lead the wise man to suspend judgement on all matters of fact and matters of value, even to the extent of the negative commitment that the Academic view represented. The Pyrrhonians adopted this stance for a moral reason. Suspension of judgement was held to lead to the inner state of unperturbednesss (*ataraxia*), which was, in differing forms, the objective of Stoics, Epicureans, and Sceptics alike. Pyrrho seems to have seen quite clearly that practical affairs require us to act as others do, and accordingly said that the wise man would accept the customs of the society in which he found himself, follow the preferences his own nature gave rise to, and treat appearances as though they were realities. But he would retain his inner calm by remaining inwardly uncommitted on the wisdom of the customs, the goodness of the preferences, or the reality of the appearances. The value of philosophy lies not in any power to lead us to truth, but in its ability to supply us with arguments which undermine commitment by showing that there are counter-arguments to every opinion.

Hume discusses scepticism in the first and seventh sections of Part IV of Book I of the *Treatise*, in Section XII of the first *Enquiry*, and in an essay, 'The Sceptic'.[6] The essay is a pedestrian exercise, but is helpful. It contains nothing by way of epistemological argument, and little serious moral criticism. Its main theme is the powerlessness of philosophical reflection to have more than a perfunctory impact on our preferences. This is the key to the sort of scepticism that Hume espouses: it has to be one that takes due account of the psychological impotence of reason as well as its inconclusiveness. The Pyrrhonian, says Hume, is refuted by 'action, and employment, and the occupations of common life' (*E.U.* 159); 'all human life must perish, were his principles universally and steadily to prevail' (160); sceptical arguments can produce only 'a momentary amazement and confusion'. He is not merely saying here that practical affairs force us to act as though sceptical arguments had no weight. A Pyrrhonian could say this too. Hume also holds that the inner suspension of judgement on which the Pyrrhonian is supposed to lean in the midst of his practical accommodations is impossible. The classical Sceptic was claiming, as the Stoic also claimed, that we have a choice whether to say 'Yes' or 'No' to appearances or desires, and Hume denies that we have any such capacity. It is as well for us that we do not have it, for it is its very absence that enables Nature to protect us from the anxiety that they were trying to escape.

23

So the Pyrrhonian is right about the lack of rational justification for our commitments, but wrong in suggesting we can cease to make them. Hume's sort of sceptic accepts his own irrationality. But there are other qualifications that Hume adds. The first is that reason's inconclusiveness does not extend to the sphere of what he calls relations of ideas, that is wholly abstract disciplines such as those of 'quantity or number'. Here certainty is possible and common.[7] The second is that although philosophical reasoning is inconclusive, and cannot affect our beliefs or desires, it is part of the nature of some men to engage in it; and he is one of them. The inevitable result of this will be an alternation of mood: for Hume does not say that we cannot have our beliefs undermined by philosophy for short periods, only that sceptical considerations cannot prevail 'steadily'. To those with a bent for philosophy the practice of it is an inevitable reflection of their natures. But it is a hazardous practice none the less. Rather than guaranteeing inner calm, it constantly tends to promote anxiety. It undermines the philosopher's confidence in those beliefs to which nature urges assent, and causes him to be perplexed about the grand questions of human destiny to which it also shows him he cannot get reliable answers:

But what have I here said, that reflections very refined and metaphysical have little or no influence upon us? This opinion I can scarce forbear retracting, and condemning from my present feeling and experience. The *intense* view of these manifold contradictions and imperfections in human reason has so wrought upon me, and heated my brain, that I am ready to reject all belief and reasoning, and can look upon no opinion even as more probable or likely than another. Where am I, or what? From what causes do I derive my existence, and to what condition shall I return? Whose favour shall I court, and whose anger must I dread? What beings surround me? and on whom have I any influence, or who have any influence on me? I am confounded with all these questions, and begin to fancy myself in the most deplorable condition imaginable, environed with the deepest darkness, and utterly deprived of the use of every member and faculty. (I 253–4/268–9)

From this predicament the philosopher is only saved when Nature reasserts herself, and engages him in society and common affairs, which submerge his philosophical anxieties. The moral is that philosophy should be practised if one has the inclination toward it, but care must be taken not to practise it to excess, or at the expense of one's engagement with society. It is Hume's considered view that philosophy should not be taken too seriously – a view which is the source of that appearance of frivolity in his work which causes such offence to those who have a loftier view of its powers and rewards.

This, at least, is the view he leaves us with at the end of Book I of the *Treatise*. In the *Enquiry* he supplements it by a third qualification, which does not improve its consistency, but is vital to the understanding of both works. Although this qualification is not stated explicitly in the *Treatise*, it is not really new, for it is a rationale of Hume's procedure in that work itself. Although the sceptic can practise philosophy for 'the immediate pleasure' it gives him, he will not pursue the ambitious enquiries of metaphysics but will bear in mind that 'philosophical decisions are nothing but the reflections of common life, methodised and corrected' (*E.U.* 162). Philosophy, then, is unobjectionable when it is descriptive and critical, but not when it is revisionary or speculative. Hume recommends this restriction to the sceptic because sceptical criticism has laid bare the incapacity of reason to resolve broader questions. On the face of it this additional restriction seems arbitrary since sceptical criticism has, equally, shown the incapacity of reason to justify the reflections of common life. Why should they now be favoured?

The answer would seem to be this: the Pyrrhonian doubts are not only unable to prevail steadily; they are also unable to prevail *universally*. This does not only mean that many men are free of them, although this is true. It also implies that there are some topics on which they *can* prevail, topics on which assent is not required of all of us by nature. If we pursue these we become a prey to that indecision which Hume, in sharp contrast to Pyrrho, finds disturbing. On these topics the revelation of our inability to arrive at knowledge should lead us to avoid philosophical reasoning altogether and change the subject. The concerns of common life can distract us from them, and we are best advised to allow them to do so, and confine our reflections to issues that common life itself raises. If we fail to do so we shall only generate anxieties and fears. Hume's targets here are 'divinity or school metaphysics' and, above all, religion. In saying that reasoning should be confined to the reflections of common life, Hume tells us to reason in those areas where natural beliefs are enforced by nature and presupposed; and he implies (and argues elsewhere) that religion is not one of these areas. The commitment to it is widespread; but it is not universal, and it is therefore due to special causes which fortunate men can escape.[8] One essential condition for escape is the acceptance of the social demands of our natures; these distract us from the gloomy speculations which otherwise increase the artificial terrors on which he thinks religious belief depends. Hume is not just an agnostic: he is a conscious seculariser. His diatribes against the ascetic or 'monkish' virtues are based on the fact that the ascetic deliberately withdraws from those protective circumstances into which nature directs us.

Two very important features of Hume's theory of knowledge have to be understood in the light of these considerations:

(1) Even when inculcating his sceptical doubts about induction, perception, or self-identity, Hume frequently confuses us by talking as though he accepts the very beliefs which he is questioning. This is especially true when he is describing in detail those psychological mechanisms whereby nature, in spite of the absence of justifying reasons, persuades us into accepting them: he seems unable to hold fast to the contention that nature is consolidating an *unjustified* belief, and talks as though it is a justified one. This sometimes leads commentators to question whether he is a sceptic at all.[9] That there is inconsistency in Hume's procedure cannot be doubted; but it is an inconsistency that makes sense in two ways. It reflects the fact he is stressing: that in spite of the lack of justification, doubt is 'vain' and belief universal. It also reflects his admonition to confine ourselves to reflections germane to common life. For common life requires us not only to make a basic commitment to the regularity of nature, or the reality of the external world, or the continuity of the self, but also to make detailed discriminations as we apply this commitment to the changing circumstances of each day; and these discriminations require that *subordinate* use of reasoning, which it is the critical task of the sceptical philosopher to systematise and correct. For example, while all inductive inferences are equally unjustified, our natural belief commits us to determining that some are more equally unjustified than others are: and this leads naturally to the formation of rules for making scientific generalisations and calculating probabilities, which Hume himself adumbrates in the midst of his sceptical doubts.[10]

(2) In his epoch-making attacks on metaphysics and religion Hume takes for granted the very standards of scientific reasoning that he has cast sceptical doubts upon in his analysis of induction. That there is inconsistency in his procedure cannot be denied here

either.[11] But it can at least be palliated by recognising that his critical position is a twofold one. His philosophical criticism is a detailed attempt to show that those subordinate forms of intellectual discrimination to which the needs of common life commit every one of us do not, if consistently applied, lend weight to the constructions of the metaphysician or the dogmas of the theologian. This is given relevance by his psychological contention that the widespread commitment to these doctrines shows only that human nature is prone to succumb to them, not that it is forced to do so. So there is some ground to hope that an exposure of the differences between natural science and natural theology will help to free men from superstitions. Hence, the only metaphysical argument that Hume takes with extended seriousness is the Argument from Design, the purpose of which is to present the existence of God as an overwhelmingly supported scientific hypothesis; he takes this claim very seriously indeed, and deserves at least as much credit for exposing its defects as for raising his more famous sceptical doubts about those modes of thought on which it depends.

Reason and the Passions

Hume argues that our beliefs are not due to reason, but that our reasoning should presuppose and follow them. He also argues that reason cannot evaluate or control action, but that the passions do these things, and reason should be content to serve them. So he draws philosophical conclusions from psychological discoveries.

A contemporary reader is apt to feel uncomfortable about the suggestion that claims about the roles of reason and passion are psychological claims. They seem to be contributions to dated and empty debates about the spheres of influence of mental faculties, from which empirical psychology emancipated itself long ago. Hume does use language that is easy to read in this way. But he is as anxious to replace armchair discussion about secret mental powers by empirical observation of the actual course of mental operations, as he is to replace speculation about secret physical powers by observation of the actual sequences of physical phenomena. So his language must be cashed into more empirical coinage.

When he says that our inductive inferences, or our belief in physical objects and self-identity, are not based on reason, he means that they lack the kinds of justification that we call rational. This does not have to mean that we do not arrive at our commitments through inference: in the inductive case we manifestly do. It means

27

that the inferences we make are not rationally compelling. He assumes, notoriously, that a rationally compelling inference is one which follows deductively from some premiss already known to be true. He takes it to be self-evident that the conclusion of an inference which does so follow is one that we are compelled, by this very fact, to accept. But if we are also compelled to accept the conclusion of an inference that does *not* follow from a premiss already known to be true, then our compulsion is *ipso facto* not a rational one: we have to look for some cause for our acceptance of the conclusion other than its relation to the premiss. The negative evaluation of each such argument is a philosophical judgement; the search for the alternative cause is a psychological enquiry. Both could be described without the use of the noun 'reason' at all.

When dealing with the practical role of reasoning, Hume has a parallel set of arguments. Our actions are caused by our wants, our preferences and our evaluations. Hume's claim that these are not due to reason can be briefly sketched as follows:[12] even when I correctly understand a situation, it does not follow that I evaluate it one way rather than another, or that I have a positive or negative desire. Hence, if I *do* evaluate it in a particular way, or *do* have a particular desire, and even if everyone in such a situation responds as I do, the evaluation or the desire cannot be called rational. Such a predicate can only apply, if at all, to the non-evaluative judgements that express my prior understanding of what the situation is. So rational justification does not belong to evaluation, and there must therefore be an independent fund of responsive sentiment or active desire in our natures that causes these practical commitments. It is a matter for separate psychological study to determine how they come about. This turns out to be a subdivision of the study of such paradigmatic examples of emotion as pride, humility, love and hatred.

Impressions and Ideas

While it is important to recognise the deep influence that continental scepticism (and rationalism) had upon Hume, and not merely to classify him as the Third of the British Empiricists, it is still true that in certain key respects he merely takes over the central doctrines of the Lockean 'way of ideas' and uses them for his own sceptical purposes. The very fact that he could see their sceptical consequences in a way that Locke and Berkeley did not, prevented him from scrutinising them sufficiently critically. They also appeared tailor-made for the requirements of his scientific psychology: what Newton had done with the motion of material particles Hume could now propose to do for ideas. So Hume is fundamentally unoriginal in certain vital respects: he merely amends, and puts to new uses, doctrines that derived from Locke.

He accepts that the human mind is occupied, in all its activities with what Locke calls ideas, which come to it from 'experience'. He further accepts that, as Locke put it, 'We can have knowledge no farther than we can have ideas'.[13] The term that Hume uses in place of Locke's 'ideas' is 'perceptions'. The principle that our knowledge reaches no farther than our ideas is refined and applied by Hume in three major ways. (1) He maintains that all demonstrative certainty, as we know this in logic or pure mathematics, is confined to propositions about the relationships between certain of our perceptions, 'without dependence on what is anywhere existent in the universe' (*E.U.* 25). (2) He maintains that we cannot understand discourse whose terms are not ultimately definable by reference to our perceptions. (3) Since most of the propositions we assent to are not about 'quantity or number', yet are intelligible, they must be undemonstrable propositions that are expressed in terms that are definable by reference to our perceptions. Hume maintains that they must in consequence be *about* perceptions, yet must make claims about them which we can understand but not justify: that they continue unperceived, have necessary connections, or form a unitary biography. He then sees his task as that of explaining the sources and ramifications of these convictions.

In this dimension of his thought he introduces a fundamentally important and novel claim that we have already touched upon. He maintains that rationalists and empiricists alike have been mistaken in thinking that the human mind has some substantial measure of control over the sequences of perceptions that occur within it. But such a belief cannot even be expressed without violating principle (2), since it implies the independent existence of a subject which *has* the perceptions and can pick and choose among them and direct their course, whereas the mind is nothing over and above the perceptions that it has.[14]

Hence the formation of our beliefs, indeed every form of mental activity, should be recognised as the occurrence of certain perceptions 'in' the mind, rather than a free activity *of* the mind. All philosophers have recognised our passivity with respect to the advent of some of our perceptions, such as our visual sensations or our

29

dreams; but both sceptics and rationalists urge us to exercise the freedom which they believe the mind has to withhold its assent to them. Hume insists we do not have this freedom, and that our beliefs are merely products of sequences of perceptions which we do not control.

So the Lockean ideal framework provides a splendid setting for Hume's deflationary account of human nature and human knowledge. But this convenience has immense and notorious drawbacks. Historically, it has lent cogency to the Reid—Beattie interpretation of his philosophy, and obscured its more positive features. There is no doubt that it makes it far too easy for Hume's sceptical conclusions to be foisted on his readers. If we are able to reflect only upon our perceptions then the belief in an independent material world has to be read as a belief in the independent existence *of our perceptions*: a belief whose irrationality needs little additional emphasis. If we are able to reflect only upon our perceptions, then our belief that they all belong to the same person is one which it is natural to represent as an ascription to these heterogeneous perceptions of a unitary simplicity they do not have.[15]

The adoption of the ideal framework is also the cause of Hume's use of many arguments which really do embody the confusion between philosophical and psychological considerations from which I have argued that his general strategy is free. Principle (1) presents a thesis about the way the propositions of logic and mathematics are established as a discovery about the psychical status of entities supposed to be their subject-matter. Principle (2) presents a thesis about the criteria of meaning as though it were a discovery about the entities meaningful discourse has to be about. Twentieth-century Empiricism has made immense advances by de-psychologising these two theses. But it is vital to the estimation of Hume's thought to recognise that even if his theses are replaced by their suitably de-psychologised counterparts (the Linguistic theory of the *a priori*, and the Verification Principle) Hume's whole general theory about reason and the passions could still be maintained. His detailed confusions about philosophy and psychology are therefore not as damaging to his system as they are commonly alleged to be.

I have so far avoided, as a detail, the division Hume makes within perceptions between impressions and ideas. Principle (1) of course, appears as the assertion that demonstrative certainty is confined to propositions asserting relations of ideas. Principle (2) appears as the assertion that all our ideas are copies of impressions. The division is generally agreed to be an unhappy one, and Hume himself is uncomfortable about the adequacy of his account of it. He explains it in Section I of Part I of Book I of the *Treatise*, and in Section II of the *Enquiry*. In his explanation he gives examples of each class, and tries to present a criterion of discrimination between them. Impressions include 'all our sensations, passions, and emotions, as they make their first appearance in the soul' (I 11/1); ideas, he says, are 'the faint images of these in thinking and reasoning'. In the *Enquiry* the examples offered are 'the pain of excessive heat or the pleasure of moderate warmth', which are contrasted with the perceptions a man has when he 'afterwards recalls to his memory this sensation, or anticipates it by his imagination' (*E.U.* 17). The criterion he offers is that of difference in force, liveliness, or vivacity. He immediately admits it to be dubious, since the ideas we have in dreams or sickness may 'approach to our impressions'; though he tries to dismiss this as a trivial difficulty.[16] Hume's problem is clear: the criterion has to be internal to the perceptions themselves, since he intends to proceed later to account for our belief in the external world as an imaginative construction from our experience of perceptions, and cannot describe the difference in terms that presuppose its existence. Yet if our impressions are actually those perceptions we have when we perceive external objects and those emotions we have in response to them, it will be at best a happy accident if a wholly internal criterion is available to sort these perceptions out from the rest that we have. Sensing the difficulty, he tries to suggest that it is merely one of nomenclature, and that we can all *recognise* the difference he is after even if we cannot name it happily.

There are two appeals in this vein. The first reads as follows: 'I believe it will not be very necessary to employ many words in explaining this distinction. Every one of himself will readily perceive the difference between feeling and thinking' (I 11/1–2). This appeal has led MacNabb, plausibly, to suggest that the distinction Hume really has in view is 'that between what we think about, the given, and our thoughts about it, or the symbols by means of which these thoughts are thought'.[17] That perception which does not have reference to some preceding perception is an impression, and that which does is an idea. This would obscure the referential character of the passions, which Hume classes as impressions, but Hume explicitly denies it to be an intrinsic feature of them in any case. It would also need to be supplemented to include those ideas which we have in imagination or dreams, that are copied from previous perceptions but are not recognised to have this origin at the time. Hume's second appeal, in the *Enquiry*, is this: 'All the colours of poetry, however splendid, can never paint natural objects in such a manner as to make the description be taken for a real landscape' (*E.U.* 17). This suggests that the difference Hume wants is that between the real and the imaginary, a difference which has to be defined in terms of the occasions on which experiences occur. The attempt to make this into an internal difference between perceptions themselves reaches its unhappiest outcome in his notorious account of belief.

This distinction, infelicitously introduced, is amended and twisted in many ways. (1) Hume sometimes talks as though an impression is a source of incorrigible information; that we are immune to error with regard to its nature. Yet the distinction between calm and violent passions in Book II requires him to say that we can have an impression that is so faint that we can fail to notice we have it. (So much for vivacity.) And his account of the origin of our idea of necessary connection requires him to claim that we all misunderstand the nature of one of our commonest internal impressions. (2) Although the division between impressions and ideas seems exclusive, his theory of sympathy leads him to say that an idea can be so enlivened that it becomes an impression. (He even says that it is enlivened by an idea — that of the self. So much for faintness.) (3) He divides impressions into simple and complex ones. Simple ones are only nameable and not describable. Yet he has to say that they can resemble one another, since their capacity for associative connections, crucial in Book II, requires this. (4) The very words 'impression' and 'idea' suggest that an impression or an idea is *of* something distinct from itself. This suggestion is not misleading in the case of ideas, but is in the case of impressions. Hume is at great pains to deny the reality of the distinction between a sensory impression and an independent object it might be thought to represent. Also passions are no more than impressions, both in the sense that they do not represent their objects, and in the sense that there is no difference between the impression (or feeling) of love or anger and the love or anger it is a feeling of. (5) Hume calls ideas images, but has to require them to be more. He needs them to be universal concepts.[18] He also needs them to be judgements. He describes the truth or falsity of our judgements as 'the agreement or disagreement of ideas, considered as copies, with those objects which they represent' (II 127/415), but the implication that judgement is the mere occurrence of one or more ideas leads him into open perplexity when he tries to mark the difference between entertaining a proposition and believing it.

Association

Hume's theory of association evokes little interest in the contemporary reader. Yet it was that feature of his system about which he seemed most vain. He singles it out for a special closing panegyric in the *Abstract*, and although he makes relatively little explicit use of it in the first *Enquiry*, he will not let it go. He was convinced that it was the major theoretical plank of the 'science of man' on which his reform of philosophy depended. While he was not the first to use the doctrine[19] he undoubtedly was right to claim originality in the nature and extent of his use of it.

He says of association that it 'is a kind of attraction, which in the mental world will be found to have as extraordinary effects as in the natural, and to show itself in as many and as various forms' (I 21/12–13). The concept of attraction had of course been used by Newton. In association Hume thinks he has found an ultimate principle of a similar sort, whose explanatory power will likewise not depend upon any allegedly deeper hypotheses, but will illuminate the familiar and observable characteristics of our mental life and outflank the pretensions of the rationalists.

But at the very outset these claims are qualified. He first offers the theory as an account of the connections between *ideas*. Leaning on the description of an idea as an image, he says association is a 'uniting principle' that explains the activity of the *imagination*. Immediately he has to concede that the principle is limited in its application, since 'nothing is more free than that faculty' – we seem able to imagine what we like. So the principle is merely one that guides imagination 'in some measure'. Hume is offering us a principle that will explain how the mind arrives at its opinions. He says these are not the work of sensation or reason but imagination, which means that they are the outcome of whatever rules govern the succession of images the mind has. But in introducing these rules he has to admit that they do not apply to the voluntary operation of imagination, namely *imagining*.

He follows this concession with another, which greatly weakens the comparison with attraction. Even where association does operate, it is only a 'gentle force, which commonly prevails'. In

33

other words it is not a universal principle which enables us to *predict* how our minds will work, but at best a source of *ad hoc* explanations. It can still be a fruitful source of such explanations; but in using it to provide them Hume embellishes it with a sumptuous proliferation of amplifications and subsidiary hypotheses.

He says the principle operates through three relations: resemblance, contiguity in time or place, and cause and effect. These relations exist between 'objects'. The associative mechanism is one that 'conveys the mind' from one idea to another, or from an impression to an idea, because the idea *to* which it is conveyed is an idea (or is an idea derived from an impression) that resembles, or has been found contiguous to, or to be the cause or effect of, the impression or idea *from* which the mind is conveyed.

The relation of cause and effect is ultimately analysed away in terms of resemblance, contiguity — and association. To expect effects to follow causes is to expect events that resemble those that have been contiguous in the past to be contiguous in the future: the expectancy itself being a by-product of the associative transition from the earlier to the later. This is as near as we get to a pure explanatory application of the doctrine of association. Although our beliefs in the external world and personal identity are also said by Hume to be due to imagination, the detailed accounts are replete with additional hypotheses. For example, it is crucial to both accounts that we are said to treat a series of resembling perceptions as though they were one and the same continuing perception, because of the smoothness of transition along them: so instead of passing from one to the other because of resemblance, the resemblance causes us, while passing from one to the other, to think we are staying with the one. Here the operative principle is the propensity for ease and smoothness, of which association is merely one instance.

Hume makes frequent and ingenious use of association in his account of the passions. To use it here he has to amend it to apply beyond the imagination, even in his stretched sense of that term. Not only is there association of ideas, but since the passions are secondary impressions, there is also association of impressions. The only possible relation to appeal to here as its basis is resemblance: one passion can lead to another that resembles it, even though they are distinct and simple. So love can lead to benevolence, and hatred to anger. Hume shows much ingenuity in illustrating the way in

34

which, in his view, the association of impressions and the association of ideas work together to produce the indirect passions, but the account is implausible because of the degree to which the mechanism requires piecemeal modification. The famous principle of sympathy is, superficially, an example of association: when I become aware of another's passion, this may generate a resembling one in myself. But since the very reverse can also happen, Hume has to introduce the opposed principle of comparison to explain the exceptions.

Belief[20]

Hume has to insist upon the involuntariness of belief, and to represent it as the product of association. He also has to represent it in the language of impressions and ideas. It cannot *be* an impression, since the occasions on which we believe something to be the case are precisely those on which the presence of that in which we believe is *not* certified by an impression. But if we say a belief is an idea, we are unable to explain the essential difference between merely imagining or considering the proposition that something is the case, and believing it to be the case. So Hume is forced to an uneasy compromise. To have a belief is to have an idea, but in a special manner: 'belief is a more vivid and intense conception of an idea' (I 105/103). Other adjectives are 'lively, forcible, firm, steady' (*E.U.* 49). The source of this special manner is custom, but Hume is unable to do more than pile on adjectives to capture the nature of this manner itself. The difficulty is reminiscent of that which attended the introduction of the distinction between impressions and ideas, and reflects similar constraints. To make it worse, the only language Hume can think of suggests that in belief an idea has characteristics definitive of impressions, which is theoretically impossible. Hume's solution, at least in the *Treatise*, is to hint that the liveliness of the idea in belief is borrowed from that of the impression which occasions it. It is hard to imagine a more ingenious, or a more unsatisfactory, solution to a self-made theoretical predicament.

The Treatise and the Enquiries

Hume presented the two *Enquiries* as more mature and stylistically improved versions of Books I and III of the *Treatise*. They are often read instead of it, as he himself went so far as to request. But many philosophers have judged them to be inferior popularisations, and have confined their attention to the *Treatise*.

The *Enquiries* are obviously easier to read. We are not dealing in them with a young genius, fighting his way through a tangled mass of complex issues for the first time, with a bewildered reader following behind as best he can. Instead we are led with elegant deliberation through a carefully prepared exposition of those results of Hume's system which could readily be connected with the issues that were the wider concern of the eighteenth-century republic of letters. Much vital detail is lost in the process. But there are gains.

The gains are greater, by far, in the first *Enquiry*, since here Hume adds the essays on 'Miracles' and 'Particular Providence'. He has been accused of adding these in order to gain notoriety, but he already had enough notoriety to displease him. Hume omits the most radically Pyrrhonian discussions of perception and personal identity, and emphasises instead the application of mitigated scepticism to the claims of revealed religion. There is far less emphasis upon the detailed application of the doctrine of association, and a relatively sparing use of the doctrine of impressions and ideas. But two things must be emphasised. First, whatever the adjustments in presentation, the crucial Sections IV to VII on induction and causation, depend just as critically as anything in those Sections of the *Treatise* to which they correspond, upon an appeal to the psychology of habit. To apply a theory in one work is not to abandon, though it may restrain one from repeating, the details of its construction in another. Second, the applications of those modes of reasoning that serve the commitments of common life, though stressed more explicitly in the *Enquiry*, emerge over and over again in the *Treatise*. Any internal stresses in Hume's scepticism in the one work can readily be matched in the other.

The second *Enquiry* shows us a similar shift of emphasis. Hume seeks to show that his naturalistic theory of moral evaluations can provide adequate answers to egoism and account for our moral commitment to justice. The main body of the work consists of a leisurely description of the nature of those characteristics of men and society which are the objects of our evaluative judgements, and of the conditions under which we approve or disapprove of them. He claims this to be an application of 'the experimental method'. In a clear sense it is: Hume is conducting systematic social observation. Yet he deliberately leaves out the deeper investigation of the emotional bases of the social evaluations he describes. In particular he is content to stress the effects of sympathy without exploring its inner mechanism. But there is no reason to suppose this, or any other of the psychological theses of the *Treatise*, to have been abandoned. Some of the more indigestible philosophical arguments, such as those against ethical rationalism, are relegated to appendices, an untidy method of exposition which militates against Hume's opinion that this was the best of his writings. I must confess to a personal view that the second *Enquiry* is, in comparison with the ethical portions of the *Treatise*, a bland and insipid document.

In the chapters that follow I assume that the *Treatise* is the fundamental source for Hume's teachings, except in the philosophy of religion. But I also assume that his teachings are not inaccurately represented in the *Enquiries*, and that an account of them can be supplemented from them without hazard. In the case of induction and causation I think the common practice of beginning with the *Enquiry* and turning to the *Treatise* to supplement what is found there is a wise one, and therefore follow it in Chapter 2.

2 Causation and Induction

The problem of induction (the problem of the epistemological status of inferences from experience) and the problem of causation (the problem of the meaning of individual causal judgements) seem to be distinct from one another. Hume, however, discusses them together at all times. This is because he holds that inference from experience is most commonly inference from effects to causes or from causes to effects; and, far more fundamentally, because he holds that the nature of causal judgements cannot be understood until we recognise the way in which our inferences from experience are actually performed and what leads us to make them in the way we do. General questions about causation set the framework for his investigation of induction; but his answers to those questions presuppose theses about the justification and origin of inductive inference. The intricate relationship between these two topics, both explored by Hume in unprecedented depth, have led to his being celebrated, and attacked, for a variety of alleged discoveries or errors. It is universally agreed that Hume has told us something of permanent and unchallengeable importance about each theme, but there is little common agreement as to what this is in each case. In this brief treatment I shall merely attempt to indicate the exact nature of Hume's argument and conclusions, as we find it in the *Treatise*, the first *Enquiry*, and the *Abstract*.

I shall proceed first by describing the argument as Hume presents it in the *Enquiry*. This is the version that most readers encounter first, and it is his most mature presentation of it. I shall then look briefly at the version in the *Abstract*, which is a succinct summary of the much more lengthy and circuitous discussion in Part III of

Book I of the *Treatise*. While I cannot follow the *Treatise* version in detail, I shall comment on some of the most significant passages which have no counterparts in the shorter works.

The Enquiry Argument

Hume begins, in Section IV, by setting up the division commonly called 'Hume's Fork'. It is a division between two exclusive and exhaustive classes of 'objects of human reason or enquiry', namely Relations of Ideas, and Matters of Fact. The distinction is fundamental, and wholly dogmatic. The doctrine that the division reflects is that any 'affirmation which is either intuitively or demonstrably certain' is an affirmation whose certainty is bought at a high price. The price is that it tells us only about relationships between ideas we entertain, and not at all about 'nature' or 'the universe'. This price, though very high, does buy us a benefit. The benefit is immunity to falsification by evidence. But Hume is not concerned to explore this benefit, or the price we pay for it. For his main concern is not with affirmations about relations of ideas, but with those that are about matters of fact. These do, of course, deal with nature, or the universe. What Hume wishes to do is make clear what price we have to pay for our ability to make affirmations of this kind. He prides himself, correctly, on being the first philosopher to recognise how high the price is. (Kant followed him in this estimate of his contribution, while thinking that Hume sets the price even higher than he should.) The price is, in Hume's view, that no matter of fact can be demonstrated.

The reason he gives for this claim is that the 'contrary' of any true proposition about matters of fact can never be demonstrated to be false; for if it could, it would imply a contradiction, and could not be 'distinctly conceived by the mind'.

Having told us this, Hume proceeds to ask about our knowledge of *some* of these matters of fact: those that we are not assured of by the 'present testimony of our senses or the records of our memory'. What is it that 'assures' us of them?

His initial answer is that we base such assurance as we have on reasonings that make use of the relation of Cause and Effect, which is one of the three 'principles of connection among ideas' he has told us of in the preceding Section. He says that whenever someone claims to know some matter of fact that is 'absent', he will do this because the matter of fact in question is the cause, or the effect, of one that is 'present'.

How, then, do we come to know about causes and effects? In Section IV there are three parts to his answer. (1) Our knowledge of cause and effect does not come from 'reasonings *a priori*'. (2) It comes, instead, from experience. (3), Inferences from experience (inductive inferences) are not 'founded on reasoning'. (1) and (2) are empiricist theses. (3) is, notoriously, a sceptical thesis.

(1) and (2). No one, says Hume, is inclined to think that our knowledge of causal relations that were once unfamiliar has been acquired without observation. This is true both of common-sense oddities that surprise us when we first hear of them (such as the fact that two smooth pieces of marble will stick together), and of causal connections that have had to be discovered by scientists or engineers (such as the effects of explosives, or the manner in which bread nourishes us). But we are easily led to overlook the fact that familiar causal connections are learned by experience also: such as the connection between the impact of one billiard ball on another and the movement of the second. If we doubt this we need only reflect that without past experience to guide us we would not be confident that the second billiard ball would move merely through seeing the first one moving towards it. If we doubt *this*, we should reflect that the event which is the cause and the event which is the effect are *distinct*, 'nor is there anything in the one to suggest the smallest hint of the other'. This in turn can be shown if we reflect that although we confidently expect the familiar effect to follow when the familiar cause occurs we can very easily, and with complete logical consistency, conceive something else to follow instead. So what must be at work is the *familiarity* of those relationships we have experienced in the past, not some piece of *a priori* reasoning which would proceed without reference to that past experience.

(3). At this point, as Part IV of the Section begins, there arise those sceptical doubts for whose emergence Hume has been preparing. If our knowledge of matters of fact which we are not now experiencing is due to our use of the relations of cause and effect, and all our reasonings about cause and effect depend on experience, we must ask how we can justify reasoning from experience. He says that in the rest of Section IV he will only give the negative part of his answer: 'that, even after we have experience of the operations of cause and effect, our conclusions from that experience are *not* founded on reasoning, or any process of the understanding'. Such phrasing is unclear: it is not easy to determine whether Hume means that we do not reason from past experience but proceed on unverbalised habit, or merely that we reason, that is perform inferences, but do so without rational warrant. In most contexts the latter is the correct interpretation, so that Hume's claim is that we do make explicit inferences, but are not impelled to do so by the existence of logical connections between the premisses and the conclusions. Even read this way Hume's point is as much psychological as it is logical: since the logical relationships are not there to impel us to conclude what we do, something else must be responsible.

The sceptical doubts hinge, of course, on the fact that no conclusion about any matter of fact that one has not observed follows validly from any premisses which state matters of fact that one has. This is unaffected by the appearance, in the premisses or the conclusion, of the language of cause and effect. For (again) causes and effects are distinct. From the fact that a particular sort of cause has always been followed by a certain sort of effect, it cannot be validly deduced that it will be so again. We regularly infer that it will be, but this inference cannot be represented as a valid deduction. We are now beginning to see the darker implications of the dogma that no matter of fact can be demonstratively certain.

Philosophers may wish to resist this conclusion. The most obvious way for them to resist it is by trying to render the inference a valid one in spite of appearances by the introduction of an additional premiss stating that causal sequences will continue in the future as they have in the past. Such a procedure is circular, for such a premiss must itself either be a proposition which it is self-contradictory to deny, which it is not, or must be established from experience in the very manner we are seeking to justify. In addition such supposed philosophical justifications are unavailable to ordinary folk, who need to make causal inferences as much as philosophers do, and therefore proceed without their assistance.

In Section V Hume tells us how they manage to do it. This information will provide us with a 'Sceptical Solution' of the doubts he has raised in Section IV. The answer is already before us if we reflect upon the critical role played in our causal thinking by familiarity. What the sceptic shows we cannot do by reasoning, we achieve through *custom*, or habit. It is this to which all inferences from experience are due. Hume introduces the principle in a way that makes it clear that he believes the very existence of the ideas of cause and effect themselves is the product of custom. A man suddenly placed in the world would observe sequences of objects, but would not call them causes and effects, and would be unable to make inferences from one to the other; it is only when we have enough experience to notice constant conjunctions and be led by them to expect their future repetition that we can classify them as sequences of causes and effects.

Custom, however, has to have something to operate upon when it generates actual causal inferences. What it operates upon will be those items of present information to which we attach the causal inferences that we make. We expect effects when we are presented with objects that resemble their previous causes; belief in the imminence of the effect is a consequence of the present encounter with an object joined to such effects in the past by 'customary conjunction'. Hume strikingly compares such belief with emotional responses:

> Having found, in many instances, that any two kinds of objects — flame and heat, snow and cold — have always been conjoined together; if flame or snow be presented anew to the senses, the mind is carried by custom to expect heat or cold, and to *believe* that such a quality does exist, and will discover itself upon a nearer approach. The belief is the necessary result of placing the mind in such circumstances. It is an operation of the soul, when we are so situated, as unavoidable as to feel the passion of love, when we receive benefits; or hatred, when we meet with injuries. All these operations are a species of natural instincts, which no reasoning or process of the thought and understanding is able to produce or to prevent. (*E.U.* 46—7)

Hume now turns, in Part II of Section V, to a subsidiary but important problem, implied in the italicised '*believe*' in the above passage. If causal inferences are to be understood as inferences from presently observed objects to expected ones, the expected ones will have, in his psychology, to be present in idea. But the way in which they will be present in idea cannot be the same as the way in which objects we imagine or dream are present in idea. It is not merely that we cannot help thinking of them when their customary causes appear before us; though it is partly this. Our thinking of them must take the form of *expecting* the ideas of them to be followed by the objects of which they are ideas. Hume feels he must give some account of the felt difference between mere imagination and such expectation. He enlarges the question to this: what is the difference between merely imagining some situation and believing it to be a real

42

one? He assumes (and he has often been criticised for this) that the difference has to be of some introspectible sort. This assumption is unaffected by his inability to *describe* the difference that introspection reveals. He is forced to content himself with remarks such as these: 'I say, then, that belief is nothing but a more vivid, lively, forcible, firm, steady conception of an object, than what the imagination alone is ever able to attain . . . belief consists not in the peculiar nature or order of ideas, but in the *manner* of their conception, and in their *feeling* to the mind.' (*E.U.* 49.)

He finds this special manner of conception in cases where our beliefs are intensified by contiguity and resemblance, as well as cases of causal inference. My idea of an absent friend is enlivened if it is occasioned by the sight of a picture that resembles him, and my ideas of my home and family become more vivid as I perceive objects close to them while approaching home. He insists implausibly that these are cases of belief, since I believe my friend and my family to exist, or to have existed. And in all cases, what generates the liveliness of the idea is the regular past conjunction of the object it represents with the present object which now calls it up.

In this way, he says, we are equipped with 'a kind of pre-established harmony between the course of nature and the succession of our ideas' which is indispensable to us in the struggle for survival and the acquisition of knowledge. No doubt the irony of these final passages is deliberate. But it should not mislead us into overlooking the fact that if Hume is correct this remark is literally true. It was this very fact about Hume's theory of causal judgements that led Kant to seek some other account of their coincidence with the realities we seek to discover when we make them.

There is a second apparent digression in Section VI ('Of Probabilities') where Hume applies his account of causal inference and belief to the understanding of probable inferences. He distinguishes between the *probability of chances* and the *probability of causes*.

The probability of chances. In a rare piece of naked *a priori* metaphysics, Hume tells us that strictly speaking, there is no such thing as chance. But as we do not always know the causes of things, we have to reason as though there is. We do this by calculating probabilities. When we predict the outcome of the throw of a die, we look to see what numbers are on its sides. If every side has a different number, we have an equal degree of expectation of each

43

number's coming up when the die is thrown. But if there is one number that is on more sides than the other numbers are, we will glimpse that number more often, and this will print the idea of that number on our minds with more force than the ideas of the other numbers, so that we will acquire something tending to belief with regard to it. The strength of our belief that a particular number will come up will be mathematically proportionate to the frequency of the occurrence of that number on the sides of the die.

The probability of causes. We sometimes find that a particular cause is followed by its typical effect some of the time, but not all of the time. Even though we may very well believe that this lack of uniformity is only apparent, and that the real causes, if we knew them, would be uniform, we adjust our expectations to the proportion of positive and negative instances we have hitherto encountered. So we expect the proportion of positive and negative instances in the future to be the same as it has been in the past. Hume therefore equates the unqualified expectation that the past ratio of positive to negative cases will continue in the future, with an expectation of future positive cases whose strength corresponds to the proportion of past positive cases alone.

In Section VII Hume returns to the analysis of the idea of causation itself. For the first time in his argument he now makes explicit use of his distinction between impressions and ideas, instead of the studiedly noncommittal language of 'objects'. Hitherto he has explained our causal inferences as mental acts that issue from a custom that is rooted in constant conjunctions. Our common notion of a cause, however, seems to contain more than this. Hume never denies that it does: indeed he has listed contiguity and cause and effect as two distinct relations, and conjunction is merely one sort of contiguity. In addition to this he has also said that our causal inferences often take place in circumstances where we may believe that the conjunctions on which they are based are not ultimate — so that they may be manifestations of 'secret' connections that we do not know about. Until the idea of causation is more fully understood we may be inclined to think that some covert reference to such hidden forces is part of the very meaning of this notion. There are philosophers who have claimed just this: among them Locke, in his doctrine of powers, or tertiary qualities. One of Hume's fundamental objectives is to locate and render harmless that feature of the idea of causation which makes such doctrines plausible.

As his comparison with love and hatred has already hinted, he wishes to do this by tracing this feature to inner, psychical, sources. But this in turn has its dangers; for philosophers are apt to suggest that there are secret powers within ourselves that our idea of causation reflects. Hume has to use the doctrine of impressions and ideas to ensure that the quest for the sources of our idea of causation is not led astray.

The element in the idea of causation which has so far eluded capture is that of 'power, force, energy, or necessary connection'. These terms are still alternative names for an undeniable element in our common, non-philosophical idea of a cause. Hume thinks that it can be traced to a clearly identifiable impression; but not one we can find if we look 'outward'. When we look at the billiard balls we do not find any impressions except those of solidity, extension and motion, and the successive events in which they are combined with each other. (If we did find a further impression of power or necessity, it would entitle us to infer the later occurrence of the effect from the prior occurrence of the cause, and we have seen that such an inference, though common, is invalid.) Let us then look 'inward'. Is there any 'internal impression' that can be the source of our idea of power?

At this point Hume feels obliged, at the cost of a further digression, to put aside two possible suggestions. (1) the suggestion that we can trace the idea of power to 'the influence of volition over the organs of the body'; (2) the suggestion that we can trace the idea of power to the ability of the will to 'direct the faculties of our mind'. (1) Regarding the first, he says that although experience does teach us that volitions[1] are followed by bodily movements, our knowledge of the connection is based on experienced conjunctions as much as it is in other cases; and our knowledge of the details of the connection is less than it is in most. It is a brute fact that our volitions can affect some of our bodily movements and not others, and we are usually quite ignorant of the immediate effects of the volition, even though we can infer that the effects we do know of are not the first in the chain. If we could detect an impression of power, such connections would not be the unexplained brute facts that they are. (2) The same is true of our ability to will changes in our mental lives. The changes we can bring about by volition are considerable, but no amount of scrutiny of them will produce an impression of power or force intervening between the volition and its effects, any more than external observation will show us such a power between two billiard balls.[2]

Hume now proceeds in Part II to identify the internal impression from which the complex idea of causation derives its element of supposed necessity or power. The impression is one that we are led to by custom or habit. When we contemplate a sequence of two events that has never occurred before, we do not say one is the cause and the other the effect. We may say we have observed conjunction, but we do not yet talk of connection. When the sequence has been observed frequently, and without exceptions, we do talk of connection, and call the two events cause and effect respectively. The mere repetition of the sequence has added nothing new to the sequence itself. But it will have added something new to our perception of it. For after many such experiences, habit makes us expect the second event after the first event occurs. The connection is in the imagination, not in the objects. But only when this habitual transition is established do we make causal inferences. So the element of necessity in the idea of causation is the ideal counterpart of the internal impression we have when we *feel* the habitual transition from the first event's occurrence to the second event's anticipated occurrence, at the time when we perceive the first event. This explanation entails that, in so far as we *ascribe power* to the first object, we are projecting our own felt expectancy on to that part of nature we are observing.

He concludes with two definitions of what a cause is. The first he states in two allegedly alternative forms: '(I). An object, followed by another, and where all the objects similar to the first are followed by objects similar to the second. (I*a*). Or, in other words, where, if the first object had not been, the second never had existed' (*E.U.* 76; numbering mine). The phrase 'or, in other words' is manifestly inappropriate. The first version, (I), is equivalent to something like 'an event, *C*, has occurred, and an event, *E*, has followed, and events like *C* are always followed by events like *E*'.

The second version, (I*a*), is equivalent to something like 'an event, *C*, has occurred, and an event, *E*, has followed, and *E* would not have occurred at all if *C* had not occurred first'.

The concept defined in (I), correctly or not, is that of a sufficient condition; that defined in (I*a*), correctly or not, is that of a necessary condition. Hume's whole account is an account of how we allegedly come to ascribe power or necessity to a cause in the sense of (I); and the implications of the appearance of (I*a*) are never explored in the *Enquiry* at all.

Hume's second definition of what a cause is, is this: 'II. An object followed by another, and whose appearance always conveys the thought to that other' (*E.U.* 77; numbering mine). He points out that in both definitions what we are saying when we call some event a cause is something that is 'drawn from circumstances foreign to the cause'.

The existence of two definitions is not a sign of confusion. The first definition concentrates on those elements in our notion of a cause that derive from external observation, and can therefore properly be ascribed to the world we observe, subject to any provisos we might wish to add about future inferences based on custom. The second definition concentrates upon that additional element in the idea which has a purely psychological source; this element, once correctly located, is one which we cannot ascribe without confusion to the objects of our observation. It is part of our common notion, but it is not a part that need intrude at all, once its source is understood, into our descriptions of nature: this is the moral of the first definition. If it does so intrude, we are attaching unnecessary metaphysical significance to a common attribution which, though a mistake, is a harmless one until metaphysicians try to capitalise upon it.

The Summary in the 'Abstract'

Corresponding to Section IV Part I of the *Enquiry* the *Abstract* has the mere assertion that 'all reasonings concerning *matter of fact*' are founded on the relationship of cause and effect. Hume then turns at once to the scrutiny of what can be found in that relationship when both cause and effect are before us. He declares he can only find contiguity, temporal priority of cause to effect, and constant conjunction. He then turns to the inference that we make from cause to effect when only the cause is before us. This inference is not a valid demonstration, and must depend on experience. Yet in basing it on experience we do not provide a rational justification of it; for to provide this we would have to be in a position to assert that the future will resemble the past, which we cannot assert in this context without circularity. 'This, therefore, is a point which can admit of no proof at all, and which we take for granted without any proof' (254). Section V, Part I of the *Enquiry* is then paralleled by two brief paragraphs in which Hume tells us that causal inference is the product of custom instead: 'It is not, therefore, reason which is the guide of life, but custom. That alone determines the mind, in all instances, to suppose the future conformable to the past. However easy this step may seem, reason would never, to all eternity, be able to make it' (254).

Hume spends considerable space (seven paragraphs) in expounding 'our author's' account of the nature of belief, as a special manner of conceiving the anticipated object, and as being independent of the will. The probability of causes nets a paragraph, as does the much more important topic (Section VII, Part I in the *Enquiry*) of the alleged similarity of mental causes to physical ones. The famous psychological account of the origin of the idea of necessary connection, or power, is very baldly, and almost hesitatingly, formulated: 'Upon the whole, then, either we have no idea at all of force and energy, and these words are altogether insignificant, or they can mean nothing but that determination of the thought, acquired by habit, to pass from the cause to its usual effect. But whoever would thoroughly understand this must consult the author himself.' (259)

The Structure of the Argument in the 'Treatise'

In Section II of Part III of Book I of the *Treatise* (recast in *E.U.* Section IV, Part I) Hume begins by arguing that it is the relationship of causation which 'informs us of existences and objects which we do not see or feel' (I 78/74). Scrutiny of the relation reveals the presence of contiguity and succession. But our idea of a cause contains more: 'production', or necessary connection. Any impression from which *this* idea is derived is not to be found in the qualities of the cause or the effect, or in their observed relationship. To find its source we must proceed indirectly, and consider two questions: 'First, for what reason we pronounce it necessary, that everything whose existence has a beginning, should also have a cause? Secondly, (i) why we conclude, that such particular causes must necessarily have such particular effects; and (ii) what is the nature of that inference we draw from the one to the other, and (iii) of the belief we repose in it?' (I 81/78; numbering mine.)

The first of the questions (that of the status of the so-called Causal Principle) is ignored in the *Abstract*, and almost, if not quite, overlooked in the *Enquiry*. In the *Treatise* Hume deals with it, though incompletely, in Section III ('Why a Cause is Always Necessary'). He concludes his discussion there by promising us that an answer to this question will be found through a consideration of the second, tripartite query — a promise on which he never delivers. The remainder of Part III is devoted to his second question.

Items (1) and (2) within it form the themes of Section IV to VI (to which *E.U.* Sections IV, Part II and V, Part I, correspond). In brief the argument is that causal inference is due to the constant conjunction of the cause and the effect. But this constant conjunction does not produce the inference through the reason; for it to do this we would have to be able to presuppose that 'instances, of which we have had no experience, must resemble those of which we have had experience, and that the course of nature continues always uniformly the same' (I 91/89). Such a principle cannot be demonstrated, since the contrary contains no contradiction; nor can it be based upon an appeal to experience without manifest circularity. So the inference must be due to the association of ideas in the imagination. It is a passage from the impression of the cause to the idea of the effect, consequent upon the association that custom has established between the ideas of the two phenomena.

Sections VIII to X (recast as Part II of Section V in the *Enquiry*) elaborate the account of belief as a lively idea (of the effect) related to a present impression (of the cause). The association between them is, Hume again insists, the product not of reason but of custom or habit. This is his answer to (3).

Sections XI to XIII are a digression on types of probability, far more complex than the cursory treatment in *E.U.* Section VI. The central feature of the argument is the same, however: the equation of the quantitative estimates of probabilities with quantitative expressions of our inclinations to expect the events that are judged probable. If Hume has given us a correct account of the origin of our belief in natural uniformities in our experience of constant conjunctions, it does not seem necessary for him to insist in addition that our calculations about less-than-constant conjunctions reflect expectations that vary as precisely as the calculations do with the quantities of past evidence. It would seem that the relatively minor weight given to these considerations in the *Enquiry* shows Hume's recognition not only of their implausibility, but of their loose connection with his basic contentions.

In Section XIV (the counterpart to *E.U.* Section VII), Hume returns to the analysis of necessary connection. He is now able to trace this idea to an impression; not an impression of the senses, but an internal impression, or impression of reflection. 'There is no internal impression which has any relation to the present business, but that propensity, which custom produces, to pass from an object to the idea of its usual attendant. This, therefore, is the essence of necessity. Upon the whole, necessity is something that exists in the mind, not in objects; nor is it possible for us ever to form the most distant idea of it, considered as a quality in bodies' (I 163–4/165–6). He follows this with two definitions of causation, which are paralleled by those of the *Enquiry*, but will receive separate treatment below. The Section concludes with a very important series of theoretical 'corollaries', which are unfortunately not matched in the *Enquiry* at all. Section XV, also unmatched in the *Enquiry*, lists practical rules for causal investigations.

The similarities between these three expositions of Hume's most celebrated doctrines are far greater than their differences. Adequate discussion of what Hume says about induction and causation is far beyond the scope of this chapter. I shall attempt merely to indicate the nature of Hume's inductive scepticism and the possible responses to it, and then make some comments on his analysis of causal relations. It is in the latter connection that the differences that there are between the *Enquiry* and the *Treatise* are most significant.

Hume's Scepticism About Induction

Hume holds that our inductive inferences are performed as a result of constant conjunction and association. If it were not for the associative mechanism which is established in us through custom and causes us to have the ideas of hitherto-inexperienced phenomena in that special manner which constitutes belief in their existence, we would not come to have the beliefs about matters of fact that we do have, but would be for ever suspended in doubt. For the alternative to having these beliefs through custom would be having them through reasoning, and this is not open to us since all such reasoning is invalid or question-begging. While custom saves us from the sceptic's doubts, his reasons for doubt are still correct. For inductive reasoning has no justification, since it is invalid.

As D. C. Stove insists, Hume's inductive scepticism depends entirely on his deductivism.[3] His scepticism is the view that no proposition which is not itself observed to be true is rendered more likely to be true by the citation of evidence from experience. His deductivism is the view that an argument gives no rational warrant for its conclusion if the inference to that conclusion is not deductively valid. Since Hume is clearly right when he tells us that inductive reasoning is not deductively valid, there can be no doubt that if one accepts his deductivism, his scepticism about induction follows.

50

Stove tries to undermine it by distinguishing it from what he calls inductive fallibilism. This is the thesis that inductive inferences are not only invalid, but incurably so: that however many observations I may add to those that already support an inductive conclusion, the inference to that conclusion will remain invalid. He elaborates this in at least two other ways: 'To say that inductive inferences are all incurably invalid is another way of saying that there is a permanent possibility of falsity in even the best-confirmed empirical generalisations and predictions';[4] and 'For inferences of that kind (i.e. inductive inferences) are what inductive fallibilism says they are, and what Barbara and *modus ponens* are not: invalid, and consequently not of the highest possible degree of conclusiveness'.[5] He holds that inductive fallibilism is true and important, but that inductive scepticism is false because deductivism is false.

My purpose here is to be as clear as possible about what Hume holds. I think that although Hume would certainly consent to what Stove calls inductive fallibilism, Stove has omitted something else which Hume does not clearly distinguish from it, and that he accordingly underestimates the complexity of Hume's argument. (I do not suggest Hume's argument becomes stronger when its presence is recognised.)

I see every reason to agree that Hume would not only accept inductive fallibilism but would regard it as a direct consequence of the formal invalidity of inductive inference – a point which Stove, from the above quotations, holds also. But as Stove presents it, inductive fallibilism is a thesis about the status of our accounts of the natural order. Hume commits himself to more than this. Consider this, from the *Abstract*: 'It is evident that Adam, with all his science, would never have been able to *demonstrate* that the course of nature must continue uniformly the same, and that the future must be conformable to the past. What is possible can never be demonstrated to be false; and it is possible the course of nature may change, since we can conceive such a change' (253–4). Hume does not say here only that Adam's science is vulnerable to refutation because it is not demonstrable. He also says that its non-demonstrability entails that *the course of nature* may change. Those scientists and laymen who have come to accept the shortcomings of Newtonian science (Stove's example of the healthy influence of fallibilism) have not thereby committed themselves to the opinion that the course of nature has altered in the period between Newton and Einstein — only that further reflection and observation has forced a redescription of it. If Hume had clearly distinguished between the vulnerability of inductive generalisations and the possibility that the course of nature might change, it would seem that he would think of each, equally, as a direct consequence of the deductive invalidity of inductive inferences.

Hume certainly holds that because inductive inference is formally invalid, it lacks rational justification. This conclusion, however, divides into at least three contentions: (1) that inductive conclusions are incurably vulnerable (inductive fallibilism); (2) that there is real possibility that the course of nature may change in the future from what it has been in the past; (3) that no evidence, however great in quantity, can contribute any likelihood to the conclusion of any inductive inference (inductive scepticism). Each is thought by him to be established by the formal invalidity of induction. Clearly (2) is more radical than (1), since (1) could be true in a world where our understanding of natural regularities was always subject to correction, though the regularities remained, Clearly (3) is more radical than (2), since (3) would imply that the proposition that nature would change had just as much likelihood when all the evidence was against it as it would have otherwise, whereas (2) only entails that it has *some* degree of likelihood. Their combination is a total scepticism about induction. That its effect is not wholly negative in Hume's own eyes is due to his view that the non-rational forces in human nature rescue us from the perpetual indecision into which the irrationality of induction would otherwise plunge us. We are lucky *not* to be rational beings.

It is accordingly possible to contest Hume's position in at least three ways; each of his three conclusions can be attacked, and each can be argued, at least, not to be a consequence of the formal invalidity of induction.

With regard to (1), the thesis of inductive fallibilism, Hume has many defenders who would reject (2) and (3). The best-known in our century are Popper and the philosophers of the Vienna Circle. Stove's formidable arguments must now be added to theirs. But it is striking that Stove accepts fallibilism to be a direct consequence of the invalidity of induction. He even says, 'To say that inductive inferences are all incurably invalid is *another way of saying* that there is a permanent possibility of falsity in . . . empirical generalisations'. It is not another way of saying any such thing. At least the inference from one to the other has been contested by those who have objected to the Positivist conclusion that inductive conclusions are always 'merely probable'.[6] Further, to say that such inferences are 'invalid, and consequently not of the highest possible degree of conclusiveness' is to treat validity as the high point on a continuous scale on which probability and support are lower down. This is also contestable.[7]

With regard to (2) Hume has been followed, at least to a degree, by Russell; critics have contended, however, that aside from a simple appeal to deductivism, a worry about the possibility of the future being different from the past must be due to conceptual confusions about the notions of past and future.[8]

With regard to (3) (inductive scepticism) what is at issue is whether rationality and likelihood are notions which Hume (in this respect a high rationalist) is correct in restricting to deductive demonstrations. This can be countered as Stove counters it, by the application of the Theory of Logical Probability and the production of counter-examples. It can also be countered through the informal and detailed examination and deployment of our notions of rationality and evidence. To call either procedure question-begging is to overlook the fact that Hume's stance on this fundamental question is a wholly dogmatic one.

I have not tried to examine the detailed relationships between the three propositions into which I have divided Hume's scepticism about induction. Nor do I suppose them incapable of further subdivision. But some separation of it into its parts is essential. For there is a widespread agreement that Hume has shown us something vital and incontestable about induction, but has drawn conclusions from it that are too gloomy. But there is no agreement on what it is that is vital and incontestable or which conclusions are too gloomy. To decide this for ourselves we need to be clearer on what his claims are than most of his readers — in spite of the lucidity of his prose, and in spite of the fact that his arguments are stated three times — have usually managed to be.

Hume's Analysis of Causation

The definitions. I have already quoted the two definitions of causation in the *Enquiry*. In Section XIV the *Treatise* has what are essentially the same two definitions, except that what I have called definition (1a) is absent. Corresponding to (1) the *Treatise* has 'An object precedent and contiguous to another, and where all the objects resembling the former are placed in like relations of

precedency and contiguity to those objects, that resemble the latter.'
Corresponding to (II) the *Treatise* has 'A cause is an object precedent and contiguous to another, and so united with it, that the idea of the one determines the mind to form the idea of the other, and the impression of the one to form a more lively idea of the other'. (I 167/172).

Once again, the first is an 'external' and the second an 'internal' definition. In the *Treatise*, however, there is an obfuscatory complication. Hume says that the first definition is of causation considered as a *philosophical relation*, and the second is of causation considered as a *natural relation*. This distinction makes no appearance in the *Enquiry*, and its absence is a benefit. But its presence in the *Treatise* is a substantial barrier to the understanding of that work, so some extended comment upon it is necessary.

The distinction appears in Section V of Part I of Book I. Hume introduces it as a distinction between two ways in which *ideas* can be connected in the imagination. His use of it in the two definitions of a cause suggests that he thinks of it as a distinction between two sorts of connection among objects. The unclarity has an easy enough explanation. Hume sees that philosophers and scientists say that things are related when plain men would not say so. Two things that occupy different places on some scale of measurement are said to be related by that fact alone; whereas in ordinary speech we might be inclined to say that we would never compare them with one another unless they were related in some other sense, such as that of being close to one another in space. To some extent, then, the distinction between what is natural and what is unnatural here is equivalent to that between what is technical and what is untechnical. But it is intended to go deeper. Hume clearly supposes that philosophical relations are relations we speak of because we find them to be present on special examination, whereas plain men do not mention them because they do not notice them. So they are really present in objects, though it is odd ('arbitrary') to draw attention to them. The relations are objective, but the objects in which we can find them are not connected in our minds as a result of this, because most men do not find them. This is why they are not 'natural': although they are real, it is unnatural to mention them. The unnaturalness of a relation is a fact about its failure to connect our ideas of the objects among which it exists. The relations which are natural will then be those, as he says, which form the basis of the association of ideas; so the existence of these relations results in the transition of the mind from one idea to another. This implies that these relations also exist in the objects we observe.

Hume then confuses us by including the three bases of association (resemblance, contiguity, and cause and effect) among the *philosophical* relations! What are we to make of this? He gives us a partial answer at the end of Section VI: 'Thus, though causation be a *philosophical* relation, as implying contiguity, succession, and constant conjunction, yet it is only so far as it is a *natural* relation, and produces a union among our ideas, that we are able to reason upon it, or draw any inference from it' (I 95–6/94). The relation of causation is a philosophical relation in that its elements (contiguity, succession, constant conjunction) are actually present in the objects. But the same relation is natural one in that it generates an associative connection; and when it is described from this point of view we must expect a different description of it.[9]

But this is not all. Hume has to leave it an open possibility that what is present in the phenomena, and produces the associative connection for the plain man, may not be quite what the plain man thinks it is. More precisely, what makes us associate objects with their usual effects may turn out on examination not to be bogus or illusory, but still to be misunderstood because of the very association it produces.

If this is correct, then Hume's second definition is parasitic on the first. The first will include that feature of the causal relation (that is constant conjunction) which explains the passage of the mind from the one object to the other. This will be a real feature of the object, but will not be the whole of the philosophical relation, and it will, moreover, be that part of it whose nature it is easiest for the layman to overlook and misdescribe (as power or necessity).

This helps us to understand the intent of the definitions and their relation to each other. Hume knows, and says, they are different. The second defines the way that the object of the first affects the human mind. This relationship makes it clear that Hume does not think he is proving the subjectivity of causation, but that he does think he is proving the subjectivity of necessary connection. Causation as described in the first definition would still be a recurrent feature of the world if no one could observe the world; but the additional element that observers add to their common concept of causation would not.[10]

Sufficient and necessary conditions. What I have called Definition (Ia) in the *Enquiry* is absent in the *Treatise*. The question naturally arises from this (and from the fact that the *Enquiry* argument does not prepare us for its appearance) whether Hume thought he had explained, or explained away, our common use of the word 'cause' to signify a necessary rather than a sufficient condition.

Flew and others have argued that Hume neglects the practical interest we all have when we consider causes. A cause, as Flew puts it, is a lever.[11] We search for causes so that we can change our environment. Sometimes we want to change our environment by finding sufficient conditions for the desired change to follow, and when this is so we can be said to be searching for causes in the sense Hume has defined for us. But, at least as often, we try to change our world by *preventing* unwanted features of it from continuing. It is in these contexts that we most commonly talk of searching for causes, as in our search for the cause of cancer. Here what we seek to identify is that without which the undesired effect would not occur — the necessary condition. In such circumstances it is enough, for success, to discover that without which the effect does not occur; we do not, thus far, care whether or not it follows on the cause always — it is enough if it never happens without it. So it is not part of the notion of a cause as a necessary condition that it should also be a sufficient one.[12] Hume's definitions seem not to have captured this sense of 'cause' at all. Except, of course, (I*a*).

If (I*a*) is to be taken seriously, Hume would seem, at least sometimes, to have thought his account comprehended causes as necessary conditions. Now he does seem to consider himself to have accounted for our propensity to infer causes when we encounter perceived effects, as well as our propensity to infer effects when we encounter perceived causes. In practice, however, his detailed analyses are always of our forward-looking anticipation of some effect, not of our backward-looking search for some cause. Indeed, his deflationary account of the idea of necessary connection depends on this restriction: when we ascribe power or necessity we ascribe it always and only to a cause, and never to an effect, even though we look backward for causes with just as much confidence, and just as habitually, as we look forward for effects. If Hume's account is intended to explain this confidence as well, he would need to give some account of why the temporal priority of causes makes us ascribe power to them alone, when the confidence and the habit are as fully operative when we look backward as they are when we look forward. But even if we can assume such an account to be available, it would do nothing to show that Hume's analysis could cover our thinking about necessary conditions as well as our thinking about sufficient conditions. For Hume's deflationary objective is one that makes him concentrate upon our belief that a cause guarantees its effect, and only a sufficient condition is thought to do this. Hume seems to settle the question himself, when in the first of the 'corollaries' in Section XIV he tells us that 'there is no foundation for that distinction we sometimes make betwixt efficient causes and causes *sine qua non*' (I 168/171). This seems to deny the applicability of the notion of a necessary condition altogether.

If all this is true, then the intrusion of (1a) in the *Enquiry* is an inconsistent relapse into one of the 'prejudices and popular errors' from which he is trying to rescue us.

'*Every event has a cause*.' The view that all, or some, effects have necessary conditions as well as sufficient conditions is not equivalent to the 'Causal Principle'. This tells us that everything that occurs has a sufficient condition; and it is of course consistent with this to believe that alternative sufficient conditions would do as well as the ones that we find. Hume is commonly thought to have tried to explain why we believe in the Causal Principle. But it is not discussed in the *Abstract* at all, and unless (1a) is a confused reference to it, it is absent from the *Enquiry* also. In the *Treatise* we have to turn for instruction on this difficult theme to the fascinating Section III of Part III: 'Why a Cause is Always Necessary.' In this Section Hume refutes rationalist arguments for The Causal Principle. He directly anticipates Kant's insistence that while 'Every effect has a cause' is analytic, 'Every event has a cause' is not. He tells us that the latter is neither intuitively nor demonstrably certain. The main weight of his argument rests on the claim that it is just as easy to imagine something's coming into being uncaused, as it is to imagine its being caused to come into being. He concludes by saying that our 'opinion' that every 'new production' has to have a cause must arise from experience. The quesion of how it does so, he says, is best dealt with as part of the question, 'why we conclude, that such particular causes must necessarily have such particular effects, and why we form an inference from one to another'. He says we may find the same answer will do for both.

But there is no reason to expect this. For although we may discover why we think that certain causes have to have certain effects, this is not a discovery of why we think (if we do) that every 'new production' has to have a cause. It might very well be that certain events have to have certain results, without its being the case

57

either that these results can only come about from those causes, or that they are unable to come about with no cause whatever.

There is a very common view about the history of modern philosophy, according to which Kant saw, when he woke from his dogmatic slumbers, that Hume had given an explanation of why we all think that every event has a cause, and then tried to give a better explanation that would preserve the rationality of this belief. Perhaps this is what Kant thought he saw in Hume, but Hume does not give us as much as this. What he gives us is an account of why we think that causes have to have the effects they have. This account, however successful, cannot be the same as an account of why we believe that all events have to have such causes. Hume tells us why we ascribe power or necessity to the relationship that holds between the sufficient condition of some event and that event of which it is the sufficient condition. He does not tell us why we think that any events, let alone all events, have to have such conditions.

But although Hume seems to lose sight of his stated objective of telling us why we believe the Causal Principle, he appears to lean on it himself. He leans on it explicitly in his treatment of probability. He also leans on it in the much more important discussion of liberty and necessity, where he says that apparent irregularities in human conduct are only superficial, and that our practical decisions require us to assume this.[13] So although it is no doubt fairest to think that Hume only believed himself to have explained that which he has explained, there are some grounds for thinking that the strange appearance of Definition (1*a*) reveals a tendency to assume he has explained more.

The corollaries. It would be unreasonable to overlook some of the implications that Hume draws in the *Treatise* from his examination of causation. He omits them from the *Enquiry*, but his later modesty is unjustified. For when we turn to Section XIV of Part III, where he draws out his 'corollaries', we can see that he was himself aware of the fundamental philosophical importance of his conclusions. Whatever their limitations, they do indeed have the importance he ascribes to them. We may therefore conclude by a brief examination of them. (1) *'All causes are of the same kind.'* This proclamation is the most important single event in the history of the decline of Aristotelian natural philosophy. Hume's account of causation requires that for one thing to be the effect of another it has to follow it in time, and have done so uniformly and without exception. This rules out all forms of causation except efficient causation, since material, formal, and final causes do not stand in the required temporal relationships to that which they are 'causes' of. For this to be more than a dogmatic rejection, Hume has to lean on the second of his definitions rather than the first, and say that the sequences he is prepared to classify as causal ones are the only possible sources of the idea of power or force or necessity, and that other temporal relationships, however regular, cannot generate it. So the material cause, though always present in a thing, does not precede that which it causes, and so cannot be felt to exert any power; the final cause is not properly called a cause because it comes after its effect, and any power we feel in the sequence works from earlier to later components. (2) *'The common distinction between moral and physical necessity is without any foundation in nature.'* Causation as Hume has defined it is, he proclaims, operative wherever there are sequences of events to be observed. So the minds of men are as much theatres of 'necessity' as physical nature is. The notion of necessity is here being robbed of its sting, or so Hume intends. Since necessity is only a subjective feature of the observer of sequences, its ascription to mental processes, when rightly analysed, implies no more real force or compulsion in the causes found there than it implies in those found in physical nature. (3) *'The distinction, which we often make, betwixt power and the exercise of it, is equally without foundation.'* If power is a subjective feature of our perception of sequences, it cannot be said to be present where the sequence that generates the idea of it does not actually occur. This is another facet of the rejection of Aristotelianism: the denial of real potentialities. It is a very radical doctrine, implying as it does that my car only has the power to kill someone when all other relevant factors (my driving it, its tank being full, the road being slippery) are also present, and that it is false to ascribe such power to it except when it is thus exercised. This corollary is the foundation of his denial of liberty of indifference, and his belief in the moral harmlessness of determinism. (4) *'We can never have reason to believe that any object exists, of which we cannot form an idea.'* Hume's target here is the doctrine of substance, which was thought, in most versions, to be the locus of causal powers. Hume's argument is that to claim something has causal properties is to claim it can play the role of cause in causal sequences. This entails some discernible properties other than the mere production of the effects which follow in the sequence. Both material and spiritual substance must be rejected if such independent

59

characterisations are not available. If they are available, then the causal claims made for them become empirically testable. (5) *'There are no objects which, by the mere survey, without consulting experience, we can determine to be the causes of any other; and no objects which we can certainly determine in the same manner not to be the causes.'* He puts this most succinctly in his next sentence, surely his best epigram: 'Anything may cause anything.' Comment on this is really superfluous, but it is Hume's most succinct and powerful expression of the consequence of maintaining that it is by observation alone that we can learn of the course of nature. When we think, as we are prone to think, that there are some events that intrinsically belong together, this is merely the consequence of our being accustomed to finding them conjoined. As Passmore has put it, in an epigram fit to be put beside Hume's, 'intelligibility is familiarity'.

3 Perception

In his account of causal inference Hume has tried to show how our natural belief carries us beyond the knowledge we derive from present impressions and memories; how the concept of a cause itself reflects the manner in which human nature generates such belief; and how philosophers, through overlooking its psychological mechanisms, have misrepresented the nature of our concept of causation and have managed to deceive themselves into claiming *a priori* knowledge of the physical world that is unavailable to us. A parallel pattern can be seen in his discussion of our perception of the external world. But there is one major difference. He believes in both cases that human nature provides its own antidote to scepticism and that his psychological investigations can show us what that antidote is. But in the case of causal inference, it is Hume himself who first clearly saw the sceptical danger for which the antidote is necessary. In the case of perception, his predecessors had been very forcibly shown this danger by Descartes, and their theories had been explicitly offered as intellectual defences against it. Hume is concerned to show their inadequacies, and to reveal the intellectual processes that lie behind them. Both here and in his discussion of personal identity he takes great pleasure in unravelling the confusions of those who refuse to accept that scepticism is, in its own terms, unanswerable. His prime philosophical target is the theory of representative perception, and its attendant doctrines of primary and secondary qualities, as these are known from the writings of Locke.

Hume's discussion of perception is found in the *Treatise* in Section II of Part IV of Book I. In the first *Enquiry* this is matched by a mere five pages in Section XII. A comparison of the two reveals that the psychological mechanisms that generate our common perceptual beliefs are not described in the *Enquiry* at all. Hume is content to point to their existence and to emphasise that philosophical reasoning can offer no substitute for them when sceptical doubts are raised. There is, however, no inconsistency between the stated doctrines of the two works, and in what follows I shall concentrate entirely on the text of the *Treatise*.

Perceptions, Minds and Objects

Hume's argument is tortuous. He begins by proclaiming that nature has not left it an open option for us to decide whether or not we shall believe in the existence of 'body': 'We may well ask, What causes us to believe in the existence of body? But it is in vain to ask, Whether there be body or not? That is a point which we must take for granted in all our reasonings' (I 183/187). He confines himself, therefore, to the first question. In order to answer it he divides our belief in the existence of body into two. The first is the belief that 'objects' continue to exist when they are not 'present to the senses' – the belief in continued existence. The second is the belief in distinct existence. The latter he divides again, into a belief in the spatial externality of objects, and a belief in their independence of perceivers[1] : of *these* two, he is the more concerned with the second. He holds that continued existence and distinct existence mutually imply each other, but need to be distinguished for the purposes of his genetic account of our compound belief.

He tells us brusquely that there is no third possibility: 'These are the only questions that are intelligible on the present subject. For as to the notion of external existence, *when taken for something specifically different from our perceptions*, we have already shown its absurdity' (my italics). He refers us to a much earlier passage, Section VI of Part II of Book I, which is entitled 'Of the Ideas of Existence, and of External Existence'. This reference is of great importance. Unfortunately the clarity of the earlier Section does not measure up to its importance for the understanding of the later one. Its main theme is that the idea of existence is not derived from a separable impression, and therefore to reflect on an object *as existing*, and to reflect on that object *simpliciter*, must be one and the same. He infers from this that no two objects can be the same in all respects except that of existence. He then moves to the idea of external existence, and says that similar considerations prove that we cannot have any idea of 'anything specifically different from ideas

62

and impressions', since these exhaust the contents of the mind. 'We never really advance a step beyond ourselves, nor can conceive any kind of existence, but those perceptions, which have appeared in that narrow compass.' (I 72/67—8)

Hume's chain of reasoning, and the exact nature of his conclusion, are obscure, but it is important to resolve the obscurity. One possible reading of him is that he is denying that the idea of external objects has sense. This reading is too strong, however, for his later notion of distinct existence would then seem to lose sense also. If this is not meant, then another, more innocuous, reading is suggested by his next sentence, where he explores the degree to which external objects can be thought 'specifically different from our perceptions': the reading would be that Hume considers we cannot form a clear idea of external objects unless they are thought of as possessing qualities that our perceptions have, such as size or shape. This would then be a point similar to one he makes about inferred causes, which have to be thought of as like familiar ones. This reading, however, is too weak; for Hume seems explicitly to have in mind that what we regard as having distinct existence can only *be a perception*. It is not merely that all the qualities that we can meaningfully ascribe to any subject are qualities that we can find in our impressions and therefore duplicate in our ideas; it is that only impressions and ideas, which collectively exhaust the class of perceptions, can meaningfully have any qualities ascribed to them. So it seems to be a basic premiss of Hume's later argument, not that the ascription of external existence apart from our perceiving is absurd, but rather that we can only intelligibly ascribe such external existence *to perceptions*; in this instance, of course, to impressions.

It is important to emphasise here that Hume[2] does not consider it logically absurd to suppose that a perception might exist independently of the mind which has it. He makes this quite clear at a later stage in Section II (I 200/207). The mind, he says, is nothing but 'a heap or collection of different perceptions'. Since every perception is a distinct occurrence, there is nothing absurd in supposing one such perception to exist independently of the mind; for this is merely to suppose it to exist without belonging to the collection with which it is now associated. Perceptions are what minds are made up of; but they might, in logic, exist alone and not form parts of minds. This does not show that such independence can *only* be ascribed to perceptions, but in the immediately ensuing paragraph Hume infers that if there is no absurdity in supposing perceptions to exist apart from a mind, the same must be true of objects, since an object's being present to a mind consists merely in a perception joining a group of others which constitute a mind's biography. This reasoning presupposes and reinforces Hume's earlier argument in Section VI of Part II. Between them they manifest the presupposition of Section II of Part IV: that to believe we perceive distinct and continuing objects is to believe the proposition that our perceptions have distinct and continuing existence. If these are not one and the same belief, then Hume is trying to account for the origin of a conviction that we do not hold, instead of the one that we do.

The Senses and the Reason

To return to Hume's argument. He has divided our belief in the existence of body into a belief in the continued existence of objects, and a belief in the distinct existence of objects. He next asks whether these beliefs are due to the senses, the reason, or the imagination. He makes fairly short work of the first two possibilities.

(1) (a) The senses cannot have given us the belief in continued existence, for to do this they would have had to present us with unperceived objects, which is absurd.

(b) This leaves the possibility that the senses might have given rise to the belief in distinct existence. He offers five arguments against this.

(b1) The senses only present us with perceptions, and cannot present us with the fact that they are distinct or external. The argument seems to be that the recognition that something is independent of ourselves is necessarily a *judgement*, not a *perception*. Perceptions only have sensory qualities, such as hardness or colour, not such complex relational characteristics as mind-independence.

(b2) If the senses were to present us with the data necessary to infer the independence of objects, then the senses would have to include among their data both the objects and ourselves, so that the separation between the two was sensorily obvious; and this is not what happens.

(b3) We cannot be mistaken about the nature of our impressions. All our impressions, 'passions, affections, sensations, pains, and pleasures' are 'originally on the same footing'. We do not think that our senses present us with independent existences when we have the passions. So we must be wrong if we think they do this in the case of external impressions.[3]

(*b*4) If we distinguish between the externality of objects and their independence, we may think that the former is given us in sensation by the presented contrast between our own body and things external to it in space. But 'properly speaking' we do not perceive our own bodies, but only certain perceptions, so that the externality that is required for the argument cannot be found in sensation at all.

(*b*5) There are three kinds of sensory impressions: those of primary qualities, such as shape and solidity, those of secondary qualities, such as colours and tastes, and those of the painful and pleasant organic consequences of our encounters with objects, such as the pain we feel when cut. Both philosophers and the 'vulgar' say the first have independent existence; the vulgar say the second do; no one says the third do. Yet all are equally perceptions; so the different judgements men make about each class must have their sources in something other than what the senses present.

These arguments are all highly questionable. They depend on an insistence that no opinion can arise from the senses unless it is an opinion about the presented qualities of a sensory image: an opinion about the visual features of that image if it is a visual image, an opinion about the auditory features of that image if it is an auditory image. This prevents consideration of the possibility that the senses could inform us of any fact that can only be noted by a judgement, as opposed to some ostensive device (*b*1, *b*2). It also prevents consideration of the possibility that our senses could give rise to an opinion about anything other than our sensory images themselves, such as that which they might be images *of* (*b*4). This insistence reinforces, though it does not follow from, Hume's assumption that what we believe, when we believe in the distinct existence of objects, is the distinct existence of impressions. This assumption is required for the other two arguments, (*b*3) and (*b*5), to have any tendency to show that our belief cannot arise from the senses.

(2) Hume makes even shorter work of the possibility that we owe our belief in the distinct and continued existence of objects to the reason. This would mean that we base it, soundly or not, on arguments. But the arguments that there are are known only to a few philosophers, even though the beliefs are universal. They are also bad arguments. And it is striking that the conclusions philosophers draw are not the same as the common-sense beliefs of plain folk in any case: philosophers believe in the representative nature of perception, whereas everyone else assumes that bodies are 'the very things we feel or see'. (This last phrase is critically ambiguous. Even

though men do assume that bodies are the things they feel or see, they may not, and do not, think that the things they feel or see are perceptions, or that perceptions are things.)

The Imagination: Constancy, Coherence, Identity

Since neither the senses nor the reason produce our belief in distinct and continued existence, the imagination must. 'Since all impressions are internal and perishing existences and appear as such, the notion of their distinct and continued existence must arise from a concurrence of some of their qualities with the qualities of the imagination; and since this notion does not extent to all of them, it must arise from certain qualities peculiar to some impressions' (I 188/194). This sentence makes it quite clear, again, that Hume is interpreting the belief whose origin he is trying to find as the belief that our *impressions* have a distinct and continued existence. The difficulty of understanding how we could come to have such a belief is emphasised by the stress upon the alleged fact that our impressions are not merely internal and perishing, but *appear as such*. Hume is overtly committed to the view that at some level of perceptual awareness we have, *and* know that we have, *only* internal and perishing impressions. From this we pass, somehow, to the belief that these impressions, or at least some of them, are not internal but distinct, and not perishing but continuous. The task is to explain how.

Hume contrasts this task with the one he undertook in trying to account for our belief in universal causal connections. In the case of our causal beliefs, custom makes us ascribe to unobserved phenomena the regularities we have constantly found among observed phenomena. But in our perceptual beliefs we ascribe to our perceptions two features (continuousness and distinctness) which we do not, and could not, find among them on any occasion. So custom may play a role in generating this ascription, but it must also be assisted by 'some other principles' (I 191–2/198).

This contrast does not merely make Hume's psychological task harder, however. It also implies that the belief whose origin he is seeking to explain is false. In the case of our causal beliefs, Hume can speak, however flippantly, of pre-established harmonies – for aside from the ascription of necessity, our belief that unobserved phenomena are like observed ones is a belief that, however groundless, might very well be true. But in the case of our perceptual

66

beliefs, we ascribe to our perceptions, according to Hume's analysis, features they patently do not have. So the belief in distinct and continued existence is ineradicable and untrue together.

Hume's account of its origin has consequently to be, and is, an account of how we come to overlook the internality and perishability of the impressions we have, and come to talk of them as distinct and continuing. We know we have impressions; we believe we perceive objects; how do we come to think that the impressions are objects? The entrenchment of such a belief has to come about because we deceive ourselves into overlooking those features of our impressions which stand in the way of holding what we believe.

It is often said that Hume is only drawing out rigorously the implications of the Lockean 'way of ideas' in the philosophy of perception, while being fully aware that they are intolerable. This may be so; but the moral may be that the way of ideas prevents a correct analysis of the convictions Hume considers himself to be explaining. From the fact that the vulgar believe that they feel and see objects, it does not follow that they do not distinguish their perceptions from objects. From the fact that they ascribe distinct and continued existence to what they perceive it does not follow that they ascribe such existence to their perceptions of it. And, most fundamentally, from the fact, if it is one, that they can only be said to know facts that they see or hear or otherwise perceive, it in no way follows that the facts they know must all be facts about visual or auditory or other perceptual images that they have. But all these are taken as given in what Hume now sets out to do; namely, to show how, in spite of the alleged fact that men's perceptual knowledge is confined to features of their impressions, they ascribe distinct and continued existence to those impressions and refer to them as objects.

Hume's account runs as follows. Those impressions to which we ascribe distinct and continued existence cannot be singled out for this by their involuntariness or their liveliness. For many impressions that have these features are not thought to be distinct and continuous — our pains or emotions, for example. What causes us to ascribe distinct and continued existence is a combination of two factors, *constancy* and *coherence*. Of these constancy seems to be more fundamental for Hume, but coherence more frequently influences the imagination. As Price makes clear, they are not features of individual perceptions, but of *series* of perceptions. (Hume's accounts of them frequently involve him in talking of objects rather than of impressions; of slipping, that is, into language suggesting the existence of the belief which is the product of the process he is describing. But this need not be regarded as anything worse than carelessness perhaps.)

Constancy is a feature of a series of perceptions when each member of the series is exactly like the preceding ones: when we look at a stable object like a mountain, then look away, and then look back, we get the same impressions that we got before. Coherence is a feature which a series of perceptions has when it contains alterations, but the alterations are regular and predictable. Hume's example is the perceptions I have of the fire in my room when I return from an outing: the impressions I receive on my return are not the same as the ones I received before I went out, but they can be connected to the ones I had earlier as earlier and later members of a series that I have often observed to be continuous (when I have stayed in the room in front of my fire and watched it burn down). These are the phenomena; and although we may think Hume's lapse into object-language when he gives the context of his examples is not accidental, the constancy and coherence themselves are features of the sequences of impressions.

When we ask exactly how the constancy and coherence produce the belief in distinct and continued existence, Hume's story becomes very complex. He begins with coherence. On the surface the account which he gives seems question-begging. He tells us that the coherence that our sensory impressions have is of a special kind — a kind that depends for its very existence on the supposition of the continued existence of objects. He gives two examples. (1) I am sitting in my room in a position where I do not have a view of the door, and I hear a noise like that of a door turning on its hinges. If I rely exclusively on the perceptions I have received, I will think it to be an oddity. For although in the past I have seen doors moving when I have heard that sound, this time I have not seen this, but have only heard the sound in isolation. I do not even *expect* to see the door move when I hear the sound, for I am not in a place where I can see it, so there is no question of my anticipating a later perception to follow the first one, as Hume's previous account of cause and effect might suggest. As long as we confine ourselves to actual impressions, what we have here is an isolated one that forms no part of a coherent sequence. To place it in a coherent sequence I have to suppose the continued existence of the door which I have seen on other occasions when I have heard this noise. (2) His other example is of

68

my receiving a letter, and fitting this otherwise isolated phenomenon into my previous experience by supposing the continued existence of its writer, and the sea, and the ship it came on. In both cases, he insists, the *coherence* is produced by the supposition of the continued existence of presently unperceived objects. Perhaps, then, the use of object-language here is deliberate: Hume's very point is that only on the supposition of continued existence could we even have the amount of coherence among our perceptions that we seem to ascribe to them. The question, then, is whether he is in a position to explain the belief in continued existence as due to coherence among our perceptions, when he seems to ascribe the very coherence itself to the postulation of continued existence. The answer seems to be that he wants to have it both ways; but in a not-unreasonable manner. His position seems to be (I 192/197) that we attribute continued existence to our impressions because of their coherence, but that once this habit is set up it has its own momentum, so that we reinforce it by ascribing continued existence whenever doing so will introduce more of that coherence which is its original source. Here is one of the additional principles that Hume has promised: custom or habit is not merely the cause of our belief in coherence; our attachment to habit is so great that we form beliefs in order to deepen its hold upon us.

This account tells us more about the way our belief in continued existence reinforces the role of coherence than it does about the way in which any coherence that we may find, rather than ascribe, first produces that belief. So it is not surprising that Hume is forced to put most of the weight of his account on to constancy, which becomes the primary principle in his genetic account.

His account begins with a discussion of identity. An object can be re-identified. We say, that is, that an object is something that preserves its identity through time. It is the same object now that it was at some earlier time. An assertion of this form seems to Hume a near-paradox: to identify two things seems to him to say both that there are two, and yet to deny it. There can be little doubt that his sense of paradox comes from assuming that when we re-identify an object we are saying that a perception we have now is numerically the same as a perception we had at some earlier time; and it is at least plausible that without this assumption judgements of identity would not appear paradoxical at all. But Hume considers that our very idea of identity contains within it these contrary elements of unity and number. He says that we combine them together by thinking of that which lasts through time as exhibiting unity and the times through which it lasts as exhibiting diversity. Such a delicate combination would be impossible if there were any feature in our perception of the object which could interfere with its apparent unity. Such interference would result in there being more differences than the mere differences in the times, and this would merely lead us to a point where we would have to say that we had a succession of different objects, rather than one continuing one. Such discordant features would inevitably be present if the object *changed* in any respect, or if it were *interrupted* during any of the times through which it lasted. So our paradigm of identity must be an object that lasts through time without change and without interruption. Hume is quite aware of the distinction between numerical identity, which is the idea he is trying to explain, and similarity, which he calls specific identity; but he insists that, strictly speaking, the successive stages of a thing to which we ascribe numerical identity have to be exactly like (specifically identical with) each other, and to be separated by no gaps. So invariableness and uninterruptedness are necessary conditions of numerical identity. This view has disastrous consequences when he considers personal identity, but it is put to work in equally dubious ways in his theory of perception.

It is the existence of the concept of identity that enables us to disguise from ourselves that feature of our perceptions which would otherwise prevent us from ascribing continued existence to them. This is their interruptedness. We are able to form the habit of doing this because although our perceptions are fleeting and interrupted some of them come in series in which the later ones exactly resemble the earlier ones – that is, they exhibit constancy. But a series of perceptions that displays constancy offers us one of the two conditions required for identity, namely invariance. When we experience invariance in a series of perceptions the observation of them is so like the observation of a series that is invariable and uninterrupted that we indolently allow the condition of identity that is present to lull us into ascribing the other condition that is not. We call a succession of exactly similar perceptions the same, and overlook the gaps between the members of the series. In Price's language constancy produces gap-indifference, and makes us speak of identity where there is none.[4]

The ascription of identity to a series of similar perceptions is not achieved without conflict. We realise with one half of our mind that we are denying the obvious gaps in our perceptions with the other.

70

We accordingly 'seek relief from the uneasiness'. We obtain it by giving up the unpleasant principle of gappiness in order to preserve the comforts achieved by yielding to the 'smoothness' of the resembling series. To give this up we 'suppose' that the perceptions that are invariable are also uninterrupted. We suppose them to continue when we are not having them, during the gaps. This supposition is not absurd: since all impressions are distinct from each other there is nothing absurd in supposing that one or more could continue to exist when detached from the mind it is a part of when we perceive it. Hume admits that it *looks* absurd, but insists it is not. It is this passage which makes it plausible for Price to suggest that we can use Russell's language of 'sensibilia' to describe Hume's view.

Supposition is not, however, the mere 'feigning' of the separate existence of perceptions. It requires us to *believe* in it. Its freedom from absurdity is not enough for this, and Hume needs some account of why we accept the truth of our invention. His answer is in the usual terms he uses when discussing belief. The idea of the unsensed but continuing impression can *become* a belief, or be assented to, when sufficient vivacity is communicated to it. Such vivacity is communicated to it by the impressions which we do have at the time when we have the idea. On having a desk-impression, for example, my memory of many earlier desk-impressions that resemble it, combined with the vividness of the present desk-impression, communicates vivacity and assurance to the idea I have formed of the intervening, unsensed desk-impression that fills the gap between the earlier ones I remember and the present one I am having now.

Coherence has dropped out of sight, but we may surmise that Hume considers constancy to give us the mechanism which coherence can then reinforce, and which can then reinforce coherence. So it is the imagination that introduces order into our perceptions by inventing a fiction to bolster a confusion. Hume insists throughout that once we have committed ourselves to continued existence the belief in distinct existence follows from it. (He ought of course to add that we make the necessary inference from the one to the other!)

Philosophical Theories of Perception; Primary and Secondary Qualities
Having explained the origin of the vulgar belief in the distinct and continued existence of perceptions, Hume now turns to philosophical accounts of perception. These arise, he says, because 'a very

71

little reflection and philosophy' is enough o show us that 'the doctrine of the independent existence of our sensible perceptions is contrary to the plainest experience' (I 203/210). It is not, let us emphasise again, that philosophical reflection can show this doctrine to be absurd. The arguments against it, which Hume explicitly says show it to be false, are empirical ones: that our perceptions will change with changes in our sense-organs, or with changes in our spatial relationships to objects that we perceive. (Hume seems not to see any oddity about raising these objections at this point in his argument, presumably because they are the familiar stock-in-trade of epistemological sceptics; but to use them at all is to presuppose knowledge of our physical bodies and of their spatial relationships to objects external to them. There is at least an appearance of circularity in his arguing in such a fashion.)

Faced with these allegedly devastating arguments philosophers reject the belief in distinct existence. Since this is logically tied to the belief in continued existence they should reject that also. But they do not; human nature is too much for them. Instead they introduce a distinction between perceptions and objects and claim that it is the perceptions that are interrupted and perishing, whereas the objects 'preserve a continued existence and identity'. This solution, says Hume, is only a 'palliative remedy'. On the surface this is an odd criticism, since his own account of the origins of our vulgar belief ascribes it also to a desire to alleviate an 'uneasiness'. But he means, of course, that the philosophical theory pretends to solve the problem to which it is a response, not merely divert our attention from it, and leads us very quickly into even more intractable difficulties. The theory requires us to say that objects cause perceptions, which is an opinion we could never form from observation, since, *ex hypothesi*, we never have access to the objects but only to the perceptions. The theory gets what plausibility it has from a quite different source – our prior acceptance of the vulgar theory, which it is a specious attempt to preserve. What makes us move from the vulgar theory to the philosophical is a set of reflective considerations which, if pursued to the end, should make us abandon the belief in distinct and continued existence altogether. What makes us come to rest in the philosophical theory and not pursue the consequences of our reflections to the end is our commitment to the vulgar theory, which comes not from such reflection, but from the influence of the imagination. So the philosophical theory is 'the monstrous offspring of two principles, which are contrary to each other'.

The solution, then, cannot lie in philosophy. It is able, on occasion, to disturb our tranquillity by revealing the confusions which lie at the root of our common beliefs: 'Carelessness and inattention alone can afford us any remedy. For this reason I rely entirely upon them; and take it for granted, whatever may be the reader's opinion at this present moment, that an hour hence he will be persuaded there is both an internal and an external world.' (I 209–10/218).

Hume's arguments against the philosophical theory of perception are very similar to those used earlier by Berkeley. He adds to them in Section IV of Part IV, 'Of the Modern Philosophy', where he launches a detailed attack, heavily Berkleian, against Locke's distinction between primary and secondary qualities. Primary qualities, such as solidity or motion, were alleged to be qualities that exist both in external objects and in our perceptions of them; secondary qualities, such as colours or tastes, were alleged to exist only in our perceptions but not in objects. Hume does not allude to the supposed scientific basis of this division: the primary qualities are clearly the quantitative features of our world which natural science was thought to concern itself with, and the secondary qualities those mind-dependent characteristics which elude precise quantification. Instead he stresses, as Berkeley had stressed, the perceptual inseparability of the two kinds of quality. The distinction is the result of a theory, and could not be suggested to us by empirical considerations.

Hume and Phenomenalism

Because Hume follows Berkeley in his attacks on the representative theory of perception it is tempting to see him also as a forerunner of twentieth-century Phenomenalism. While much of his psychology of perception could be pressed into the service of such a theory, the differences between it and Hume's views are greater than the likenesses.

The phenomenalist holds that statements about physical objects can be analysed into statements, or sets of statements, about sense-data Sense-data can be equated, reasonably enough, with Hume's impressions; and, like the phenomenalist, Hume rejects the philosophical view that we are entitled to believe in the separate existence of physical objects on the one hand and impressions on the other. But phenomenalists regard it as a necessary condition of a successful sense-datum analysis of physical-object statements that their truth is unaffected by the proposed translation. Hume makes no pretence of preserving it. Indeed he is at one with the representative theory in holding that our vulgar perceptual beliefs, if interpreted beliefs about our impressions, are false. His problem is to explain their hold upon us. It is of the essence of his explanation that it is an account of these features of our perceptual experience which deceive us into overlooking their manifest incompatibility with the evidence. It is also of the essence of his attack on representationalism that he agrees with its major premiss: that our perceptions do not exhibit the distinctness and continuity that we believe the objects of perception to have. Hence the constancy and coherence of our perceptions, which might well appear in a phenomenalist theory as part of the analysis of the continuity and distinctness we ascribe to perceived objects, appear in Hume's psychology as characteristics which lull us into overlooking their absence.

Where Hume agrees with phenomenalists is in assuming that the vulgar system of perception is one in which the continuity and distinctness of objects are ascribed to perceptions: that it is impressions alone that are the subject-matter of our perceptual beliefs. It is this assumption alone that makes scepticism of the senses possible in his system; for the manifest falsity of our perceptual beliefs on this interpretation is indeed something that we would need elaborate mechanisms of self-deception to conceal from ourselves.[5]

4 The Self

Hume's views on personal identity have not only left his readers dissatisfied. They failed to satisfy Hume himself. The very arguments that Hume has used to explain how we come to believe that causes necessitate their effects, or to believe that we perceive distinct and continuing objects, require him to ascribe certain habitual tendencies and purposes to the human mind; he says that we follow these tendencies, and subscribe to these purposes, to consolidate those natural beliefs about our perceived environment which would otherwise fall before the attacks of the philosophical sceptic. When he turns to examine our belief in the continuing identity of the mind itself, however, he finds it to be as vulnerable to sceptical attacks as our belief in the distinct and continued existence of material objects. But to represent our belief in the continued existence of ourselves as the product of self-deceiving fictions looks, on the face of it, like assuming and denying the belief at one and the same time. The dissatisfactions that Hume and his readers have felt have been deepened by the sense that they concern the viability of his whole epistemological procedure.

I shall attempt an outline of Hume's arguments concerning personal identity, and then offer some considerations with regard to the defects that it has, and other defects it has erroneously been thought to have.[1]

'Of Personal Identity' 'Of Personal Identity' is Section VI of Part IV of Book I of the *Treatise*. (There is no corresponding passage in the *Enquiry* at all.) It is preceded by the less interesting but important Section, 'Of the Immateriality of the Soul', in which Hume, with less subtlety, but almost as much effect, as Kant in the Paralogisms,

lambasts the pretensions of *a priori* psychology. He exposes the unintelligibility of the doctrine of mental substance, and the untenability of rationalist claims that matter cannot think or that mind cannot produce physical effects. In Section VI he gets to work on the much harder task of confronting the limits that experience places upon the extent of our self-knowledge.

They are severe ones, at least in Hume's system. For just as the philosophical doctrines of representative perception are the result of misguided attempts to justify the vulgar belief in distinct and continued existence, so empty philosophical theories of substance and inhesion are the result of a common belief that our perceptions belong to a continuing self. And just as the vulgar belief in the distinct and continued existence of our perceptions lacks justification and derives its power from sources other than reason or the senses, so our belief in personal identity is found by Hume to lack rational or observational warrant, and its strength also has to be accounted for by psychological methods.

Perceptions are distinct from one another. Hume has argued, when discussing existence, that there is no logical absurdity in supposing a perception to exist without belonging to anyone's mind. What relationship, therefore, do those perceptions that *do* belong to my mind have to one another, or to me, that justifies me in saying that they all are had by the same person? Hume has already dismissed as vacuous the metaphysical thesis that there is a spiritual substance in which they all inhere. At the outset of Section VI he dismisses a supposedly empirical version of the same theory, which he ascribes darkly to 'some philosophers': this is the claim that each of us is intimately aware in his own experience of 'what we call our *self*' — which is 'that to which our several impressions and ideas are supposed to have a reference'. The idea of such a self he declares to be without content, since no impression can be found, on introspection, from which it could be derived. When each of us looks within, he will only find thoughts and feelings and wishes; he will not find *himself* — unless perhaps Hume's own inability to find himself within is not matched in the case of the proponents of the theory.

The consequence of this failure to found the unity of a person's mind upon reason or experience is that each of us is 'nothing but a bundle or collection of different perceptions, which succeed each other with an inconceivable rapidity, and are in a perpetual flux and movement' (I 239/252). Again:

The mind is a kind of theatre, where several perceptions successively make their appearance; pass, repass, glide away, and mingle in an infinite variety of postures and situations. There is properly no simplicity in it at one time, nor identity in different, whatever natural propension we may have to imagine that simplicity and identity. The comparison of the theatre must not mislead us. They are the successive perceptions only, that constitute the mind; nor have we the most distant notion of the place where these scenes are represented, or of the materials of which it is composed. (I 239–40/253)

Our ascription of identity to the life-history of a mind is without foundation in the contents of the mind, and there is nowhere else to look in order to justify it.

We must therefore pass from the question of philosophical justification to the question of psychological origins: 'What then gives us so great a propension to ascribe an identity to these successive perceptions, and to suppose ourselves possessed of an invariable and uninterrupted existence through the whole course of our lives?' (I 240/253). It is immediately noteworthy here that Hume talks, as he did in his discussion of the ascription of distinct and continued existence, as though the entities to which identity is ascribed are *perceptions*. Since he has shown, to his satisfaction, that there is no evidence for the existence of something distinct from the perceptions, to which they belong, there is a formal consistency about his assuming here that when we ascribe identity, we must ascribe it to the perceptions themselves. But although this is consistent, it is hardly plausible. It would require far more than negative arguments to establish that when we speak of ourselves as identical through time, we are ascribing identity to the *perceptions* we have at different times. Such an ascription would be so very blatantly contrary to the facts.

Hume reinforces this error by another, far more serious, which he also imports from his discussions in Section II. This error lies within his analysis of the idea of identity, which he tells us again is the 'idea of an object that remains invariable and uninterrupted through a supposed variation of time'. If the problem is to offer an account of how we could ascribe identity, thus understood, to perceptions that 'succeed each other with an inconceivable rapidity', it is clear that the account has again to be a story about how we disguise the rapid succession from ourselves. It is such an account that Hume offers, though in very general terms.

We are able to distinguish an identical object (in his sense) from a succession of distinct but related objects: although the latter is clearly an example of diversity, the closeness of the relation between the members of the series 'facilitates the transition of the mind from one object to another, and renders its passage as smooth as if it contemplated one continued object'. We are accordingly lulled by the similarity of the experience of the two types of object(s) into thinking of the related series as one identical object. He speaks of this as a 'mistake', and an 'absurdity': but one of which we cannot rid ourselves, and which we consolidate by the invention of 'some new and unintelligible principle' such as soul, self, or substance, just as we 'feign' the continued existence of perceptions to disguise the interruptedness of our sensory experience. This last analogy suggests that Hume thinks that all men, not just philosophers, are prone to succumb to theories of substance. Even if he does not think this, it is plainly out of the question to interpret him as exempting the ordinary man from the alleged confusion between identity and succession. He tells us that the fact that philosophical fictions hover close by is a reason for not thinking of disputes about identity as harmless verbal arguments. Presumably such fictions provide the only plausible justification for a mistake that none of us wishes to admit that he makes.

In order to justify this account of the origin of our belief in identity through change, Hume thinks that all he needs to do is to show that all objects to which we ascribe identity 'without observing their invariableness and uninterruptedness' consist of a succession of 'related objects'. To show this he takes various kinds of changing thing, claiming in each case that the relation of the change that takes place to the phenomena to which it occurs is of a sort that would encourage us to overlook its occurrence and call the objects the same in spite of it. The change is, for example, small in proportion to the whole, or takes place only gradually, or leaves the function of the whole object unaffected. The same principles are at work in the case of persons; he particularly instances the relationship of resemblance that holds, he says, between earlier perceptions and the later memories of them, and the causal relationships that exist between the various perceptions that chase, draw after, and expel each other during our life-histories. The function of these relationships is to help us to ignore the reality of the successions and the differences that we experience. So the identity of persons, like the identity of all changing things, is 'fictitious'.

Hume concludes by saying that most disputes about identity are merely verbal ones. Since 'identity depends on the relations of ideas, and these relations produce identity by means of that easy transition they occasion', when these relations and the ease of transition lessen, so does the tendency to ascribe identity. His point here seems to be that in the history of all entities there comes a time when we are more affected by the differences between the perceptions we have now and the ones we had before than we are by the similarities between them, so our tendency to overlook the numerical diversity of our perceptions is at last arrested, though not removed altogether. Disputes about whether we have the same thing or not then become merely verbal ones. (Is the house still there when the roof blows off, or the car still there without its wheels?) Such disputes are of no consequence, unless they tempt us to resort to metaphysical principles to reinforce the answer that we give.

This last does not of course mean that Hume considers us to be justified in ascribing unity to changing objects *before* we encounter a reluctance to do so. It is just that the barriers we have erected to the recognition of change eventually begin to wear thin, even without the aid of philosophy. The only standard of identity that Hume admits is violated at *all* stages.

Identity, Diversity and Perceptions

Hume has argued two things: (1) our belief that the mind has identity is a mistaken belief. In fact it is a mere bundle or collection of *different* perceptions between which there is no real bond. Philosophical attempts to justify our belief by inventing a substance or self which would provide such a unity are understandable consequences of a recognition of its absence, but are either unintelligible, or have no basis in the evidence of introspection. (2) Our belief, though false, can be accounted for as the result of a confused manner of apprehending and reflecting upon the perceptions that we have. Since they resemble one another, and are at times causally related to one another, we overlook their numerical diversity and ascribe identity to them when it does not exist. There are limits to this gullibility, but they are merely limits on our ability to be lulled by these relationships into overlooking the diversity in our perceptions. It is essential to recognise that Hume does not think that the associative connections of resemblance and causation

79

constitute real bonds among the perceptions that they connect. They merely provide an explanation of our *overlooking* the numerical distinctness of those perceptions from one another; they do not *remove* this numerical distinctness. (Presumably a real bond between them would do just this; in which case it is not surprising that Hume does not tell us what a real bond might be like, and seems content to agree with his metaphysical opponents that the absence of one is enough to falsify our belief in personal identity.)

Fortunately the reasons that Hume offers for the falsity of our belief in personal identity are confused in themselves and inadequate for their conclusion. Many of the factors he subsequently offers as causes of our holding this belief are misunderstood because of the mistaken use to which he has put them. This is partially concealed by the fact that, in a manner reminiscent of his treatment of our belief in the external world, he sometimes speaks as the Section proceeds as though the belief whose origin he is explaining is one which is in fact true.

Hume's fundamental error is his assertion that the idea of identity is the idea of an object that persists without changing. There is a sense of 'same' or 'identical' in which we do require an object to which it is applied to remain unchanged: this is the sense which he himself refers to as the specific sense of these words. If two things are said to be identical in the specific sense they are said to be exactly alike in some respects: a sort of sameness which does not negate, but rather requires numerical diversity. If one object is said to be the same in this specific sense it is said to be unchanged at one time from what it was at another time. Specific sameness in one and the same object does indeed *mean* unchangedness, at least in one or more respects. This sort of sameness is distinct, however, from numerical sameness. The numerical sameness of an object through time does not entail the specific sameness of that object at an earlier time and at a later time, any more than the specific sameness of two objects at one time entails their numerical identity at that time.

Numerical identity does entail specific identity in *some* cases, however. Among these cases, catastrophically for Hume's understanding of these themes, are many *perceptions*. If a sensory impression, or an image, changes its character, we would usually say it is another one, rather than say it is the same one altered. If the sound or scent or memory-image I have changes, then it is succeeded by another. At least it is natural to say so, even if it is not necessary. So if we assume, with Hume, that when we ascribe identity to the mind we are ascribing identity to the perceptions it has, it is clear that our ascription is absurd, and elaborate devices would indeed be necessary for us to continue it in the face of such an obstacle.

In fact, however, this assumption is false, and no absurdity is present in our ascription. When giving his account of our alleged confusion between identity and diversity, Hume abandons the terminology of perceptions, and talks instead of 'objects'. It is indeed true that there is as sharp a contrast as there can be between an invariable and uninterrupted object, and a succession of distinct but related objects — but only if the same *sorts* of object are in question on both occasions. Yet if they are, there could be no possible confusion. We do not, and we could not, confuse an invariable and uninterrupted note with a succession of distinct but related notes. But we could, unconfusedly, say that a succession of such notes constituted one continuing tune. We do not, and we could not, confuse an invariable and uninterrupted perception with a succession of distinct but related perceptions. But we could, unconfusedly, say that a succession of such perceptions constituted one continuing mind.

Our language is full of class-terms which are applied to a succession of object-stages whose distinctions and difference are quite open to us and do not prevent us from ascribing identity to their totality.

When we do this, however, we do it because of the relations between the items that form the time-stages of the whole continuing object. A wholly heterogeneous succession of items would not have identity ascribed to it. On Hume's 'strict' view, the relationship we discern between the successive parts of changing things are relationships which enable us to overlook their diversity and ascribe identity to them where there is none really present. What he should have said is that the relationships we discern between the successive parts of the changing things are the relationships which ground our ascription of identity to the temporally continuous wholes to which they belong — or, in contemporary philosophical parlance, they are the relationships which supply our criteria of identity for continuing objects of those kinds. Hume has located these relationships as accurately as one could reasonably expect in a very general survey — resemblance, gradualness of alteration, causal interrelatedness, conspiracy to a common end. But he has failed to see that they can constitute real bonds between the parts of things, and has been forced by his misunderstanding of the concept of identity to class them as factors which distract us from the numerical diversity of those parts, which they do not do.

When this is recognised, some at least of Hume's perplexity about personal identity can be seen to be groundless. Our mental history, he says, is a mere bundle, to the parts of which we mistakenly ascribe unity because of the resemblance and causation between them. But these relationships do not distract us, as he claims, from the diversity of the perceptions we have. They may, instead, be adequate grounds for saying that these constitute the life-history of one person, or at least of one *mind*. Hume may have found the relationships that ground our ascription of identity, even while misdescribing their function. Certainly he has done nothing to show that the relationships between our perceptions are not the real bonds that would justify it.[2] For the absurdity that he thinks these relationships obscure from us is one that none of us commits. There is no demonstrated occasion for the scepticism for which he claims our carelessness and inattention are the cure.

In short, Hume says that the identity of a person is not something that really belongs to the perceptions that make up his mental history, but something that we attribute to them because of the union of their ideas in the imagination when we reflect on them. We read it into the phenomena without warrant from them. But he supports this contention by representing the ascription of unity as the ascription to the variety of mental phenomena of an invariance that fits a paradigm of identity which is conceptually mistaken. It is one, ironically, which he shares with his philosophical opponents. In adopting it he credits a strict accuracy to the sceptic which belongs, for once, to the ordinary language-user.

Mental Unity and Individuation

So far I have argued that Hume's perplexity about personal identity derives in part from a mistaken interpretation of identity in general. Hume has also been subjected to many criticisms for alleged defects and incoherences in his theory as an account of the identity of *persons*. Some of these may well have been at the root of his own dissatisfactions with his theory, and they need to be considered before it is possible to decide how far his difficulties about the self are of fundamental importance in his philosophical system.

Persons and minds. The question that Hume addresses himself to in Section VI is a question about the unity that he thinks we ascribe to a succession of perceptions. Although he writes as though this is a question about the unity of persons, it is really more restricted than this: it is a question about the unity of *minds*. This restrictedness is of great importance. For one thing, the 'inconceivable rapidity' with which our perceptions change is not matched by the changes in our bodies, so the heterogeneity that strikes Hume as an obstacle that our ascription of identity has to overcome, is much exaggerated when we consider only that part of us which we can find when we look within, and ignore that physical part of us that can be discerned from without. For another, if one holds that the discernment of common relationships between our perceptions is, in whatever manner, a necessary condition of ascribing them all to one person, it is at least possible that their common connection with one continuing body is the only relationship many of them have to one another. But to press this difficulty further is to attack Hume from the standpoint of another theory, rather than to uncover internal difficulties in his. In spite of Hume's Cartesian identification of a person with his mind, I shall proceed as though what is at issue is merely the viability of Hume's account of our belief in the unity of the mind alone.

Identity and individuation. This very concession seems to sharpen another difficulty. For if we allow Hume to ignore the role played in our judgements of identity by our awareness of human bodies, it looks as though Hume has no way of individuating minds from one another. He cannot, it appears, answer the question: 'How do I distinguish the series of perceptions that constitute *my* mind from the series of perceptions that constitutes *your* mind?' For we seem to distinguish ourselves from each other through our perceptual capacity to distinguish between human bodies. Worse still, when he raises his puzzle about our judgements of our own identity, does he not presuppose the very discrimination that he now has no way of explaining? How can he raise the question he raises about the unity each of us ascribes to his own mental history without assuming some way of distinguishing between one mental history and another?[3]

To assess this criticism we must first note that the question Hume poses is not itself the question about individuation just mentioned. The question he raises is rather, 'What makes me think that I am entitled to ascribe unity to the perceptions that make up my mental history?' This looks quite distinct. The difficulty is whether or not it can coherently be raised without there first being some answer to the problem of individuation. We must also note that there is a certain oddity about the problem of individuation: as I have formulated it, it suggests that each of us is presented with a large number of perceptions, some of which are his own and some of which are not, and has the task of deciding which is which. This is clearly absurd, and Hume is innocent of supposing it otherwise. What he seems to suppose is rather that I am presented with a series of perceptions, and then perform two tasks. One is the imaginative construction of a world of distinct and continuing physical objects. The other is the generation of a firmly entrenched ascription of unity to the total sequence of perceptions out of which the world of physical objects has been constructed. Hume does not raise the question of how we generate the belief in a community of perceivers. No doubt he should have done so; but not to raise a question is not to presuppose an answer to it which is inconsistent with those questions that one does try to answer. Had Hume raised this question I suspect that he would have claimed that the generation of the belief in other perceivers is an extension of the construction of the external world, and would have suggested that we are aware of the mental lives of others by inference from our supposed perception of the behaviour of their bodies. (This is indeed what he seems to presuppose in his account of the knowledge we have of the feelings of others in the mechanism of sympathy.) If this speculation is sound, it would mean that the generation of the belief in the existence of other selves would be subsequent to the generation of the belief in the unity of one's own self and the belief in the existence of external objects, and is not presupposed by either.[4]

Self-identity and self-awareness. The most fundamental criticism of Hume's Section, however, is one which raises the possibility that his whole philosophical method may founder when it is applied to our self-knowledge. It has been suggested that Hume cannot use his usual technique of psychological explanation when what is to be explained is the belief in the identity of the mind. For in order to show how this belief comes about, Hume has to tell us how it feels to perceive one sort of sequence of impressions, and how it feels to perceive another sort, and how the perception of the one can be confused with the perception of the other. Such a story can only be true, it is said, *if there is something* that perceives the differing sequences and can notice that they seem the same, or fail to notice that they differ. And does this not presuppose the actual existence of the very self-identity that he claims to expose as the fictitious product of the process he is describing? How can a mere series of discrete perceptions make judgements, even erroneous ones, about its own contents? This criticism, if it can be sustained, is one that strikes at the procedure Hume follows to answer the question that he does raise, and does not depend upon foisting upon him some answer to a question with which he does not concern himself.[5]

We can dismiss the suggestion that Hume is committed by his procedure to the existence of the substantial self of his opponents. That could only be shown if it could be proved that only a self of that kind could perform the functions that Hume has to ascribe to us. We must also put aside the tempting suggestion that we can assist Hume here by supposing him to be giving a logical analysis of our talk about minds, and not to be offering a piece of psychology.[6] That interpretation fails in the face of the fact that Hume considers himself to be explaining a false belief, whereas the statements about individual perceptions into which a reductive analysis would translate such a belief would presumably be true ones. We are still left with the awkward fact that Hume's account hinges on the way the sequences of our perceptions *seem* to us: upon the existence of apprehensions, or misapprehensions, of the sequences that we have. These apprehensions at least must exist, in addition to the sequences apprehended. In admitting this, are we admitting that the mind has to be the sort of unitary entity that Hume denies it to be?

There is an unwelcome element of speculation in any answer. But an answer of sorts is available. It is available if one recalls that Hume tells us that the mind is nothing but a bundle or collection of perceptions; so that any apprehensions of the kind Hume's account needs will have, in their turn, to be (or to be, *strictly speaking*) merely additional perceptions in the bundle. So Hume's psychological task becomes that of showing how it is that the sequence of perceptions that I have comes to include within it mistaken judgements about a supposed unity that the series possesses. This task he attempts to fulfil by claiming that such mistaken-judgement perceptions are the outcome of other perceptions in the series, which are in their turn mistaken apprehensions of the nature of other sequences, that is apprehensions of them as identical when they are diverse. No doubt in offering such an account Hume would fall into the trap of using common forms of speech that embody convictions that he questions; but this could be construed as mere carelessness. Strictly speaking, it is individual perceptions which are the units of mental activity that generate the fiction of mental unity — and also, of course, the fictions of the distinct and

85

continued existence of those objects that we consider some of our perceptions to be perceptions *of*.

It seems to me that Hume's procedure, if not all his language, is fully consistent with this reading of Section VI. If so, it would seem to provide a plausible defence of that Section against the criticism that in order to carry out genetic psychology he has to assume the truth of the very beliefs he considers to be false. For on this account, the series of perceptions that I have neither is, nor includes, anything other than atomic perceptions themselves.

If this is Hume's programme, it still runs into an objection. In order to evade the criticism that Hume ascribes mental acts such as apprehensions and misapprehensions to an entity that has a kind of unity he denies the human mind to have, it is necessary to say that mental activities can be ascribed to perceptions; or, more exactly, that they *are* perceptions. It is a matter of considerable difficulty to decide whether or not such a claim is intelligible. Those who have felt that Hume must presuppose a continuing mind when he tells us why we believe in one, have presumably felt that it makes no clear sense to talk of individual apprehensions and misapprehensions, or of such mental acts as simply being impressions or ideas. There seems no doubt that in order to evade their criticism, Hume's theory has to be expressed in a manner that clearly commits him to this, even though his theory is designed to account for the fact that our common-sense convictions ascribe such mental acts to continuing minds. I rest content here with the insistence that Hume can only be shown to be guilty of incoherence on this matter if it can be shown that the ascription of mental acts to perceptions is unintelligible.

The self and the passions. In Section VI Hume makes a distinction between 'personal identity as it regards the thought or imagination, and personal identity as it regards the passions, or the concern we take in ourselves'. Although he makes little use of this distinction in Book I, the idea of the self is prominent in two important ways in Book II of the *Treatise*, where he analyses the passions.[7]

The first place where the idea of the self attains prominence in Hume's treatment of the passions is in his account of the origins of the indirect passions of pride and humility. Pride is that emotion which results when some agreeable fact does not merely give me pleasure, but is connected with myself. Humility results when some disagreeable fact does not merely displease me, but is connected with myself. Hume says that the self is the *object* of these emotions.

However this doctrine is to be interpreted in detail, it is clear that he holds the idea of oneself to be an indispensable ingredient in the associative process that gives rise to these two emotions. The second place where the idea of oneself is important is in the account of the mechanism of sympathy. When this operates I become affected myself by an emotion that another person has. This happens when my recognition that he has some emotion is turned into a parallel emotional state in me. This comes about because the idea which I have of the other's passion is enlivened until it has the vivacity of an impression. What enlivens it in this way is, surprisingly, the idea of the self. Hume seems to be drawing our attention here to the fact that emotions are contagious because of our capacity to understand that others feeling them are like ourselves — a capacity which he says can be greatly increased when they have other connections with us such as blood relationships.

It has been suggested that in Book II Hume makes use of the idea of the self in ways that are inconsistent with what he says about it in Section IV of Book I. The alleged differences have even been thought to lend weight to the view that Book II was composed first.[8] There is no doubt that Hume's language in Book II does not reflect the caution that one might expect: he even goes as far as to refer to 'the idea, or rather impression, of ourselves' (II 41/317), which would lend credence to the view that he is proceeding as though he thinks that we have the very impression of a pure ego that he begins Section VI by denying. But whatever such slips may indicate about Hume's manner of composing the *Treatise*, his theories in Book II do not commit him to the denial of what he has said in Book I. Aside from the phrase just quoted, there is no evidence whatever that when Hume speaks of the idea of the self in Book II he means the idea of a pure ego or spiritual substance. Indeed there is very definite contrary evidence. When he defines the object of pride and humility, he says it is 'self, or that succession of related ideas and impressions, of which we have an intimate memory and conciousness' (II 5/277). What Hume needs to be able to use in the accounts of the indirect passions and the mechanism of sympathy is primarily the idea of oneself as distinct from others. This means that Hume has to take for granted that there is some answer to the problem of individuation. He has not supplied such an answer, but his failure to do so merely leaves a gap in his system, and does not reveal any inconsistency within it. His theories seem quite consistent with the sort of account of the origin of the distinction between one mind and another that I have earlier suggested his discussions in Book I would permit him to construct.

But it would be misleading to pretend that Hume's psychology of the emotions has need of no more than the ability to distinguish between one person's present state of mind and another's. For we can be proud or humble about our pasts and our futures, as well as about our presents; and the complex associative processes that he describes when he gives the histories of our emotions require the ascription of their successive parts, at least in normal speech, to one and the same sentient mind. So his theory of the emotions involves him in ascribing unity through time to the beings which have them. But this is at most merely one instance of Hume's taking for granted in another place the propriety and correctness of a belief that he has previously argued to be baseless but has also insisted is ineradicable. As a piece of psychology the account of the passions merely requires him to show that we use the idea of the self, not to show it is epistemologically sound for us to do so. And even if it required more, we have seen that Hume's arguments for its baselessness are mistaken.

Hume is forced by his mistaken analysis of our concept of identity to interpret all ascription of identity to changing things as a mistaken ascription, and to regard the relationships that occasion it as distractions which make us overlook the diversity of their successive stages. He accordingly considers our belief in the unity of the self to be a commitment to a fiction. It is hardly surprising that he adopts the alleged fiction himself when describing the role which the idea of oneself has in our emotional life – indeed, throughout his account of human nature in all its aspects. But it is not clear that his strict view is one that cannot be stated without incoherence. I have tried to indicate the forms that attempts to adhere to it in detail might take. These are unappetising primarily because the belief he attacks is not false; or at least it is not shown to be by the analysis of identity he chooses to adopt. There are more inspiring tasks than that of demonstrating the inner coherence of view there is every reason to consider untrue. But it is only just to convict a philosopher of confusions he actually commits.

5 The Passions

Hume's Method of Analysis

Everyone who has heard of Hume knows that he says reason is, and ought only to be, the slave of the passions. When this statement is so famous, it is a pity that so little attention is usually paid by Hume's readers to his detailed account of the passions in the second Book of the *Treatise*. It is admittedly tedious reading after what has preceded it, mainly because of the prominence in it of his associationist mechanics. But their very prominence is a sign that their inventor thinks he is displaying the constructive power of his psychological system; and an understanding of his account of the passions is essential for a grasp of the moral theory of Book III.

The very fact that it is intended as a psychological disquisition has led some scholars who have examined Book II to dismiss it as confused, since it has seemed to them what Hume is in fact engaged in is not psychological exploration, but conceptual analysis.[1] This criticism is sometimes sound. But here, as elsewhere, Hume proceeds very self-consciously, and if he treats a question as a psychological one when others would not so treat it, he does so by deliberate choice. In several places in Book II he explicitly rejects suggestions which, if followed, would shift the analysis from the psychological to the conceptual plane.[2] It is a healthy exercise for those of us who have opposite instincts to follow his account in detail.

In analysing the passions Hume is concerned with three questions, even though he does not list them separately. In the case of any passion that he treats, he is concerned to know (1) what its nature is, (2) how it arises in us, and (3) how it affects our mental lives and our conduct. A contemporary philosopher might think that the first question is not clearly distinguishable from the other two: that, for

89

example, it would be logically incorrect to say that someone loved another unless this were manifested in certain ways. Hume explicitly disagrees with this position. He insists that the passion *causes* its manifestations, and that the relationship between the cause and its effects is here, as elsewhere, a contingent one. This of course entails that a passion be recognisable independent of its usual results, and can occur without them, so that our first question must have an answer that is independent of that given to the third. Passions also have a distinctness from their causes that parallels their distinctness from their effects. It is therefore unsurprising to find Hume saying that every passion is a unique simple impression. Those who deny one can understand the nature of a passion without knowing its usual origins or manifestations are tempted also to deny that there are such independently identifiable inner states, or that their occurrence is necessary for the occurrence of the passion. But neither view follows. Even if an anger-feeling cannot be the whole of anger, this does not show it does not occur, or even that it is not essential. It is certainly important if the feeling is not enough alone; for if it is not, then even though the feeling should occur without its usual causes or results, we could not say correctly that the man who felt it was angry. But if its occurrence is necessary to anger, the analysis of that passion will have to involve both causal and conceptual analysis, since certain causal sequences will be necessary conditions of the application of the name of the emotion. So Hume's psychological enquiry could still form a part of a conceptual one, and need not be replaced by it. That something accessible only to the person himself *cannot* be a necessary condition for the application of a psychological description is a fashionable dogma that is at least as open to question as Hume's assumption that it must be.

Hume's understanding of his investigation does, nevertheless, have one deep difficulty. His doctrine that passions are impressions does not seem to allow us to apply the distinction between *feeling* and *being* to them. We do sometimes want to ascribe a passion to someone when he does not feel it, or to refrain from ascribing it to him even though he has the appropriate feelings. Hume's doctrine does not seem to allow for either, except perhaps in the case of a man who has one passion and mistakes it for another. It might be possible to preserve the distinction we need by reference to having the appropriate feeling by itself, and having it together with its usual causes or results: at least this would offer some framework to preserve it. But it cannot be preserved at all if the occurrence of the feeling is all that the passion consists of. For then the question whether someone has the passion and the question whether he has the feeling would be the same question, and they are not.

The Passions as Simple Impressions: Calmness and Violence, Strength and Weakness

Hume holds that every passion is a simple impression. This sounds like a depressingly Butlerian thesis, that every passion is what it is and not another passion. Hume does to a large degree believe this, but it is not as tongue-tying a thesis as it may seem. He clearly thinks that we can only know the meaning of the names of the various emotions by experiencing the impressions themselves, and that each is unique, much as the impressions of the colours are. But he does not take this as precluding all description of particular passions, any more than he draws the parallel conclusion about the colours. He clearly thinks the passions can be compared with one another, since he accounts for their genesis in terms of the association of impressions, which depends on similarity. So he has to consider it possible that one passion is in itself like or unlike another, apart from their respective causes or results. While this may be less plausible than Hume thinks, it is not obviously absurd. When he says, for example, that grief and disappointment lead to anger, anger to envy, envy to malice, and malice to grief again, 'till the whole circle be completed' (II 10/283), it is not absurd to suggest that this happens because each member of the circle feels at least a little like the ones each side of it. So although the simplicity of the impressions precludes their analysis, it does not make it impossible to make at least crude comparisons between them. In addition to this intrinsic sort of comparison Hume holds that passions resemble each other in being pleasant or unpleasant, even suggesting sometimes that this is their sole mode of similarity. He never attempts any analysis of this; his occasional use of 'pleasant sensation' to mean 'pleasure' suggests pleasure and passions must be distinct, but he writes at other times as though pleasure and pain are non-separable tonal features of the emotional impressions themselves.

There is another, more important, way in which we can qualify the ascription of a passion to someone, without commenting on its circumstances. We can distinguish different degrees of *intensity* within it (II 4/276). It can be so 'soft' as to 'become in a manner imperceptible', even though the word 'passion' tends to call to mind very intense emotional disturbances. Hume says that this usage reflects a 'vulgar and specious division', which hides the fact that one and the same emotional experience can be either intense or mild. This capacity for variation is the basis for Hume's critical distinction between *calm* and *violent* passions. A calm passion is one that is usually (though not necessarily) mild in its felt emotional quality; a violent passion is one that is usually (though not necessarily) intense in its felt emotional quality. Although Parts I and II of Book II are about violent passions (Pride, Humility, Love, Hatred) the concept of a calm passion is essential to Hume's theory of human motives.[3] His assaults on rationalist theories of conduct rely critically on the claim that we are motivated, indeed exclusively motivated, by passion, even if we pride ourselves on thinking otherwise. The main reason we are inclined to think otherwise is that we assume that if a passion were strong enough to lead to action it would register as having a high degree of intensity, and we often manage to exercise moral choice without this happening, or even to exercise it in the face of contrary passions. But this assumption confuses the strength or weakness of a passion, which is a matter of its capacity to affect our thought or action, with its intensity or mildness, which is a matter of its felt emotional quality (II 130/419). When this confusion is made, we are apt to think that something other than passion, namely reason, is determining our action, simply because we see it has not been determined by a violent passion. In fact, says Hume, it has been determined by a calm one.

For this distinction to be successful, Hume has to be right in insisting that an emotion's felt intensity is logically independent of the emotion's effects. To test this we have to look at the cases he uses the distinction to interpret. These fall into two classes. The first class contains those cases where we act in the absence of any intense emotion. Hume's interpretation here involves an extension of the word 'passion' (which can be seen if we reflect that the phrase 'calm passion' is slightly paradoxical); against this disadvantage we have his arguments that no alternative motivating forces can be responsible. I must defer comment on these until we reach his discussion of reason and the will. The second class contains those cases where we act contrary to some intense emotion. The difficulty here is that one of the criteria we use for determining the intensity of an emotion is the degree of difficulty we have in suppressing its manifestation. Emotions are like pains in this respect: we seem to make a necessary connection between their intensity and what he calls their strength. In his favour, however, is the fact that we also wish to hold that men vary in their capacity to resist passions as well as in the intensity with which they feel them – though of course we express this in terms of their varying strengths of will.

As examples of calm passions Hume mentions benevolence, resentment, the love of life, kindness to children, the general appetite to good and aversion to evil (II 129/417), the sense of beauty and deformity in action, composition and external objects (II 4/276), and moral approval and disapproval.[4] Examples of violent passions are desire, aversion, joy, grief, hope, fear, despair and security, (II 4/277; also II 148/439), pride, humility, love, hatred, ambition, vanity, envy, pity, malice, generosity 'with their dependents' (II 4/277), the desire of punishment to our enemies and of happiness to our friends, hunger, lust and 'a few other bodily appetites' (II 149/439). The mixed character of this list illustrates the catholicity not only of Hume's concept of passion, but of the distinction between the calm and the violent within them. We can therefore illustrate previous comments from the above list. (1) A normally calm passion can be violent on occasion, as when the 'sense of beauty and deformity' turns into 'the raptures of poetry and music' (II 5/276). (2) A normally violent passion can be calm. An example Árdal quotes is that of a 'calm anger or hatred' (*Letters* I 19, 46; Árdal p. 95). (3) The moral sentiments of approval and disapproval are, if Árdal is right, calm passions, but like the sense of beauty and deformity they can presumably become violent, as when a man burns with moral indignation (my example). (4) When we say that 'reason' has overridden a passion, especially a violent one, we are misdescribing an occasion when a calm passion is showing its strength. The passion in question is presumably the 'general appetite to good and aversion to evil', or prudence (III 279/583).

The Causes of the Passions: Direct and Indirect Passions, Sympathy and Comparison

I turn now to the second theme in Hume's analysis of the passions, that of their causes. When we reflect that passions can cause one another, it becomes clear that this question cannot be separated from that of the effects of the passions without some artificiality.

It is as a contribution to the account of the origin of the passions that we have to understand Hume's divisions between *direct and indirect passions*. His classification is not wholly clear, since he uses the term 'direct' in two slightly differing ways (II 4/276; 148/439). When he first introduces it in Section I of Part I he says the direct passions 'arise immediately from good or evil, pain or pleasure', whereas indirect passions are 'such as proceed from the same principles, but by the conjunction of other qualities'. But in the Section 'Of the Direct Passions' he adds that 'Besides good and evil, or, in other words, pain and pleasure, the direct passions frequently arise from a natural impulse or instinct which is perfectly unaccountable'. This sentence does not, in the absence of other evidence, mean that pleasure and pain are themselves passions, though if not they are presumably still impressions; but it does make clear that some passions are not merely direct in being aroused without 'other qualities', but can be aroused without pain or pleasure either. Kemp Smith, and Árdal following him, call this group primary passions. They seem to include the desire of punishment to our enemies and happiness to our friends, hunger, lust, 'and a few other bodily appetites' (149/439); and another list yields benevolence and resentment, the love of life, and kindness to children, these also being said by Hume to be calm passions. These lists include some very important determinants of conduct, especially if we add to the latter list of primary passions 'the general appetite to good and aversion to evil, considered merely as such' (129/417) – which I have some inclination to do, in spite of Árdal's comments. Most or all of these items are inclinations or desires. Hume is clearly applying here his basic principle that one must accept, and not insist on trying to explain, the correlations one finds in nature. But he is doing more than this. He is suggesting that the unaccountability of the primary passions is of a sort that those arising from pleasure and pain do not show. A hint seems to be given when he says that the primary passions 'produce good and evil, and do not proceed from them, like the other affections' (149/439). This suggests that the pleasures and pains involved are merely anticipated ones, and not present ones. But this does not seem enough to distinguish them from the other direct passions, which include desire, aversion, joy, grief, hope and fear and are said to arise, at least often, from future pleasures or pains 'conceived merely in idea', which must refer to the pleasures of anticipation. Hume just might mean that the primary passions can be aroused by the presence or prospect of that which they are impulses towards or away from, without this presence or prospect having to register itself as pleasant or painful; but the text does not really support this. The theoretical purpose of the separation of the primary passions is probably to reinforce Hume's conviction that psychological hedonism and psychological egoism are false. The falsity of the first would be proved by the insistence that the primary passions can produce pleasure, but are not generated by it; the falsity of the second would be proved by the inclusion of benevolence. But the difficulty of providing a causal differentiation of the primary passions from the other direct ones remains when Hume extends his theory that pleasure and pain cause emotions to cover all intentions to seek future goods. This makes some of the primary passions as dependent on pleasure and pain as the other direct ones. I will comment on this in my general comments at the end of the chapter.

Primary passions aside, the *direct passions* are aroused by pain and pleasure, which here must mean perceived things or events that are painful or pleasant, or the ideas of their past, present, or even future occurrence.[5] Hume lists desire, joy, hope, and security on the pleasant side, aversion, grief, fear and despair on the other. Their arousal, he says, being due to (another) 'original instinct' (II 148/438) does not 'merit our particular attention' (II 149/439). He does, however, spend about eight pages of Section IX of Part III in unhurried speculation on the genesis of hope and fear. This is as good an example as any other of the rather creaky mechanics he employs to fill out his genetic explanations. He sees that joy and grief are occasioned not only by past or present pleasures and pains, but also, at times, by anticipated ones – only, however, when these are judged to be certain. He cannot simply say that joy and grief are caused by past and present pleasures, and hope and fear by future ones. He has to enquire why future pleasures and pains that are thought to be certain cause joy and grief, whereas those that are merely possible or probable produce hope and fear. His answer is that when faced with uncertainty the understanding fluctuates between accepting and rejecting the future existence of the object; in so fluctuating it causes the mind to fluctuate between the attendant passions of joy and grief. These do not each vanish at the onset of the other (since the passions are more 'slow and restive' than the understanding is), nor cancel one another out to yield a passionless equilibrium (as they would if the object contained an even mixture of good and evil features, expected with equal confidence); instead they mingle. The resulting mixture is either hope or fear, depending on the relative dominance of joy and grief. If the probability gives way to certainty, then the mixture gives place to one of the constituent passions in its pure form. There are apparent counter-examples: for instance, where men still fear calamities they regard as certain. Hume insists that in this case the presence of fear rather than grief is the result of the fact that the certainty of the calamity is rejected by the understanding: men deceive themselves into thinking of the calamity as merely probable (II 153—4 445). This move unfortunately explains the fear as being due to the self-deception, and reverses the common and more plausible view that the self-deception is due to the fear. It is also clear from this account that in order to head off the suggestion that the nature of the expectation is an integral part of the passion, Hume has had to compromise his claim that the passions are simple impressions: it is hard to see how hope and fear, if they are mixtures of joy and grief, can also be simple, any more than the mixture of oil and vinegar with which he compares them can be a simple liquid.

Hume says far more about the aetiology of the *indirect passions*, which occupy him in Parts I and II of Book II, concerned respectively with Pride and Humility, and Love and Hatred, and subsidiary passions (or 'dependents' as he calls them). It is in these accounts that he distinguishes between the *causes* of emotions and their *objects*, and introduces the two principles of *sympathy* and *comparison*.

The distinction between the cause of an emotion and its object is introduced at the outset of the account of pride and humility (II 5/277). It is important, especially if one is criticising Hume, not to read what he says anachronistically. A distinction between the same terms is now a commonplace in the discussion of emotions, even though its exact nature and the extent of its utility are in dispute. On the surface it is made now much in the way Hume appears to make it: 'With regard to all these passions, the causes are what excite the emotion; the object is what the mind directs its view to when the emotion is excited' (*DP*. 144). This looks very much like the distinction between what brings about (say) my anger or delight, and what I am angry or delighted with, or at, or about. But it is not the same. There are two main reasons why the distinction is used by contemporary philosophers. First, it is common to hold that a person must, in logic, be aware of that at which he is angry or delighted, whereas he can be wholly ignorant of what *causes* him to feel the anger or delight — as when he complains about a misplaced comma because he is liverish. Second, the object of the emotion may not in fact exist, as when I am angry at the insult contained in a statement that was never actually made; in such cases it is still said to be the object of the emotion in spite of its non-existence, since the emotion is unintelligible without the mention of it. In consequence the objects of emotions are sometimes called intensional objects; these have, it is said, to be distinguished from causes, which cannot not-exist.

Neither of these considerations are offered by Hume when he makes his distinction; for both are irrelevant to it. To Hume the passions are *secondary impressions*: 'arising either from the original impressions, or from their ideas' (II 3/276). Whatever problems there may be in defining the originality of the original impressions, there is no doubt that Hume thinks the secondary ones are caused by them or by the ideas they give rise to. Hence the causes of passions are all *mental* causes, a point which should not vanish from sight even in those contexts where the physical reality of the external world is taken for granted, as it is in Book II. So he would not include unknown physical causes among the origins of the passions; and even though he occasionally speaks as though one can have an impression without being aware of it, this is not his standard view, and is not appealed to or presupposed when he separates causes from objects. This separation is expressed in the *Treatise* in a way that makes its purely psychological character obvious: it is a distinction 'betwixt *that idea* which excites them, and that to which they direct their view when excited' (II 6/278; my italics). It is implausible to suggest that the idea which excites an emotion is one I might be unaware of having. On the other hand it is not implausible to suggest that the idea which excites my emotion might be an idea of something that does not in fact exist. So emotions caused by false beliefs do not require the distinction of cause and object at all, in Hume's theory.[6] We have to look in quite another direction for the purpose of *his* distinction. He makes it quite clear. In the case of the direct passions one can infer him to believe the cause and the object are the same. In the case of the indirect passions they differ because these passions are not brought about only by the perception of some thing or quality, but require my awareness of the person to whom it is related: with pride and humility this will be myself, with love and hatred some other person. It is these that are the objects, as distinct from the causes, of these passions.

He argues the need for the distinction (II 5–6/277–8) by saying that awareness of myself is not alone enough for me to feel pride or humility, since it could not alone determine which of the two I should feel; and awareness of another person is not enough for me to feel love or hate, since again it would not decide between them. There has to be something additional, as the person himself is not 'sufficent alone to excite them' (II 5/277). This clearly implies that the object is still *one of the causes* of the passion, though not the determining one. This is borne out further when Hume distinguishes between the genesis of joy, as a direct passion, and pride, as an indirect one. In the former case the emotion is no doubt due to *some* relationship between the cause and myself for the cause to affect me, but it is not a relationship that has to register with me; whereas 'in order to excite pride, there are always two objects we must contemplate', the cause and the self (II 18–19/292). This again implies very clearly that the idea of oneself acts as *one* of the causal antecedents of pride, and justifies us not only in regarding the cause—object distinction as the basis of the separation of direct and indirect passions, but in regarding it as a distinction *within* the causal elements that go to generate the indirect ones.

It has to be admitted at once, however, that his description of the associative mechanism that leads to the indirect passions is not wholly consistent with this in its details. It runs as follows. Pride arises when (1) some perceived quality of a thing or person, or the thought of it, leads to (2) 'a pleasant sensation' (II 15/288), and this in turn leads to the arousal, through the associative factor of resemblance between impressions, of (3) the similarly agreeable impression of pride, which in its turn, 'by an original and natural instinct' leads to (4) the idea of oneself, the passion's object. (This is supposed to show how it is that when I think of the well-appointed house which I own, the pleasure it generates causes me to feel pride as its owner, not merely delight in its proportions.) Should item (1) be disagreeable, it would lead not to a pleasant sensation but to a 'painful' one; so the story of humility differs from that of pride in that (2) is a painful sensation and (3) is, of course, the similarly painful impression of humility. In the case of love, the idea of some other person replaces item (4), the idea of myself; and in the case of hatred we have the same pattern as in that of humility, except again that instead of (4) we have the idea of the other. Hume offers this summary:

When an idea produces an impression, related to an impression, which is connected with an idea related to the first idea, these two impressions must be in a manner inseparable, nor will the one in any case be unattended with the other. It is after this manner that the causes of pride and humility are determined. The quality which operates on the passion produces separately an impression resembling it; the subject to which the quality adheres is related to self, the object of the passion: no wonder the whole cause, consisting of a quality and of a subject, does so unavoidably give rise to the passion. (II 16/289.)

This account is open to severe criticism. Hume's summary clearly identifies item (1) as an idea, though in the discursive passages preceding it he frequently talks of the cause as though it is the external thing and its qualities rather than the idea of them, and indeed implies the same in the last sentence of the summary. This is perhaps not serious, but it hides an additional obscurity, namely that of the status of the pleasure and pain which are so important in the story. If the first item in the story is read as some external thing, then the second is easy to read as a pleasant or painful sensation of that thing; but if, as the summary requires, the first item is the *idea* of the external thing, then item (2) has to be the pleasure or pain itself, which now becomes not a mere tonal quality in some other impression, but a specific impression on its own account. This makes it harder to interpret the view that item (2) generates item (3) (the pride- or humility-impression) just through resemblance, since the resemblance is said to consist solely in the pleasantness or painfulness of each, and it can hardly do this while remaining the whole of the content of either. Hume is very definite that the causes of pride and humility produce, in each case, a 'separate pleasure' or 'separate uneasiness' (II 12/285), but this now cries out for interpretation.[7] The main difficulty, however, lies in the fact that the direction of attention to the alleged object arises, on Hume's extended account, as the last item, (4), in the causal chain.[8] If this is taken literally, it can only mean that the fact that the cause of pride is related to myself plays no part in the generation of pride, any more than in that of joy, but is something that engages my interest *after* I feel the pride. Hume's summary, with its 'no wonder . . .' shows that he does not really believe this, and it is in any case clearly false. It is true that pride can itself generate more self-absorption, but equally clear that a man's awareness of the fact that a pleasing thing is related to himself is a necessary condition of his feeling pride in it. Since both are true, however, a mere re-ordering of items (3) and (4) in Hume's sequence, though an improvement, would not be enough. The implausibility of the story arises because of Hume's rigid separation of the emotion and its object, and the consequent impossibility of their relationship being other than contingent and external. To describe the relationship as internal would probably force us to introduce the notion of the intensional object which, if I am right, has not made its appearance in Hume's text.

I now turn to *sympathy*. This concept is of great importance in Hume's ethics, and makes its first appearance in Section XI of Part I of Book II. I shall confine myself here to Hume's use of it in his account of the genesis of the passions.[9]

In these contexts at least, it is clear that Hume is using the word 'sympathy' in a technical way. It is also clear that it is not the name of a passion, in particular not the name of those passions like pity, compassion, or benevolence, which might be thought to be named by it in its non-technical use.[10] Hume refers to sympathy as a *principle* (II 137/427). It enables us to 'receive by communication' the inclinations and sentiments of others. It works as follows: (1) We become aware of the feelings of others through observation of 'external signs'. In Hume's language, we have an *idea* of the other's passion. At this stage we are merely cognisant of his passion and are not moved by it. Passions are notoriously contagious, however; so some other factor must be at work to produce the contagion. To Hume this passage from the mere idea of the other's passion to the arousal of the parallel one in myself is just a matter of the 'conversion' (II 43/320) of the idea of it into an impression, for ideas differ from impressions, as we know, merely in liveliness. So what we have to search for is something that will suitably enliven the idea. (2) He claims that what does it is the 'idea, or rather impression, of ourselves' (II 41/317). Quite apart from any problems this claim may raise for his views on self-identity, it is unattractive, for it offers no reason why sympathy should operate on passions rather than on (say) beliefs, nor does it explain why we are influenced so much more by some men's feelings than by others'. (3) Hume would say in response that we do sympathise with the beliefs of others, which are passion-filled phenomena in any case; and the fact that some men's passions move me more than other men's is due to the standard associational factors of resemblance, contiguity, and causation which operate between those men and myself. Since all men are somewhat similar, we are able to share the passions of all men; but the other relationships, plus the greater resemblances that tend to result from them, explain our greater readiness to share the passions of those specially connected with us.

100

(4) As a consequence of this enlivening force, the idea of the other's passion becomes an impression, and I then sympathetically *have* the passion he has. This in turn can lead me to have other passions, such as pity, and intensify passions I may already have, such as love. This account is unconvincing. (*a*) The idea I have at stage (1) is of another's passion; the impression I end up with in (4) has to be my own passion, not just a more vivid awareness of his, or the account loses its point. Hume's account entails the view that my original recognition of the other man's passion in (1) amounts to my feeling the passion, faintly, myself; but this is false, since I can surely be aware that he has it without feeling it, even faintly, myself, and can feel it, faintly or strongly, myself, without being aware that he does. (*b*) The only place where the transfer of ownership of the passion can be plausibly explained in Hume's story is in stages (2) and (3), where Hume tells us that the idea is enlivened by the idea of myself, reinforced by my associations with the other. But this would surely only serve to turn an idea of *his* passion into a passion of *mine* if it involved *explicit reflection* on the fact that I am like him, or am connected to him. Such reflections do arouse parallel feelings in people. But such reflections only occur in some of the cases Hume is concerned with, and he seems to be committed to the view that the associative mechanisms, here as elsewhere, may be unconscious ones.[11] (*c*) Since all my ideas are copies of impressions *I* have had, the idea of the other man's passion that I get at stage (1) when I interpret the 'external signs' can only arise if I myself have previously experienced the passion he is now having. This can be made to seem less damaging than it looks if we reflect that the sympathy Hume is talking about is not sympathy in the ordinary sense, and that a technical term can be restricted as its inventor may choose. But this is a very limited defence. For if sympathy in his sense is restricted in this way, the same restriction will apply to the genesis of any passions which depend upon it. One of these is compassion, which is the most likely candidate for identification with sympathy in the non-technical sense. So that Hume is committed to the view that one cannot feel compassion for someone else without actually having had the very emotion that he is having. And this is false.

Two passions that Hume explicitly accounts for by using the sympathetic mechanism are the love of fame (in Section IX of Part I) and compassion (in Section VII of Part II). The love of fame is not strictly a passion on its own account: Hume is actually describing how pride is reinforced by the good opinion of others, and humility by their bad opinion. The sympathetic process generates in myself the approval that I recognise in the other, and this merges with my pride, and strengthens it.[12] The same process occurs when my humility is matched by the low opinion held of me by others. When a proud man is shocked by the low opinions of others, this shock is due to the collision between his own sentiment of pride and the contrary sentiment generated in him by sympathy. The fact that sympathy is greatly strengthened by close relationships accounts for our being more distressed by the low opinion of those close to us than by that of strangers, and finding it easier to hold up our heads where we are unknown. (This account seems to make pride and humility into approval and disapproval directed to oneself, and implies that approval and disapproval are themselves passions. This is important for Hume's moral theory, though this convenience is bought at the price of blurring the distinction between approval and love, which is sometimes revealingly replaced in Hume's exposition by 'esteem'.)

Compassion, or pity, though not identical with sympathy in Hume's sense of the word, is brought about by it. It is a 'concern for ... the misery of others ... without any friendship to occasion this concern' (II 86/369). It arises because the relationship of resemblance which joins us all together is enough to re-create sympathetically in us the unhappiness of others. This suggests that the pity is identical with the re-created distress, which would be plausible if we take pity to be concern *at* another's unhappiness, but the most natural reading is one which makes it a passion aroused by that re-created uneasiness. This reading seems required by his usual interpretation of it as a concern to *relieve* the distress of others, which seems to be the point of his saying that pity 'counterfeits' benevolence, or the desire for the good of another. Given Hume's views on the distinction of passions from their causes and results, he is not entitled to rest, as he seems to do, on the fact that the word 'pity' has both senses.

The example of compassion faces Hume with other difficulties that force him to introduce two other principles. The unhappiness of others can lead not only to distress, but also to joy, so that we show malice rather than compassion. And even when it does lead to compassion, this is sometimes not proportionate to the distress that occasions it: I may be moved to great compassion at the sight of a misfortune that the victim is far less distressed by than I would be, so that there is little or no passion in him for the sympathetic mechanism to communicate to me. The former difficulty requires the *ad hoc* discovery of another principle, that of *comparison*; the latter Hume tries to deal with by the appeal to *general rules*.

Comparison has the opposite effect from that of sympathy; it tends to arouse in us emotions opposed in their nature to the ones we detect in other people. Hume's examples are malice and envy. Hume speaks of malice in different ways, sometimes as a pleasure deriving from the unhappiness of another, sometimes as a desire to produce such unhappiness in another in order to get this pleasure. It is in the latter interpretation that malice 'counterfeits' anger (or the desire for harm to another) as pity counterfeits benevolence. Envy is more vaguely described, and is said to arise from 'some present enjoyment' that another person has. Whereas in sympathy the awareness of another's passion leads to its duplication in myself through the enlivening of the idea of it, in comparison I am affected by the *contrast* between his state and mine. This is due to a general epistemological factor: the estimate of the magnitude or intensity of a quality is increased by the contrast with a nearby instance of its opposite. There seems no reason why this should not increase my sense of the man's distress if I am serene myself – and indeed it often does, but Hume at this stage disregards this. He fastens on the fact that the contrast heightens my awareness of my own well-being, and therefore produces a pleasant emotion in me, even though 'considered in itself' his pain is painful to me. And if I discern well-being in him, this will heighten my sense of my own burdens, producing a painful emotion in me. The former process is supposed to give us malice, and the latter one envy. One wants, however, to say that although they may be good enough accounts of some familiar feelings, they are not accounts of *these*. I may get some happiness from reflecting on my own felicity when I see the unhappiness of others, but although this pleasure results *from* their misery, it certainly need not be pleasure *at* their misery, which is what malice amounts to. And although comparison with the more fortunate may increase my self-pity, self-pity and envy are not the same. Hume says, interestingly, that I can get pleasure by recalling my own past pain because this heightens my present happiness; this is true, but he is surely incorrect to call this malice against oneself, for one does not have to be glad that one suffered thus to get the pleasure he refers to. But if we put aside the mis-identifications, what he says is often perceptive, as when he tells us that I can become uneasy when I compare my good fortune with the sufferings of a friend,[13] or that the pain of guilt may be increased when I think of the ease I still enjoy in spite of it, so that I come to crave punishment in order to lessen the contrast.

The appeal to *general rules* is something Hume undertakes in order to deal with a different sort of exception to the principle of sympathy. Here he says that the exceptions do not point to another competing principle, but merely show the strength of sympathy itself. We feel greater-than-normal compassion for someone who suffers calamities but has a 'greatness of mind' which elevates him above the distress which usually follows them (II 88/370). Here the sympathetic mechanism can still work, for the imagination is carried from the sight of his calamities to the thought of their usual effect, and it forms a 'lively idea of his sorrow', even though *he* feels none. This lively idea sets the usual sympathetic mechanism in motion. It is not very clear how far this is supposed to involve a belief in the existence of the sorrow he does not feel. On Hume's accounts both of belief and of causation it is hard to see why it should not, but the facts of such cases make it impossible for him to say this unambiguously. (Another example he uses in the same passage seems clearly to require explicit knowledge of the absence of the appropriate passion in the other persons: this is the case where we feel embarrassment at the foolish behaviour of those who are unaware of their foolishness, which Hume analyses as a sympathetic participation on our part in the shame that they *would feel if* they understood their own behaviour accurately.) Hume says, unhelpfully, that sympathy makes us overlook the victim's greatness of mind, or only consider it 'so far as to increase our admiration, love, and tenderness for him'. If 'tenderness' is compassion, then we have an emotion which is alleged to be generated by overlooking something and is then strengthened, not destroyed, by the recognition of it![14] If Hume could resolve such apparent conflicts in his account, he would have, of course, one more example of the effect of custom upon human thought. The difficulties arise, however, because custom is supposed to yield emotional results that depend on the absence of the beliefs that it normally generates, even the presence of contrary ones. It would seem that either the theory of sympathy or the theory of belief need to be modified.

The Effects of the Passions: Passion and Desire.

When we turn from the causes of the passions to their results, we must first note again that the passions can cause one another. Their doing so comes about through the association of impressions, which operates through resemblance, this being usually understood as a matter of pleasantness or unpleasantness. This mechanism is one which is assisted by the parallel association of ideas, though his account of this process is unsatisfactory. He even goes so far as to say the one cannot operate without the other: 'In order to cause a transition of passions, there is required a double relation of impressions and ideas; nor is one relation sufficient to produce this effect' (II 97/381). But this may only refer to the indirect passions – and of course it only refers to a *transition* of passions. There is no doubt that Hume is right in saying that we are more prone to fall into a second passion when the appropriate objects present themselves if we have already been in an emotionally similar state; but it seems unnecessary to restrict this claim to cases where there is some association between the ideas that arouse the first passion and those that arouse the second.

Passions do not only lead into one another, they also clash. This takes a variety of forms, which it is hard for Hume to do much to explain. To use examples that we have previously considered: when the proud man learns of the low opinion others have of him, his sympathetic humility collides with his pride, and produces an unpleasant shock, thus, one supposes, temporarily reinforcing the humility. If a future event is firmly expected and contains an even mixture of good and evil, the anticipatory joy and the anticipatory grief cancel each other. If the future event is all good, or all bad, but its arrival is uncertain, the joy and grief mix to yield hope or fear. Hume spells out all these complexes, but it is hard to see how his theories enable him to make them more predictable.

But it is not the effect of the passions on one another that has drawn most readers' attention. It is Hume's views of the relation of the passions to conduct. He insists that it is only the passions that can motivate action at all, and sets out to demolish the competing claims of the reason and the will. His position is in self-conscious opposition to the rationalist tradition, which we can trace back through the Stoics, and which was to receive its most sophisticated expression in Kant, according to which a man can rise above his emotional nature, and even show his metaphysical separateness from it, in the making of moral judgements and the taking of moral decisions. Hume tries to offer an alternative view not only in his account of the passions but also in his theory of the self and his account of moral judgements. I am concerned here only with the way in which his theory of the passions is constructed to fit this wider purpose.

We all know that we act from passion. We contrast such behaviour with rational behaviour, even going so far as to suggest sometimes that when we act from passion we are not ourselves, that our passions have enslaved us. The shock-value of Hume's theory comes from his attacking this view of human conduct in its own language. He insists that only passion *ever* motivates conduct, and that choices which seem to be exceptions to the rule of passion are in fact instances of it. Such a position, as Hume says, requires a widening of the customary use of the word 'passion' and a narrowing of the understanding of the word 'reason'. To the jaded modern ear such linguistic rearrangements do not merely lessen the shock-value, but tend to remove the interest. I think such a response is too simplistic; but in the present context I must confine my comments to an examination of some of the problems that Hume's rearrangements give rise to in his theory of the passions itself.

We have already seen how he uses the distinction between calm and violent passions to cover cases where we are apt to say it is reason and not passion that moves us. But this is only part of Hume's story, which he tells in the famous Section 'Of the Influencing Motives of the Will'. He insists that reason, as he interprets it, can only inform us, not move us. We have to *want* what it tells us of before we will choose it. Seen in this light, Hume's claim that reason must be the slave of the passions comes to little more than Aristotle's opinion that reason, of itself, moves nothing, and that man, to act, must first of all desire the end of his action. When we think reason does move us, it is really a desire that moves us, and a desire is a passion — in this case a calm one.

Now we sometimes think of our desires as passions: to be overcome by sexual passion may be to be overcome by sexual desire. But it may also be to be overcome by sexual jealousy or frustration. Clearly not all the passions that move us are desires, and Hume does not attempt so to classify them. But it also seems natural to deny that all desires are passions: if I go in to lunch, I may be moved by desire, but hardly by passion. But to make passions the only source of action, Hume has to extend the concept of passion so that all desires are instances of it, and he here shows no less conceptual confusion than his rationalist opponents. So all desires become passions, though not all passions are desires.

The list of direct passions (II 4/276) begins with 'desire and

106

aversion', which presumably appear here as generic terms. But the most important indirect passions are very sharply distinguished from desires. Pride and humility (II 97/382) are only 'pure sensations, without any direction or tendency to action', which could hardly be more definite. In the case of love and hatred, the position is more complex, but still quite clear. It is natural to think that love involves the adoption of the happiness of the beloved as an end, and that hatred involves the adoption of the misery of the hated as an end. But Hume explicitly denies these propositions, insisting that there is no contradiction involved in supposing love and hatred 'unattended with such desires' (II 85/368). That they are regularly so attended is a contingent fact, due to 'the original constitution of the mind'. The attendant desires do have names, but the names are not 'love' and 'hate': they are 'benevolence' and 'anger', which thus become desires for the happiness or misery of others.

What Hume has done, therefore, is to commit himself to the view that all desires are passions but not all passions desires; and he has done this to the extreme extent of taking passions that manifest themselves *in* desires and classifying these desires as *separate passions* from those they manifest. The result is certainly odd, both as an account of love and hatred, and as a story about benevolence and anger. But this is what the theory is: love and hate are impressions, which regularly, but contingently, precede benevolence and anger, which in turn, regularly but contingently, precede those actions which they are desires towards.

The oddity is compounded further. One would expect Hume to say that the consequent desires could arise at other times, without these antecedents, but although the classification of them as direct (or primary) passions would certainly require this, he seems oddly reluctant to accept it. When he discusses compassion and malice, he notices that the actions these lead to are the same as those that love and hatred lead to. He sees this as a problem, and sets about his account of sympathetic generation to show how such parallel desires arise. But he does not express this by saying that pity and malice are *feelings* that can be attended by benevolence and by anger in the same way that love and hate can. Apart from the oddity of calling the hostile desire 'anger', this would be plausible. Instead, he classifies pity and malice as themselves consequent *desires* for another's good or evil, and says that they 'counterfeit' benevolence and anger. Thus he ends with two pairs of desires that differ only in their causes, not their natures, and it requires the lengthy and implausible discourse of Section IX of Part II to explain why they have different names. The real reason of course is that the connections between the passions and the desires in these cases cannot be represented as merely contingent sequences: a fact which he senses but cannot locate in the right place. He should say we cannot have love without benevolence following; instead he says we cannot have benevolence without love preceding. So when we seem to practise it towards people we do not love but are sorry for, he has to give it another name, and misappropriates the name of the sorrow for the purpose.

Hume resorts to *ad hoc* devices to deal with these troublesome conative manifestations of the passions by saying that impressions may be related when they have similar 'impulses or directions', and that the character of a passion is not a mere matter of a present sensation, but also of 'the general bent or tendency of it from the beginning to the end' (II 97/381). But though he is right to suggest that our passions are gifted with these features, it is hard to see how they can be if they are impressions.

So much for Hume's treatment of the passions that are not desires, and their relationships to the desires that manifest them. Even deeper difficulties arise when we consider what he says about the desires themselves; for by classifying them as passions he forces them into the associationist mould, and although this no doubt seemed to him an advantage, it leads to confusions. Hume's account of how emotions arise is at its most plausible when we think of those emotions that are felt responses to happenings or persons that have already taken place, or are before us; and it is here that his separation of the emotion from its consequent wishes and actions causes least discomfort. But in the case of desires, their very essence is to point us towards the future. This might not seem to be a problem: the desire is not caused by the future event it is a desire for, but by the present idea of that future event. This is not enough, however; for one can very well think of the same event without desiring it. The theoretical temptation is now irresistible: the idea of the future event has to be accompanied by pleasure or pain in order to yield desire or aversion, as the idea of the past event has to be accompanied by pleasure or pain to generate joy or grief.

So desire is caused by future pleasure, and aversion by future pain. But this of course is not the same. For the future pleasure or pain is not here now, only the idea of it. It may be that the pleasure of anticipation and the anticipation of pleasure are the same thing, as Bernard Williams has suggested;[15] but even if this *bon mot* is true, it does not follow that either is the cause of the desire whose satisfaction it looks forward to. Both in fact are obviously *effects* of it. Hume is clearly not a psychological hedonist: he does not believe that it is always pleasure that we desire. Árdal has pointed out that Hume is not even committed to this position in the case of those desires that he says are caused *by* pleasure, since it does not follow from the fact that pleasure causes a desire that pleasure is the *object* of it. But those who have thought Hume to be a psychological hedonist have probably thought this because of his wish to make maximal use of the explanatory power of pleasure and pain as psychological causes, and his consequent failure to see that the pleasure one looks forward to is not itself the cause of one's wants. To quote Prichard:

> It seems not only possible, but common, to hold that there are a number of things other than pleasure which we desire for their own sake, and then when the question is raised, 'How is it that we desire these things?', to reply: 'Only because we think they will give us pleasure.' In my opinion, the reply is mistaken, and is made only because we are apt to think of the gratification necessarily consequent on the thought that something which we have desired is realised as that the thought of which excites the desire.[16]

Prichard goes on to say that the mistake is an insidious one, and to attribute it to Aristotle, Mill, and T. H. Green. I think we can also attribute it to Hume, even though he was not a psychological hedonist.

He could have avoided it, and it is easy to see how. I return here to the ambiguity in his characterisation of the direct passions. This group includes some that merely produce pain and pleasure, but do not proceed from them, and some that proceed from them. All of the former (or primary) group are desires, and it even includes hunger and lust. The latter group are desire and aversion, grief, joy, hope, fear, security, and despair. A coherent principle of division is impossible to delineate if we reject Hume's attempt to treat anticipated pleasure as a cause of desire, for then desire and aversion are in the wrong list. But if we accept it, hunger and lust are in the wrong list. The solution is this: to switch desire and aversion to the first list, as generic names for all the primary 'passions', to recognise that these are all desires and that it is misleading to classify desires as passions at all. The second list, the direct passions, would then contain only emotions that are *responses* to pleasant or unpleasant facts. The pleasures and pains of anticipation would attend the members of the first list, but these would be desires for, or aversions from, their natural objects, such as food, and not for the pleasures they would lead to. Hume's theory is that all desires are passions, and that many passions lead, contingently, to desires. The truth rather is that few, if any desires are properly called passions, but that it is in desires that many passions are, necessarily, manifested.

Summary

At the end of the *Dissertation on the Passions* Hume says: 'I pretend not to have here exhausted this subject. It is sufficient for my purpose, if I have made it appear, that, in the production and conduct of the passions, there is a certain regular mechanism, which is susceptible of as accurate a disquisition, as the laws of motion, optics, hydrostatics, or any part of natural philosophy' (*D.P.* 166). The *Dissertation* is merely a brief résumé of the arguments of Book II of the *Treatise*, but even if we look to the longer work, it cannot be said that the phenomena Hume examines fit at all readily into the mechanism he says will explain them. There are too many *ad hoc* adjustments of facts to theories, and piecemeal inventions of subordinate theories to cover awkward facts; there are too many cases where logical connections are denied where they exist, and causal connections discerned where they do not. These defects take away the impact of the many interesting and perceptive observations that Hume offers in the course of his argument. But the plausibility of Hume's most shocking dogma, that reason is the slave of the passions, hinges upon the degree to which he can illuminate the passionate side of man's nature; and his inability to begin to do this in the sphere of human desire is hardly an encouragement to his readers to imitate him in the reclassifications that this dogma requires.

6 The Will

Hume's general position on the nature of the forces that govern human conduct is clear and well-known, even notorious. He holds that we are always moved by passion, never by reason, and that those choices we are prone to describe in common speech in ways that seem inconsistent with this, can be seen, on closer inspection, to conform to it. There is therefore an inevitable artificiality involved in separating what he says about the passions from what he says about the will: indeed, his account of the will in the *Treatise* is merely the first half of the third Part of Book II, the Book devoted to the Passions, and not a separate investigation. It is necessary to discuss it in its own right, however, in order to see how far those phenomena that other thinkers have treated separately are incorporated into Hume's description of the passions and their effects. Such a separate enquiry soon reveals considerable untidiness and apparent confusion about details. It should be stressed that the questions I shall turn to first are not treated in the *Enquiry Concerning the Principles of Morals*, but only in the *Treatise*. In the *Enquiry Concerning Human Understanding* there is a famous discussion of the problem of the freedom of the will, which differs very little from what Hume says on this theme in the *Treatise*; but Hume does not return, save for incidental remarks, to the obviously incomplete treatment in the earlier work of the psychological mechanism of our choices. I shall begin with a survey of what he says about it.

Volitions

I will first recapitulate Hume's views on the relations of the passions to conduct.

Reason never moves us to action: only passions do. Whether we are moved, on some occasion, by one passion rather than another, is a question about their relative degrees of strength, not their relative degrees of violence. In non-philosophical discourse we often fail to distinguish these, thus fostering the mistaken opinion that to act from a passion is always to act from a violent one. Actions often spring from calm passions, but our common inattention to this fact causes us to describe such occasions as though they are occasions when passion is supplanted altogether.

The relation between a passion and the action that it generates is of course a causal one. Since the relation between a cause and its effect is contingent, Hume infers that it is never part of the essence of any passion that any sort of action should actually follow from it. It is, for example, not a necessary feature of the passion of love that it should lead to action that tends to the good of the person loved, even though it often does this. This point, which is emphasised more than once, is not clearly separated from another: that there is no necessary connection between the passion of love and the distinct passion of benevolence (which he interprets as the desire to do good to another), or between the passion of hatred and the distinct passion of anger (which he interprets as the desire to harm another — what we would more naturally call hostility). This seems to show that Hume thinks the indirect passions of pride, humility, love, and hatred generate actions by first generating other, direct, passions: though they do not have to do so.

Not all direct or primary passions lead to actions, of course.[1] Presumably none need do so, and some usually do not — joy and grief would seem to be in the latter class. But it is among the direct and primary passions that we find the ones that lead immediately to action, every time we act. These will be, at least in most cases, the desires and aversions; and it is through these that the indirect passions affect our conduct.[2]

In addition to ascribing actions to the desires and aversions, however, Hume seems to have a theory, or the fragment of a theory, about the phenomenology of choice, about the mechanism whereby the desires and aversions bring actions about. He appears to assume the need for one when he says at the end of Section II of Part III of Book II of the *Treatise*: 'Having proved that all actions of the will have particular causes, I proceed to explain what these causes are, and how they operate' (II 125/412). What actually follow this promise, however, are arguments that are supposed to demonstrate the practical impotence of reason. This in its turn might suggest that

Hume has no real need of any phenomenology of choice; that he could quite well hold that when we choose, all that occurs is a desire or aversion, followed by the action. Indeed Hume might well have maintained this to advantage. For those philosophers who have felt that more is needed to account for human actions have tended to offer volitions, or acts of will, as the immediate causes of action; and the occasions where such a claim has most plausibility are the cases where we act against, or in apparent independence of, some desire, and Hume has the doctrine of calm passions to explain such occasions. Hume might have said that the word 'will' is merely a convenient label for the process of choice, but insisted that the process named is merely a contest between desires. But he does not say this. We find a fragmentary, vestigial doctrine of volitions instead.

'By the will, I mean nothing but the internal impression we feel, and are conscious of, when we knowingly give rise to any new motion of our body, or new perception of our mind. This impression, like the preceding ones of pride and humility, love and hatred, it is impossible to define, and needless to describe any further' (II 113/398). So Hume introduces the notion of the will, saying it is one of the immediate effects of pleasure or pain, but is not 'strictly speaking', one of the passions. The definition Hume gives, or rather the form which his refusal to define the word 'will' takes, is one which leaves us unclear whether he thinks that volitions are processes of which we get some indefinable impression, or whether the volition is the impression itself. The distinction is empty in the case of passions like love and hatred, since the emotion *is* an internal impression; but it is not self-evidently empty in the case of volition, where we are apparently referring to the passage from internal impressions to action. This question, which is probably unanswerable, masks another: does the impression play an indispensable role in the initiation of actions, or can they occur without it? This question is also hard to answer, and its difficulty is not lessened by the vagueness of the phrase 'knowingly give rise', which seems on the one hand to apply only to deliberate actions, but might be construed as well to include all cases where we act in knowledge of what we do, including such cases as acting in a rage.

What follows this introduction in Sections I, II, and III of Part III of Book II is a discussion of what causes lead us to give rise to such 'new motions', and Hume's main concern is to insist that the causes are passions. What they influence is variously referred to as action, the will, or volition. In these passages there is little to guide us if we

113

are in search of some account of the mechanism by which the will operates: indeed, were we to attend solely to these arguments, they would make us disinclined to think that Hume felt any need to postulate such a mechanism, and merely thought that these terms served to mark the occurrence in human nature of a transition from passion to performance. But his reference to an impression of the will does show that he thinks there is some discernible process involved in such transitions, at least sometimes, and this is reinforced by his remark at II 167/458 that passions, volitions, and actions are 'original facts and realities, complete in themselves'.

We get a little more information in two passages in Section IX of Part III of Book II. The first passage lists volition among the direct passions, in spite of the fact that in Section I it has been said 'properly speaking' not to be a passion at all. 'The impressions which arise from good and evil most naturally, and with the least preparation, are the direct passions of desire and aversion, grief and joy, hope and fear, along with volition. The mind, by an original instinct tends to unite itself with the good, and to avoid the evil, though they be conceived merely in idea, and be considered to exist in any future period of time' (II 148/438). His saying 'along with volition' instead of 'and volition' suggests an uneasiness about including volitions among the passions, but the inclusion is there. After some comments on the indirect passions Hume tells us how grief and joy, hope and fear come about. They come about when I am presented with pleasure or pain understood to be certain or probable on the one hand, or uncertain in varying degrees on the other. The former leads to joy or grief, the latter to fear or hope. When these qualifications about the likelihood of the pleasure or pain are not added, we get desire, aversion, or volition: 'Desire arises from good considered simply: and aversion is derived from evil. The will exerts itself, when either the good or the absence of the evil may be attained by any action of the mind or body' (II 148/439). This paragraph suggests that when I become aware of something pleasant, and do not consider its likelihood, I will experience desire; and when I am aware of something unpleasant similarly unqualified, I will experience aversion. When, in either case, I judge that my actions can help me get it or avoid it, then volition occurs. This picture most naturally corresponds to thinking one would like or dislike something, and exerting oneself to get it or avoid it: or perhaps to a situation where we take some step which in itself we do not desire, in order to achieve something that we do, so that the desire for the

114

end is enough to generate the choice of the undesired means. Whatever the range of cases the distinction fits, Hume cannot intend us to infer that we can ever act without our action being due to the prodding of *some* passion. So if we refrain from executing the dictates of one desire, it has to be because we are moved by another contrary one. The existence of the activity of the will is always to be incorporated into a causal sequence that proceeds in the first instance from some passion or other.

For in spite of his willingness to admit volitions, Hume vigorously denies that we have an impression of an *undetermined* will. While he does believe we have impressions of volition, he considers it confused to interpret them in this way. In both the *Treatise* and in Section VIII of the first *Enquiry* he insists that 'the actions of the will arise from necessity' – that is, they are determined by motives with the same regularity that the movements of bodies are determined by external forces. We resist this opinion largely because we think we have inner evidence against it in our own case. Hume traces this opinion to a 'false sensation or seeming experience' of liberty in our actions. I think his account of this seeming experience is as follows. To hold that actions are not subject to necessity is not to deny that they are determined by the will, (or chosen); it is to say that the will itself when it chooses them, is free of determining causes. The will is not in fact free in this way. But the seeming experience of such freedom can be generated if, when we are challenged to show that we could have acted differently on some occasion from the way in which we did act, we find ourselves easily able to think of ourselves in imagination as making alternative choices, and easily able to imagine them issuing in overt actions. Hume may be referring here, especially in the *Enquiry* version of this argument, to the recollection of actual processes of indecision before a choice is made, processes during which we experience alternative competition inclinations, or velleities. He insists that such imaginative exercises do not show that we could ever have chosen otherwise than the way we in fact did choose. Nor is this shown if in order to prove the point, we actually *do* the alternative action that we did not do before. For such a demonstration is motivated, as the earlier action was not, by the desire to prove that we have liberty: so the earlier action and the later one have different originating motives.

This argument, though its purpose is not that of drawing attention to the processes of choice, does imply that there is an

115

inner perception of choice: also, perhaps, a distinct perception of inclination. But it tells us nothing more about it than Hume does in the sentences introducing the notion of the will with which we began.

A related argument is used by Hume in Section VII of the first *Enquiry*, to prove that there is no impression of power to be derived from the investigation of the acts of the will. Here Hume's argument is of course designed to reinforce his account of causation as constant conjunction, and necessity as a feature of our perception of it rather than of the items conjoined. He is therefore anxious to deny that in the case of acts of will we are able to perceive the necessity or power in the volition itself, and to insist that any necessity that there is, is a feature of the observer's mental life, not one of the items in the mental life that he scrutinises. To this end he insists that the connection between the act of will and the bodily movement it is said to cause is a connection, like all others, which we learn of through the conjunction of the two, not through the impression of the one. So he admits that 'we are every moment conscious' (*E.U.* 65) of the fact that 'the motion of the body follows upon the command of our will', but this consciousness is the consciousness of a regular sequence, and does not involve the perception of power in the first member of the sequence. The efficacy of the act of will consists, then, in its being the first member of such a regular pattern, and has to be learned through the observation of it.

From these scattered comments we can try to sum up Hume's views about what volition is. He seems to hold that even though every action is motivated by passion, that is by a desire or aversion, this influences our actions through a volition or act of will. We are, in other words, aware not only of the impression that constitutes the passion that moves us, but also of an impression succeeding it that constitutes the choice of the act to which the passion motivates us. The inclusion of the volition in the sequence is due to purely empirical considerations: to Hume's belief that there is an introspectible phenomenon of choice of which the words 'will', 'volition', and the rest are the names. He does not, at least 'properly speaking', classify it among the passions, even though it is an internal impression, since all actions would seem to involve volition, and we invoke the passions to explain why we perform one such action rather than another. Hume is extremely anxious to confine his account of volitions to those elements which are empirically required, and to insist that the presence of volition does nothing to support the view that anything other than the passions moves us, and nothing to support the view that the actions we will to do are exempt from causal regularities. Far from volitions being postulated to fufil theoretical requirements in Hume's philosophy, they are mentioned only to be denied any theoretical significance whatever. The will is not reason become practical; nor is the will undetermined. It is just that volitions are part of the mechanisms which the investigation of human nature uncovers.

Freedom

Hume's position on the freedom of the will is very close to the position sometimes called soft determinism. This is the theory that human actions have causes, and are susceptible in consequence of scientific explanation, but that this does not prove that they are not free. Sometimes they will be free, and sometimes not, but this is not a function of whether they have causes or not, since they always do. Such a view involves a claim about our ability to give causal explanations of human action, and a further claim about the way the concept of freedom is to be interpreted. Hume's discussion is highly polemical, and it is important as one reads it to be clear about his targets. He does not consider himself committed to denying that our actions are free, merely because he holds that there can be a science of man as well as a science of inanimate nature; but he strongly attacks those libertarian philosophers who hold that because we *are* free, such a scientific understanding of human nature is impossible. In doing this, he says things that it is easy to interpret as attacks on free will itself.[3]

This happens when he tells us that the actions of the will arise from *necessity*, and attacks the 'doctrine of liberty'. What he insists upon is that human actions are necessary in the same sense that the motions of natural bodies are. This, however, is a sense which he has been at great pains to interpret in his account of causation. According to this account, observation reveals merely a constant conjunction between those natural events which we say are causally connected. The idea of necessity arises from the observer's tendency to infer from the one to the other: from our awareness of this tendency we *feel* the necessity (II 119/406). The fact that our notion of causation contains more than the awareness of the conjunction is not to be read as implying that we observe, or are otherwise cognisant of, hidden forces in the objects conjoined; it

117

merely reflects the tendency of our own mind to infer the one from the other after the conjunction has become familiar. The necessity is in the observer, not the phenomena. When the claim that the will functions of necessity is interpreted this way it merely amounts to saying that the acts of the will occur as members of regular sequences, that we infer them from their antecedents in those sequences, and can, accordingly, explain them as being due to those influences (in Hume's view, of course, the passions) that give rise to them. The necessity of the actions of the will is as much in the observer of *these* sequences as the necessity of the movements of bodies is in the observer of physical sequences. In each case we find not hidden compulsions, but discernible causes. It is important to stress that Hume feels that the moral harmlessness of his determinism is a benefit deriving from his general theory of causation, which enables him to show that the science of physical nature and the science of man have the same logical structure, and yet to hold that our moral estimates of human actions can go on as before.

In order to show that the actions of the will occur by necessity, in this sense, Hume has merely to argue that they are attributed by us to causes in the same way that the movements of bodies are. We discover regular sequences in human nature as well as in the physical world. In so far as we fail to find such regularities, our failures can be matched by parallel ones in physical science, which (presumably) do not undermine our conviction of necessity in the physical world. His arguments here require little interpretation. They are mostly different ways of emphasising that there is a constant union and connection between actions and the 'situation and temper of the agent' — that our choices will vary with our sex, age, character, social status, physical needs, and the like. At this stage Hume makes no attempt to lean on his theory that actions are always caused by passions; at this point in Part III of Book II this claim has yet to be made, and in any case it is easy to hold that other determinants of action affect it through the passions which immediately occasion it. His contention here is that we are able to predict human actions with confidence from our knowledge of men's character and conditions, and that our ability to do this is due to our having observed regular conjunctions between these things and the choices men make.

It is natural to object to this that human actions are not readily predictable. Hume retorts to this, as one might expect, that when we are unable to predict with assurance, this is because of our ignorance of the conditions, not because of their absence. Our position here is the same as it is in the case of physical phenomena that we do not yet understand. He offers the case of the madman, whom we all judge not to be a free agent: his actions are unpredictable, but we do not infer he is free on that account. Hume says this is evidence of an inconsistency in our thinking about madmen as compared with sane men; in the context he might better have said that in the case of the madman we infer there are causes for his actions that we do not understand, but which would be found to be instances of natural regularities if we uncovered them. He stresses further that our use of what he calls moral evidence, that is the estimate of the likely behaviour of persons with whom we have to deal in our practical decisions, presupposes that human behaviour exhibits regularities, and that people in certain social situations can be expected, on the basis of past experience, to act in one way rather than another. In other words, we have to take for granted that there are regularities in human behaviour in order to make prudent decisions. Our decisions require necessity, not liberty.

Hume's arguments have been imitated by many philosophers since, and I cannot enter here into a deep analysis of the problems to which he is addressing himself. But there is one oddity about the structure of Hume's argument that deserves mention. His major anxiety is to show that if we extend the sphere of scientific enquiry to include human nature, the only sort of freedom that we require in daily life and moral reflection will not be denied. We have not yet examined his analysis of what sort of freedom that is. But it is unfortunate that he chooses to argue his case in terms of *necessity*, even though he is careful to interpret that notion in a way designed to render it harmless. For the upshot of his argument is, presumably, that the same sort of harmless necessity can be ascribed in the case of actions as can be ascribed in the case of physical events. Perhaps it can; but it is not. We do use our concept of causation to include more than mere regularity; if the additional element of supposed power or compulsion is generated by the mind's inferences, then Hume may be right that when we attribute the same regularities to human actions, there is no reason why we should not also ascribe necessity in the same way to them as we do to physical events. He therefore urges us to do so and not fear the consequences. But if his account of necessity is the right one, why do we need to be urged? Why do we not do this already? It is not plausible to suggest, as he seems to do, that this is the result of *philosophical* confusions that

119

conceal from us that the regularities present in the one case are also present in the other. He says we know this anyway. So if we are to insist that there are laws of human nature as there are laws of physical nature, we have to do so in the face of a reluctance to recognise them that is reflected in ordinary discourse, not merely in philosophical theory.

It is not, however, his attempt to use the concept of necessity in the analysis of human actions, but his criticism of the doctrine of liberty that has been most influential. His arguments here are of immense importance and great simplicity.

First, we have the major argument that the supposed opposition between freedom of action and the existence of predictable regularities in human conduct is the result of a verbal confusion. This is the confusion between 'liberty of spontaneity and liberty of indifference'.

Liberty of indifference is a philosophical myth; it is the supposed freedom from determining causes in human choice. The alleged empirical evidence for it does not confirm its existence, as we have seen, and the continual increase in our knowledge of the regularities that exist in human behaviour shows it to be contrary to all other evidence. Liberty of spontaneity is the only kind 'which it concerns us to preserve', and this is the kind of freedom we ascribe to one another in common speech when we distinguish those actions which are free from those that are not. In the *Enquiry* he defines it as 'a power of acting or not acting, according to the determination of the will' (*E.U.* 95). This is a freedom that we have if nothing hinders us from executing the choices that we have made. Its presence or absence is nothing to do with the question of whether these choices have themselves been brought about by prior causes. In fact they have: but what makes us free agents at any time is that we can then put these choices into practice without anything preventing us. So freedom, thus understood, is not opposed to the existence of causes, but is opposed to 'violence'. To be free is not to be prevented from doing that which you choose to do.

Hume then argues that moral and religious considerations do not require that we believe in any other sort of freedom than this; indeed they require that we reject the doctrine of liberty of indifference as actually inconsistent with our moral judgements. For how else can we rationally administer rewards and punishments, but by assuming that we can learn the ways in which human conduct can be influenced by pleasant and unpleasant causes? And how can it ever

120

be just to praise or blame someone for his actions if we are not able to assert with confidence that the actions of which we approve or disapprove can be traced with some confidence to reasonably stable states of character? On the occasions when we do not feel this, and an action is *out* of character, we do not go out of our way to praise or blame the man who has done it. We do of course need liberty of spontaneity before we can praise or blame an agent, since moral appraisals require that what he has done has proceeded from a choice which he has made and not been hindered from executing.

In the *Enquiry* Hume answers two possible religious objections to his position. The first is that if our choices are the results of causes, then it is not sufficient, in assessing our actions, merely to consider whether our choices were capable of execution. For even if they were, they can be traced in their origins back through prior causes, on and on into the past, until one reaches God as first Cause. Hume ironically points out that the supposed perfection of all things which seems to follow from this is not a helpful consideration in daily life, where what interests us is the relative merits of individual actions and situations, not the overall perfection of the whole. The second argument is that if our actions do not exhibit liberty of indifference, and can be traced back to God, God is the author of our sins as well as of our good actions. To this Hume again replies ironically, this time that these matters are too deep for us.

It is noticeable, however, that in presenting these objections in a supposedly *theological* form, so that what is supposed to undermine our freedom is a remote First Cause, Hume avoids facing a more difficult version of the same argument. This is the version we get when we point out that although the agent is shown to have immediate control over his present action if we can show that nothing prevents him from executing his choice, the causes of his choice, namely his dispositions and character, are themselves the products of causes over which he had no comparable control; and although it is no doubt a necessary condition of praise or blame that we consider the agent to have liberty of spontaneity, it is not sufficient. In particular we are increasingly prone to withhold blame if we find his character to be the result of social or economic deprivation. Hume is at liberty to deny our thinking to be sound in this; but he cannot then argue that the liberty his doctrine preserves is the only kind we make use of in our moral reasonings. His form of determinism is not, in this respect, innocuous even if it is true.[4]

He is also open to contemporary objections based on the analysis of the vocabulary of agency. If Hume is correct, then we are never free in the sense that we could have *chosen* differently, if the same set of influences had been at work upon the will. His analysis of volitions makes this clear.[5] So if he is right we never have real powers of choice that are not exercised, except when some outside force or violence prevents our doing what we have chosen to do. Yet it is frequently argued by contemporary moral philosophers that when we say someone has acted freely we imply that he could have done other than he did, meaning by this not merely that he has the necessary skills or strengths to do otherwise if he should *choose* otherwise, but that he might very well, on that occasion, with all the same inner and outer influences at work, have *chosen* otherwise. If these arguments are sound, then Hume could still claim that liberty of spontaneity is the only sort of liberty there *is*, but he cannot claim that it is the only sort that we presuppose ourselves to have in our moral reflections.

Reason as the Slave of the Passions

Although Hume's analysis of freedom is of great interest and historical importance, it is for him a mere part of a much wider argument. It prepares the reader (at least the reader of the *Treatise*) for the subsequent dethronement of reason as the cause of conduct and the source of moral choice. Hume wishes to destroy the rationalist conviction that free action, and especially moral action, is action taken in defiance of passion, or at least without reference to it. He holds instead that all conduct is moved by the passions, however it is evaluated. This view, however we understand it in detail, runs into a major difficulty. The rationalist view (however it, in turn, is understood) is an attempt to express a conviction that all of us have, long before philosophical sophistries affect us. This is the conviction that when we act from passion we do not, in the fullest sense, *act* at all; that we are, on the contrary, mastered by the passions that move us instead of being masters of ourselves. To act from passion is to behave *passively*, to be *affected* in our doings by forces that we do not control and in our best moments can put aside. However absurd some of the rationalist expressions of this conviction may be, it cannot be said to be a philosophical invention. Hume has to undermine it. Although he never explicitly uses it for this purpose, his theory of the self helps to undermine it by its denial that the self which has ideas, passions, and volitions has any existence of its own which is distinguishable from them; so that there can be no metaphysical basis for the suggestion that the self can demonstrate its freedom by rising above the passions that it has. His account of volition serves to undermine it more directly, because of his attack on the suggestion that undetermined choice can be verified by introspection. His analysis of freedom carries his purpose forward in two ways: first, by showing that the actions we regard as paradigms of self-mastery are just as much subject to scientific understanding and prediction as others are; and second, by showing that the only concept of freedom which we use in practice, as distinct from philosophical theory, is one which applies solely to the execution of our choices, not to their formation. But even with all this behind him, he still has not undermined the common belief that there is a clear distinction to be drawn between those of our actions that are caused by the passions and those that are caused by reason. Whatever we say about their relative effectiveness or predictability, the distinction between the two seems wholly familiar, and of the greatest importance in assessing conduct.

The doctrine of calm passions is Hume's major positive contribution to his argument at this stage. Its interpretation is controversial, but I have expounded it in a way that makes Hume's principal application of it the major factor in determining its content. He distinguishes between the degree of violence a passion has, and the strength that it has. There is no passion that is calm *per se*, though some are normally calm and some normally violent. A passion is violent when its felt intensity is very great, calm when it is faint. A passion is strong or weak if it is effective or ineffective in determining action on particular occasions. So the same passion can be strong at one time or in one person and weak at another time or in another person. The use that this distinction has in the present context is clear. The most familiar examples of self-mastery are those cases when we act in the face of an intensely felt passion. Hume says that on this occasion we do not have action undetermined by passion, but action determined by calm passion. A calm passion, by definition, is one that it is easier to miss than a violent one; so it may very well be that the only passion we are clearly aware of at the time, or in recollection, is the violent one. But in spite of this the calm one has determined the action because it is stronger. The belief in the passivity of action done from passion comes from overlooking the presence of the calm but strong passion in such instances. It also comes from the fact that a violent passion is, again by definition, a disturbing or agitating one, which will crowd out reflective considerations and long-term policies.

For this distinction to serve the purpose, Hume has to enlarge the list of passions to include some normally calm ones that would not be classed as passions by most of us (such as benevolence, resentment, and the general appetite to good and aversion to evil). This is not in his view a disadvantage, but a confirmation of the fact that our customary restriction of the word 'passion' to cases of violent emotional disturbance is one which obscures the much more important similarities which exist between those occasions and others where, on his analysis, the calm passions are operative.

There is an obvious difficulty about the distinction between violence and strength. There seems no paradox about the suggestion that a passion can be strong but calm, so that it may determine our conduct but be overlooked on introspection; unless of course there is a paradox about the implied view that there can be an impression which is still an impression and not an idea, but so faint that we do not notice it. The suggestion that a passion can be violent but not effective is more difficult, if it is to be used to explain the special character of those occasions when we are agitated in our behaviour by the passion's violence. For such occasions are surely examples not only of the inner vividness of the passion, but also of its causal efficacy. Hume does say (II 147/437) that 'generally speaking, the violent passions have a more strong influence on the will', but this obvious truth is surely not the mere inductive generalisation that he considers it to be.

The doctrine that calm passions move us when violent ones do not has to contend with more problems than this. The occasions when we are moved by calm passions will be of at least two sorts: those where there is no violent passion for the calm one to contend with, so that there is no emotional disturbance at all, and those where there is such a violent passion to contend with, and the violent passion loses the contest. Many cases of the former kind will be cases where we have a settled and habitual preference for a certain course of action: 'It is evident, passions influence not the will in proportion to their violence, or the disorder they occasion in the temper; but on the contrary, that when a passion has become a settled principle of action, and is the predominant inclination of the soul, it commonly produces no longer any sensible agitation.' (II 130/418)

Suppose we ask how we arrived at some such settled preference. Or suppose we ask what gives the calm passion its strength, or arouses it, on those occasions when it successfully opposes a violent one. In each case we are likely to answer that our preference is a *reasoned* one, or that the victory of the calm passion is the result of reflection. The total destruction of the common conviction that self-mastery is mastery over the passions can only come about when these answers are either shown to be false, or shown to require an analysis which still makes it clear that it is passion and not reason which is really in control of the choices that we make. Hume chooses the second way, not the first. His own summary of his position (II 147/437) contains this sentence: 'Generally speaking, the violent passions have a more strong influence on the will; though it is often found that the calm ones, when corroborated by reflection, and seconded by resolution, are able to control them in their most furious movements.' This does not say that reason has no role in the genesis of action. What it does do, however, is to insist that its role is wholly subordinate. Reason is the *slave* of the passions. There are many things that we can do with the aid of a slave that we cannot do without him; but that does not mean he is in charge. Reason is the slave of the passions even on those occasions which we describe in common speech by saying it has overcome them. Even our most paradigmatic exercises in self-mastery are still occasions where passion rules and reason serves. I turn now to the arguments which Hume offers in direct support of this notorious contention.

They are to be found in Section III 'Of The Influencing Motives of The Will', and there are four of them. The first two are designed to show that 'reason alone can never be a motive to any action of the will', and the second two are designed to show that 'it can never oppose passion in the direction of the will'.

(I) The first pair depend on a division between the two functions of reason: its *a priori* ('demonstrative') function, and its empirical function. (*a*) Hume argues that in its demonstrative function reason is concerned only with the relations of ideas. In so far as this has any practical relevance, it is confined to its usefulness in enterprises that employ reason in its empirical function. Mechanics and arithmetic, in themselves *a priori*, are used in practical enquiries because they help us in directing our judgements about causes and effects. So any value reason has in its demonstrative function will be derivative from the value it has in its empirical function. (*b*) Turning to this, Hume argues that our obvious practical need to know about causes and effects does not show that the reasoning which discovers their connections is what prompts our desires. He admits that when we desire or shun some object, we will also desire or shun that which causes it or is caused by it, and that objects that have not aroused desire or aversion will come to do so when they are shown to have connections with objects that have. But it is not the reasoning which causes the derivative desire or aversion. It can only arise if there is already present a desire or aversion for the original object. Reason, then, only 'directs', or re-channels, desires or aversions that it finds, and cannot generate any on its own account. If such concerns are not already present, the response to what reason shows us is that of detached intellectual interest, not a desire to attain or avoid anything.

(II) (a) Given these arguments it follows that when a passion is apparently in contention with reason it is really in contention with another passion. For nothing can oppose one force ('impulse') but another. Since reason has been shown to have no power to originate such forces on its own account, its activity during occasions of conflict must be a mere adjunct to a desire or aversion which is the real competitor to the passion we say reason is opposing.

(b) So far we have concentrated on reason's limitations. But there is another reason why reason and passion cannot oppose one another. It is that the passions in their turn lack a feature which is a precondition of anything being said to be opposed to reason. What is it for something to be so opposed? Hume's answer is that such opposition consists in 'the agreement or disagreement of ideas, considered as copies, with those objects which they represent' (II 127/415). This language, and his examples, make it clear that he is thinking here of reason in its empirical function, but he would probably, in view of his first argument, wish to extend what he says to cover the practical use of *a priori* truths also. What makes a judgement 'contradictory to truth and reason', then, is its not agreeing with the objects it is about. Its being able so to agree, and also to disagree, is a consequence of the fact that in formulating judgements the understanding operates upon its *ideas*, and ideas are *representative*. They are copies, and have 'reference'. The truth and falsity, and the reasonableness and unreasonableness, of our judgements are the result of this. The passions, by contrast, are not representative. To be possessed by a passion, even a desire,[6] is not to have 'reference to any other object'. It is just to have a unique, simple, secondary impression, and this will not agree or disagree with anything. Such agreement or disagreement is possibly only for ideas.

Of course passions are occasioned by judgements, and give rise to them, and these judgements can be true or false, reasonable or unreasonable. It is merely the passion itself that cannot. So when we say, as we often do, that an 'affection can be called unreasonable' we must merely mean that it is accompanied by a judgement that is so characterised. This happens in two ways: when a passion is founded on a false belief, and when we mistakenly think that something is a means to the satisfaction of a desire that we have, and come to seek it as a result. 'In short, a passion must be accompanied with some false judgment, in order to its being unreasonable; and even then it is not the passion, properly speaking, which is unreasonable, but the judgment' (II 128/416). When these conditions are not satisfied we do not even have this derivative unreasonableness.

It is in connection with this point that we find these famous sentences: 'It is not contrary to reason to prefer the destruction of the whole world to the scratching of my finger. It is not contrary to reason for me to choose my total ruin, to prevent the least uneasiness of an Indian, or person wholly unknown to me. It is as little contrary to reason to prefer my own acknowledged lesser good to my greater, and have a more ardent affection for the former than the latter' (II 128/416). In spite of the rhetoric in this passage, Hume's examples are carefully chosen to include absurd selfishness, absurd altruism, and self-conscious imprudence. It is easy to overlook that Hume means exactly, and only, what he says: that these preferences are not contrary to reason in the way this has been defined. They are not contrary to reason in themselves, because no passion can be and they are not contrary to reason in the derivative sense, because they are not the result of any false judgements. If I think that the only way to stop my finger being scratched is to press the atomic button, and choose to do so, then if I am right that my finger will get scratched if I do not press the button, my choice is not based on a false judgement, for I have judged the situation correctly. The same is true when I give all my funds to a charity which I correctly think will use them all up in administrative costs except for a small amount which will buy someone I do not know a small meal. And it is wholly familiar to us that people knowingly choose immediate lesser goods in preference to known greater ones, as any smoker or drinker can testify. Hume insists, however, that none of these preposterous choices are unreasonable. He does not deny that we disapprove of them. Nor is he unaware of his philosophical obligation to tell us what such disapproval comes to. He is preparing the way for just such an account, by denying that it is the detection of such unreasonableness.

The immediate results for Hume's argument are clear. Reason generates judgements. These have no power to initiate actions. It is passions exclusively that have the power to initiate actions, but in their turn they are not susceptible to appraisal in the language of rationality and irrationality as judgements are. So neither is capable of opposing the other.

These arguments raise the most fundamental questions in the philosophy of mind and action, and to assess them adequately here is out of the question. I will content myself with some comments that relate them particularly to their context in the *Treatise*.

Hume is fully aware, indeed he stresses, the ease with which immediately attractive goods can take precedence in our choices over our long-term interests. But it is clear that his insistence that reason can only act in subordination to the passions, as we find it in the first two of these arguments, depends upon the fact that we do not always choose against our long-term advantage. For he has to convince us that we will always find desire to be dominant, even in cases where at first sight it seems not to be; and it is very significant that when he lists the 'calm desires and tendencies' that we mistake for the operations of reason, he includes 'the general appetite to good, and aversion to evil, considered merely as such'. The last four words may be intended to contrast with 'considered as certain or uncertain', and point forward to Section IX with its special treatment of hope and fear, but it is at least plausible to read them where they appear in Section III as contrasting instead with 'considered only in the short term'. For the detection of a desire in those cases where reason is customarily thought to be dominant is only possible if we include a general desire for our long-term good, or prudence, to be the desire that we can detect. Indeed the settled preferences that Hume offers as natural examples of calm passions are often examples of preferences that we have judged likely to lead to our long-term good if pursued regularly. So it is critically important for his argument that the concept of a passion be widened to include this motive.

But Hume has still to allow reason more power than he seems to do. When he explains how we come to call some passions unreasonable, he tells us this is because they are accompanied by mistaken judgements; and one case of this is the occasion when we have mistakenly judged something to exist when it does not. It is interesting that in the passage in Section III, 'Of the Influencing Motives of the Will', where he first draws our attention to this possibility, the list of examples he gives of this derived unreasonableness does not include a desire. When he repeats his argument in Section I of Book III he does use a desire as his example. He offers here (II 169/460) as an instance of this kind of error my supposal that a fruit I see at a distance is a pleasant-tasting one, a supposal which prompts a desire for the fruit. For his views about the unreasonableness of desires to be plausible, such cases have to be included. But if they are, we have to recognise that whether the judgement I make is false or true, the desire I come to have is the outcome of the judgement. But then the claim that reason cannot cause actions looks much weaker. It can only mean that reason cannot cause actions except when it makes calculations in the interest of a desire, *or when it prompts a desire*. It is not plausible to suggest that its prompting the desire in such instances is the result of a pre-existing desire for good considered merely as such; or if it is judged plausible to say this in view of the obviously hedonic element in the example and Hume's equation of good with pleasure, then it would seem to be impossible for Hume to allow the same desire for good to *restrain* me from choosing the fruit on that same occasion — and this possibility has to be retained if Hume's account of prudential conflict is to be plausible in turn.

When we turn from his arguments about the impotence of reason to his arguments about the a-rationality of the passions, we can see that Hume is leaning heavily on his own theories about what a passion is. Certainly his theory is more at odds with our common convictions than he thinks it to be. He seems to be convinced that the only cases where our common moral judgements seem to require the ascription of rationality or irrationality to the passions are the cases that he analyses as due to false judgement. But this is not so, as scrutiny of what he says about these very cases can show. We might, by transference, say that a desire or aversion that is due to a mistaken or false judgement, is itself mistaken or false, but we do not call it unreasonable. On the contrary, as his most famous examples make quite clear, the ones we call unreasonable are the ones that are not excusable in this way. If a man is found to be pursuing some objective that is harmful because he mistakenly thinks it is beneficial, his conduct is shown by this to be reasonable, and not unreasonable after all. The falsity of the judgement *preserves* the rationality of the action in such cases, The choices for which we reserve the epithets 'unreasonable', and 'irrational' are the ones not covered by this kind of explanation: cases where we judge the desire the agent is trying to satisfy as being in some way inappropriate to the situation *as the agent conceives it*.[7] His preference may be the wrong one to feel; it may be excessively strong in the circumstances; but the basic category of judgement that we apply is that of appositeness or inappositeness to the circumstances as understood.[8] To admit this as a mode of rationality into his analysis Hume would have had to admit a general desire for the reasonable as well as for the good.[9] It is not obviously absurd to admit this; indeed Spinoza, and Kant, make it central to moral psychology. It is not even absurd to call it a passion, and one that was very prominent in Hume's own personality. But Hume does not admit its existence. It would seem that a real victory over our instinctive rationalism has to come, if at all, from the positive attractions of Hume's alternative account of the ways in which we disapprove of those disreputable choices which he himself declines to call irrational.

7 Morality and Society

Hume's ethics is a twofold psychological enquiry into human nature. He is concerned to ask in what way we make the moral discriminations that abound in our discussions of human affairs, and he is concerned to uncover the ways in which these discriminations influence our actions. These enquiries are not the same as those which philosophers undertake in what are now often called Normative Ethics and Meta-Ethics, even though many of Hume's arguments have been put into the service of each of these enterprises, and can often be adapted to them without much change. Reforming or defending our moral opinions, and analysing the meaning of moral terms or the relationship moral statements have to other statements, are not part of Hume's programme, even though he may commit himself incidentally on such questions as he goes about the pursuit of his own objectives. He would of course have insisted that, in so far as these philosophical tasks were known to him through the works of his contemporaries, they could not profitably be pursued except in subordination to the science of man. But it is one thing to relate our concerns to his, and quite another to translate his claims into the language of ours.

The distinction I have drawn between the two aspects of Hume's ethical theory is itself somewhat misleading, since it suggests that moral behaviour is the result of our applying the distinctions that we make use of in our evaluations. Hume does not hold this, but to a large extent maintains just the opposite. He does, however, spend the greater part of Book III of the *Treatise* on those cases where moral behaviour does have this source, because these cases seem to him to raise special problems. He does, that is to say, recognise the existence of a specifically moral motive, or sense of obligation, but

131

examines the mode of its operation partly because he does not think that morally praiseworthy conduct is in the first instance produced by it.

Moral Evaluations and Reason

Book II of the *Treatise* prepares Hume's readers to find him saying in Book III that moral action is action that we are moved to perform by certain passions, not by reason. It does not so obviously prepare them to find him saying that moral *distinctions* are not derived from reason, but are in their turn derived from the passions. It might, after all, be maintained that although we are unable to pursue what we judge to be good or obligatory, or to shun what we judge to be evil or wrong, it is reason that discovers these to us. But Hume insists that it is the passionate side of our nature that is at work when we make our moral discriminations. The judgements that express these discriminations are prompted by impressions of reflection, not impressions of sensation.

This thesis requires for its support arguments that do more than establish reason's impotence in the sphere of action. But although Hume does offer some, his case is bolstered by the repetition of those which he used to establish the earlier contention. It is clear that for him the two theses are closely connected. He makes the connection himself in this way in Section I of Part I: 'Since morals, therefore, have an influence on the actions and affections, it follows that they cannot be derived from reason; and that because reason alone, as we have already proved, can never have any such influence. Morals excite passions, and produce or prevent actions. Reason of itself is utterly impotent in this particular. The rules of morality, therefore, are not conclusions of our reason' (III 167/457). And again, even more simply: 'Reason is wholly inactive, and can never be the source of so active a principle as conscience, or a sense of morals.' (III 168/458) It is difficult to be impressed by this argument, even if we are prepared to gloss over the fact that our moral judgements frequently fail to generate actions. For Hume's theory of the passions requires him to say that many passions do not lead to action of themselves, but only lead to it indirectly by stimulating desire or aversion; and he also appears to hold that although reason never generates actions, it can prompt passions that do generate it (as he seems to admit even here when he says that reason '*of itself*' is impotent). If one admits these two things, then the fact that reason does not lead to action directly, or of itself, is not a sufficient ground for his insistence that it must be passion and not reason that is at work when we make our moral discriminations. The most it would show is that reason would have to be attended by a desire for that which it showed us to be good before our actions would reflect the judgement that it had made.

It is only fair to notice here that Hume seems in these passages to have had certain unnamed opponents in mind, and that his arguments have some force against their positions, even if not enough to establish his.[1] Samuel Clarke had argued that reason can inform us of the eternal and unchanging fitness or unfitness of actions of certain types to situations of certain types, so that morality has the same certainty and necessity attached to it as mathematics does. This view was not only supposed to provide for certain moral knowledge, but also to explain why moral judgements are felt to have binding force in our actions. It is reasonable for Hume to use his arguments for the inability of reason to generate action on its own account, against this theory: but such arguments only defeat it by destroying its pretension to account for the efficacy of conscience, and do not prove that it can only be the passions that produce our moral evaluations.

Hume also re-introduces his earlier arguments for holding that a passion cannot be judged to conform to reason, or to be contrary to it, and that such judgements can only be applied to statements of fact. He now extends his ban to include the actions that our passions generate, and insists that any merit or demerit that they have cannot consist in conformity to reason or opposition to it. One can only agree to this result if one has already accepted Hume's veto against applying the concept of rationality outside the sphere of judgements of fact. Hume's easy satisfaction with a dogmatic thesis of this sort is probably due here also to the existence of an unnamed opponent. In this case it seems to be William Wollaston, who held that moral wickedness should be construed as a kind of falsehood in actions. If one is merely concerned to expose the defects of this, it is enough to point out that the moral criticism of actions cannot take the form of calling them true or false. But Hume's position is far less innocuous than this: it is that it cannot properly take the form of calling them rational or irrational. This presupposes, as Wollaston's view does, that to call an action irrational is to say it is either itself false, or is the practical manifestation of a false judgement; and this is not so. The dubious status of Hume's veto reveals itself in an interesting way when he goes on to make a detailed concession. He repeats his earlier

133

admission that we can call desires unreasonable in a transferred sense if they are prompted by false judgements; but he insists that although this is true (which I have argued it is not) it is irrelevant to the moral criticism of actions. For when we criticise an action on moral grounds, we blame it, yet when a man acts because of a mistaken judgement of fact, we do not blame him – we pity him. I have argued that in such situations the man's action is not irrational at all. But aside from this aspect of Hume's concession, the fact that we pity and do not blame in such circumstances does nothing to show that our moral evaluations are not made by reason. For if a man acts from a mistaken understanding of what is *right,* we do not blame him either. Hume's example suggests a likeness between mistaken moral judgements and mistaken factual ones, not a contrast.

Hume is of course correct that decisions or actions cannot be called true or false, whatever we may think of his allowing that a decision taken on the basis of false information can be called unreasonable. But this merely emphasises another respect in which the contrast he draws between the criticism of judgements of fact and the criticism of actions and decisions fails to show what his theory requires. For although we do not ascribe truth or falsity to decisions, we do ascribe them to our moral evaluations – or seem to. A rationalist can quite easily argue, on the basis of this fact, that moral evaluations lead to actions in much the same way that judgements of fact do, whatever detailed differences we may find when we examine actions caused by moral error and actions caused by factual error. Hume tries to ward off such suggestions: 'Should it be pretended, that though a mistake of *fact* be not criminal, yet a mistake of *right* often is; and that this may be the source of immorality: I would answer, that it is impossible such a mistake can ever be the original source of immorality, since it supposes a real right and wrong; that is, a real distinction in morals, independent of these judgments. A mistake, therefore, of right, may become a species of immorality; but it is only a secondary one, and is founded on some other antecedent to it' (II 169–70/460). This argument has no force at all unless one already accepts that moral judgements do not discover real right and wrong for us. Hume's arguments for this come next.

Hume argues that if reason discovers moral truths, it must do so either in the discovery of relations of ideas, to which of course reason in its *a priori* function is confined, or in 'the inferring of matter of fact' – a phrase which I quote as he presents it, since it is not inference but perception that he discusses when he comes to deal with it. He spends most of his space on the first alternative, and seems again to have Samuel Clarke and his followers in mind as he writes. It is only on this understanding of reason's powers that it is possible to hold that 'morality is susceptible of demonstration': or so Hume says, relying for justification on his own theory of knowledge, a reliance which he winningly admits to by saying that 'it is allowed on all hands that no matter of fact is capable of being demonstrated' (III 172/463).

Given this bifurcation of reason, Hume goes on to argue that if moral truths can be demonstrated, vice and virtue must consist in relations about which it is possible to reason with the same exactness that we find in mathematics. But, Hume says, there are only four such relations: resemblance, contrariety, degrees in quality, and proportions in quantity or number; and all these relationships can exist among inanimate objects, to which moral judgements cannot be applied. Here again Hume draws on his own theory of knowledge, and indeed draws on one of its more obviously dogmatic tenets. All he adds by way of justification is that if anyone thinks that in moral evaluation one can discover another relation he should point out what it is. A natural retort is that the sort of relation that moral philosophers have in mind is the sort that holds between agents and situations in which they find themselves when duty beckons, that is, obligation. It appears that Hume has this retort in mind as he proceeds, for he goes on to say that anyone who believes that he can find this special moral relation that is the subject of ethical reasoning must point out a relation that satisfies two conditions. (1) The first condition is that the relation must hold between states of mind on the one hand and external objects on the other. For if it ever held between 'internal actions considered singly' it would follow that we could be guilty of 'crimes in ourselves, and independent of our situation with respect to the universe' – a possibility Hume seems to regard (though it is not clear why) as self-evidently absurd. And if the relation ever held between external objects, even inanimate beings would be subject to judgements of 'moral beauty and deformity'. (2) The second condition such a relation must satisfy is that it must have an inescapable connection with the will, so that whenever we find this relation one of the beings between which it holds must be an agent who is obliged by it to act in a particular way. As he says, he has already argued that no relation reason

135

discovers could meet this condition, since relations of ideas cannot of themselves lead directly to action in the required way.

He supports these arguments with two examples. The first is the evil, or vice, of ingratitude, of which his instance in the first Appendix to the *Enquiry* is Nero's matricide (*E.M.* 290). The second is incest. Both these crimes, he says, have analogues in the natural world. The first is like what happens when a sapling destroys its parent tree; the second is like sexual intercourse between animals that have the same parentage. Hume's argument is that we would all agree that between humans these are crimes, and that between plants or animals these are not crimes; yet the discernible relations are the same in both. The conclusion is supposed to be that the two necessary conditions for the existence of a specifically moral relation that reason could discern are unsatisfied. (1) The first condition is unsatisfied because the relation we can discern is in every case external to the minds that are present, since it is still present even when no mind is involved at all. (2) The second condition is unsatisfied because the relation that we can discern is one that is still there even when no *will* is involved at all.

We can object, I think, to Hume's application of his first condition on the ground that relationships between rational beings are not the same as parallel relationships between non-rational beings, just because of the presence of rationality. He tries to counter this possibility by saying that the situation of the human beings cannot be held to differ from that of the non-humans through the humans' ability to discern obligation, since such an ability presupposes the existence of real obligations to be discerned, and this is just what is in question. It is; but this hardly deals with an objector who insists that the relationships between the humans is different because of *other* abilities that they have, and that it is these which create the obligations. We can object to Hume's application of his second condition on the grounds that what is supposed to influence the will is not a relation one discerns but one's discernment of it.

Hume's most fundamental argument against the rational basis of evaluation comes, however, when he passes to consider the view that reason does not function in morality by demonstrating moral truths, but by discovering moral matters of fact in some non-demonstrative way. How could reason recognise such matters of fact? 'Take any action allowed to be vicious; wilful murder, for instance. Examine it in all lights, and see if you can find that matter of fact, or real existence, which you call vice. In whichever way you take it, you find only certain passions, motives, volitions, and thoughts. There is no other matter of fact in the case. The vice entirely escapes you, as long as you consider the object' (III 177/468). If you examine any virtuous or vicious actions, all you find are the agent's deeds, plus his passions, motives, volitions, or thoughts. You do not find his virtue or his vice. Hume's appeal here is of the same kind as those others where he invites us to present to him the impression of necessity, or of the self. And he makes the same suggestion: that the idea we have is one that has an origin within us, rather than in the object or person whose qualities we can observe. I turn now to this positive suggestion.

Moral Evaluations as Passions

Hume's heading for Section II of Book III of the *Treatise* ascribes it to a moral *sense*. To modern readers this suggests at first sight that Hume may believe in moral intuitions which inform us of the rightness or wrongness of individual actions by some form of moral perception; but of course he has just been vigorously arguing against such a view, which in the language of Book III would amount to ascribing the power of moral evaluation to reason in one or other of its manifestations. He makes his position unambiguously clear when he tells us that morality is 'more properly felt than judged of' (III 178/470), and that vice and virtue are discoverable 'by means of some impression or sentiment they occasion'. In the first Appendix to the second *Enquiry*, the title 'moral sentiment' replaces 'moral sense'. The moral sense, then, is our capacity for a certain kind of inner feeling.[2]

What kind? He tells us at once that it is a special kind of pleasure or pain, namely 'that *peculiar* kind which makes us praise or condemn'. This is a little difficult to square with his saying, just before, that 'the very *feeling* constitutes our praise or admiration', but it seems reasonable to interpret Hume as saying that there is a special sort of feeling which constitutes moral admiration, and another special sort of feeling which constitutes moral condemnation; that the former is a special sort of pleasure, the latter is a special sort of pain; and that it is the former which we have on those occasions when we sincerely *express* praise, and the latter which we have when we sincerely *express* condemnation, in the form of those sentences which philosophers classify as moral judgements. I do not at this point wish to place too much emphasis on any particular understanding of what it is to express the praise or condemnation. Hume also tells us that 'the case is the same' for aesthetic judgements as for moral ones.

Perhaps this does not entail, thus far, that moral evaluations are passions. It does entail that they share with the passions the characteristic of being unique secondary impressions, which means that they cannot, in his system of human nature, be analysed. All we can do is to describe what generates them, and what their effects are. It is to this description that Hume's very important claim about the *disinterestedness* of moral evaluations belongs. Moral evaluations come about when we consider their objects 'without reference to our particular interest' (III 180/472); we denominate them virtuous if they 'give pleasure by the mere survey' (III 285/591) – that is, in themselves rather than in relation to ourselves. It is also to this description that Hume's theory of the place of *sympathy* in moral evaluation belongs: for it is sympathy that enables us to feel that pleasure or pain in the object of our evaluations without which they could not occur. Hume recognises, indeed he makes much of, the fact that we can confuse moral evaluations with other attitudes that do not come about the same way, as when we confuse our hatred for our enemy with moral disapproval of him. But he regards this as an error we make in identifying which of two distinct and unique impressions we have, through overlooking its origin. It is a contingent and not a necessary truth that disinterested scrutiny of a man's character leads to moral disapproval and interested scrutiny leads to hatred.

Hume does, however, commit himself to the view that moral evaluations are passions. This appears most explicitly in Section V of Part III of Book III: 'The pain or pleasure which arises from the general survey or view of any action or quality of the mind, constitutes its vice or virtue, and gives rise to our approbation or blame, which is nothing but a fainter and more imperceptible love or hatred' (III 306–7/614). This supports the interpretation of Árdal, that moral approval and disapproval are calm forms of the indirect passions of love and hatred.[3] There are, however, difficulties in reading Hume this way. One difficulty is the implausibility of the theory itself: we are quite familiar with the experience of loving someone of whom we disapprove, or approving of someone whom we are quite unable to love. But if Hume fails ever to distinguish love and esteem, he is unlikely to distinguish love from moral approval. It could in any case be argued that if (however contingently) the emotions of love and approval differ in their origins, this would be sufficient to explain the phenomena mentioned; so that I could approve of someone I do not love just because the attitude I have is that of detached objectivity. Another, and more awkward difficulty, is that if approval and disapproval are calm versions of love and hatred, it is hard to understand the suggestion that someone who mistakes his hatred for moral disapproval is confusing one emotion with another. This hardly seems the same as being confused between two differing degrees of violence of one and the same emotion — though if it could be construed this way, there would be little difficulty in understanding how the error could occur. Finally, if approval and disapproval are forms of love and hatred, then their objects would have to be persons. Yet in the very sentence just quoted Hume seems to say (though admittedly the sentence is not without ambiguity) that we approve or disapprove of actions and qualities of mind. Certainly we all speak of approving or disapproving of actions and qualities of mind, as well as of their owners, whereas it is not natural to speak of loving or hating actions, and if we talk of loving or hating qualities of mind, it would seem to be in a derivative sense. In spite of these difficulties, I think it is clear that Hume would like to assimilate his account of moral evaluations to his general theory of the passions as closely as possible; and identifying moral approval and disapproval with calm love and hatred is an ingenious way of doing this. It also does a good deal, as Árdal says, to explain Hume's largely unsupported insistence that moral evaluations are never directed at actions individually, but only at actions 'as a sign of some quality or character', so that actions that are not such a sign (presumably those done out of character) 'are never considered in morality' (III 272/575). The only reason he offers for this strange opinion is that such actions 'not proceeding from any constant principle, have no influence on love or hatred, pride or humility'.

But if this is what Hume intends, then he does not succeed in making his account of moral evaluations fit the genetic pattern that is characteristic of love and hatred in his account of the passions. It will be recalled that when I love someone there has to be an independent pleasure that I derive from some quality of his, which leads by association to the pleasant impression of love, as the idea of the quality leads to the idea of the man who has it. On this analogy, when I feel moral approval, some action, or some state of a man's character, would have to generate in me an independent pleasure

139

that leads on to the approval of the man himself, as the idea of the quality leads on to the idea of the man as its owner. So far so good, but Hume uses language that makes it unclear whether or not he does in fact restrict approval to the owner of the quality. He takes as the terms expressing the approval or disapproval the words 'virtuous' and 'vicious'; these are in fact applied equally to the agent himself, to his character, and also to the acts he performs when manifesting it. Of course the simple fact is that we do express, and feel, approval and disapproval of all three, even though Hume's assimilation of them to love and hate would require him to restrict them to the first alone.[4] I would judge that it is indeed Hume's general view that approval and disapproval are calm forms of love and hatred, and are consequently restricted in their application to agents rather than to their actions or their personalities, but that the facts of the moral life make it inevitable that he should make statements that are inconsistent with this, and treat actions and character-traits as objects of moral evaluation also.[5] There is of course no reason in *logic* why one and the same passion should not be aroused by all three sorts of object; but Hume makes no use of this.

It is now possible to give a reasonably clear outline of Hume's views on the origins of moral evaluations. I draw upon Sections I to III of Part III of Book III of the *Treatise,* and on Sections V to VIII of the *Enquiry.*

(1) I am able to recognise that a particular state of character generates pleasure or pain in one of four possible ways.

(*a*) It may be immediately agreeable or disagreeable to other persons. Examples of qualities of which this is true are 'wit, and a certain easy and disengaged behaviour' or, on the disagreeable side, excessive pride (III 285/590; *E.M.* 261–7).

(*b*) It may be immediately agreeable or disagreeable to the agent himself. In this category fall all the passions that derive from love or hatred (III 296–9/602–6; *E.M.* 250–60).

(*c*) It may be useful to others – that is, indirectly productive of pleasure or pain in them; examples of traits that are useful in this way are generosity, humanity, fidelity, benevolence and meekness. It may on the other hand be harmful to others, that is indirectly productive of pain for them; the most obvious example being cruelty (III 271–86/574–91; *E.M.* 212–32).

(*d*) It may be useful to the agent himself, as are prudence, temperance, industry and dexterity. It may be harmful to the agent himself, as are indolence, inconstancy and irresolution (III 271–86/ 574–91; *E.M.* 233–249).

(2) In each case what we fix our attention on are the actual or possible *effects* of the character-traits in question. In each case these effects are pleasing or displeasing, either to the agent or, more usually, to others. Hume sometimes speaks of the tendency of states of character to lead to the happiness of their owner or of others, and in the *Enquiry* the notion of utility is prominent.

(3) When I become aware of the pleasing or displeasing effects on the agent or on others, these effects can be paralleled in me through the mechanism of *sympathy*. This claim entails that sympathy is not only a mechanism that generates parallel passions in me to those that obtain in others, but can do the same with regard to all pleasures or pains. Here it is essential to stress that sympathy is not itself one of the virtues; nor is it my capacity to be moved by the pleasures or pains of others; it is the mechanism that Hume resorts to to account for this capacity, which he does by saying that in sympathy I come to have a pleasure corresponding to the pleasure another has, or a pain corresponding to a pain another has.

(4) The pleasure or pain that sympathy generates in me is not itself my approval or disapproval. The latter arises from it by association: approval in the case of pleasures, disapproval in the case of pains. It is clear that even if we insist on making the object of the approval and disapproval a moral agent, the parallel with love and hatred cannot be exact, since inevitably the approval and disapproval are not directed toward the person whose pleasure or pain I sympathetically share; they must be directed toward the person who caused them to have it. The parallel is only exact when the same person happens to be both the producer and the recipient of the pleasure or pain.

(5) It is this emotion of approval or disapproval which constitutes (*is*) moral evaluation. The *expression* of it takes the form of our use of the terms 'virtue' and 'vice', and their associated adjectives, to describe the state of character which has the pleasing or displeasing effects, or, derivatively, to describe the actions which manifest it. It is of course possible to hold, however implausibly, that one expresses approval or disapproval *of the person* by calling his character-traits virtuous or vicious. The fact that these adjectives are applied to his character rather than to him does not mean that the approval or disapproval I feel, and express by so applying them, is directed at anything other than the man himself.

Conditions of Moral Evaluation: Objectivity, Utility, Sympathy

This outline of Hume's theory of moral evaluation needs to be supplemented in three important respects. More needs to be said about the cognitive preliminaries to our evaluations, and Hume's view that these have to be undertaken in a disinterested manner. More needs to be said about the fact that our approval and disapproval is directed towards men and their characters in virtue of the effects which we see them to have − to the apparently utilitarian thrust of Hume's ethical theory. And further understanding of the nature of the role played by sympathy in the arousal of the moral passions is also of importance. In each case the key to comprehension of Hume's quite complex position is the recognition that what is at issue is the psychological genesis of the moral passions.

Objectivity. Hume says that for us to feel moral approval or disapproval, as distinct from love or hatred or some other emotion that could be confused with the moral ones, it is necessary that our scrutiny of the facts should be disinterested. He seems to hold both that the moral sentiments are distinguishable in themselves from their non-moral relatives, and also that these can be confused with them if the cognitive preliminaries that lead to them are thought to be objective when they are not. In another idiom this could be expressed by saying that disinterestedness is a feature of the moral emotions as well as of the thinking that leads to them; but Hume could not put his point precisely in this way, since the notion of a disinterested (or interested) impression is not obviously meaningful.

Disinterestedness is not indifference. For what it leads to, on Hume's account, is a special sort of emotional involvement. It is rather an attention to those features of a man's character and actions that affect his feelings or the feelings of those with whom he deals, in abstraction from any connection they may have with *myself* or others close to me. It is a fact of human nature that, although sympathy is much enhanced, and much more likely to operate, when the persons whose feelings I attend to are connected with myself, it can still be put in motion by the mere fact that they are also persons as I am. When sympathy is put into motion by this most general of all resemblances, Hume calls it extensive sympathy. If this is admitted to be a fact, then all that Hume has to explain is why we are able and willing to pay heed at all to the feelings of those who are not connected with us, it being assumed that when we do this, sympathetic processes will follow.

In order, perhaps, to avoid injecting any specifically ethical

142

notions into his account of the preliminaries to evaluation, Hume treats this last question as a wholly epistemological one. He answers it in terms of our capacity to correct mis-estimates that are due to nearness or to distance. He points out that we are not unwilling to judge a face beautiful merely because we only see it at a distance, and we are not unwilling to admire the noble qualities of the heroes of antiquity merely because they are remote from us in time; this is because we realise that we would admire them without effort if we were able to have a closer view (III 278–9/582–3). This would seem to equate disinterestedness with imagined closeness, which is certainly not indifference. In these cases of course we would have no inclination to confuse our approval with love. The requirement of objectivity must also take a detached view of those close to us, and evaluate them morally instead of loving or hating them. The doctrine of extensive sympathy is obviously supposed to provide for this possibility also, but the necessary cognitive preliminaries would have to be more like cases of imagined distance when the danger to objectivity comes from actual closeness, so Hume's explanation of its possibility is not very helpful. He really needs to account for our willingness to be objective, which is itself a moral attitude. What he offers is merely an account of how we achieve objectivity when this attitude is already taken up – and his account only covers cases where we compensate for distance, not cases where we compensate for closeness. This is especially unfortunate, since it is the latter compensation that is needed when there is real risk of our feeling love or hate instead of moral approval or disapproval.

Hume also has to account for the fact that we approve or disapprove of men's characters as they are in themselves, even when they do not have actual effects that we like or dislike. A man may be judged virtuous or vicious, even though he finds himself in circumstances that prevent him from exercising his good or bad inclinations. Hume appeals here to the influence of general rules. We judge men, he says, by the general tendency attaching to the sort of characters they have: that is, we recognise that someone's character is of the sort that usually has beneficial or harmful results. Hence 'virtue in rags is still virtue' (III 280/584).

Utility. The cognitive preliminaries to evaluation, then, direct our attention to the effects of those characteristics that we evaluate. Because Hume insists that it is the effects of the objects of evaluation that lead, via the mechanisms of sympathy, to approval or disapproval of those objects, he has been generally regarded, with some justice, as the ancestor of Utilitarians such as Bentham and Mill. To turn Hume into a Utilitarian, however, one would have to transpose all that he says into the key appropriate to normative ethics. It is tempting to do this, especially in the light of his statement in the *Enquiry* that 'The end of all moral speculations is to teach us our duty; and, by proper representations of the deformity of vice and beauty of virtue, beget corresponding habits, and engage us to avoid the one, and embrace the other' (*E.M.* 172). But against this we have to balance not only the avowed psychologism of the whole of the *Treatise,* but the statement, also in the *Enquiry,* that his purpose is to 'find those universal principles, from which all censure or approbation is ultimately derived' (*E.M.* 174), a task which he insists is a 'question of fact' to be decided 'by following the experimental method'. Hume is not, in general, trying to make moral recommendations by means of a supreme moral principle, but giving a psychology of ethical evaluation. So his objectives are not the same as those of Bentham or Mill. Of course he does have to allow, in his description of our evaluative psychology, for the kinds of ethical discriminations that form the basis of the Utilitarian ethic. This he does, as we have seen already, through his doctrine of disinterested moral contemplation, which enables us to attend to the effects of men's actions and characters on society as a whole, rather than on ourselves exclusively. In the *Enquiry* it is these effects that are insisted upon most, rather than the effects on those immediately influenced by a man's actions, so that we find Hume referring frequently to 'the interests of the species' or 'public good'. This enables him to account, on grounds that certainly fit a Utilitarian ethic, for those occasions where we disapprove of the exercise of a tendency which is in most circumstances one of which we approve: his example being that of generous actions that do not benefit society as a whole, like those of a prince towards his favourites (*E.M.* 180).

Hume's account of the genesis of approval is one that allows him to include among the virtues such things as quick apprehension; a quality like this is usually regarded as a natural ability rather than a virtue, but he argues (*Treatise,* Book III, Part III, Section IV) that this distinction is really an empty one, since we admire both, and we admire both because both are equally useful. The only excuse philosophers have for distinguishing between the two is that it is useless to try and change a man's natural abilities by reward or punishment, whereas this is not true with regard to what we usually

144

classify as his virtues or vices: again, a Utilitarian standard of discrimination. It is interesting that he has no patience with the suggestion that the basis for the distinction between abilities and virtues lies in the fact that the virtues are acquired voluntarily. This voluntariness is in his view mythical, and he insists that moral approval or disapproval, being based on our perception of the usefulness or harmfulness of character-traits, and not being directed at individual actions, do not presuppose some alleged liberty of indifference in the acquisition of the character-traits that we contemplate. Many would regard this as placing doubt on his analysis of evaluation as well as on his analysis of freedom, but Hume clearly regards each as supporting the other.

On this last point Hume is on the edge of passing over from the descriptive to the normative. Even if he does not pass over it here, he certainly does in another place. In the *Enquiry* we find the following diatribe, which would have done credit to Bentham:

> And as every quality which is useful or agreeable to ourselves or others is, in common life, allowed to be a part of personal merit; so no other will ever be received, where men judge of things by their natural, unprejudiced reason, without the delusive glosses of superstition and false religion. Celibacy, fasting, penance, mortification, self-denial, humility, silence, solitude, and the whole train of monkish virtues; for what reason are they everywhere rejected by men of sense, but because they serve to no manner of purpose; neither advance a man's fortune in the world, nor render him a more valuable member of society; neither qualify him for the entertainment of company, nor increase his power of self-enjoyment? We observe, on the contrary that they cross all these desirable ends; stupefy the understanding and harden the heart, obscure the fancy and sour the temper. We justly, therefore, transfer them to the opposite column, and place them in the catalogue of vices; nor has any superstition force sufficient among men of the world, to pervert entirely these natural sentiments. A gloomy, hair-brained enthusiast, after his death, may have a place in the calendar; but will scarcely ever be admitted, when alive, into intimacy and society, except by those who are as delirious and dismal as himself. (*E.M.* 270)

Obviously here Hume is no longer saying merely that we approve of certain things and disapprove of others. He is saying that *men of sense* approve of certain things and disapprove of others. Utility is

145

now not just a consideration that is always, or usually, paramount in our evaluations. It is the only consideration that *ought* to figure in them.

A purely psychological account of our evaluations is one that can, in principle at least, reveal that the same set of effects, equally clearly discerned, can lead to different evaluations in different people. This is one such case. With this example in mind, John Kemp says: 'Hume's argument for his general thesis seems to beg the question. If the thesis to be proved is that all qualities which are genuinely virtuous promote human well-being, then a counterclaim that qualities X, Y, and Z are virtues cannot be refuted by pointing out that they do not promote human well-being. Nor will it suffice to say, rhetorically, that they are "everywhere rejected by men of sense"; a philosopher must be prepared to prove that his opponents are not men of sense, not simply assert it.'[6] This is not, I think, quite what is wrong with Hume's outburst. In itself there is nothing wrong with a less-than-universal result, if what we are interested in doing is seeing what human beings approve of and how. We may very well get disagreement from time to time. In fact we obviously do, and it is a strength not a weakness in a theory that it can allow for it. What a purely psychological theory cannot do is *resolve* the disagreement. Nor should it be expected to do so. Such disagreement is of course a *moral* problem, and the resolution of such disagreements is a basic aim, one supposes, of normative ethics. Utilitarianism is a theory in normative ethics, not a proper part of a science of human nature.

It is noteworthy that Hume is in any case barely aware of the possibility of widespread moral disagreement, and does not discuss it. He seems to assume throughout that human nature is constant in its evaluations. This seems to imply that where disagreement surfaces it is as the result of insufficient knowledge, or insufficient objectivity, in the scrutiny of the facts of the case disputed. In the language of C. L. Stevenson, Hume seems to take for granted that disagreement in attitude is always the result of disagreement in belief.

Although it is a mistake to read Hume as though he were engaged in normative ethics, he lapses into it often enough for such a mistake to be excusable. When he does his sympathies reveal themselves clearly enough to be similar enough to those of the later Utilitarian moralists, except in one basic respect. The Utilitarians were moral reformers and radicals. Hume's whole description of the way human

146

nature encompasses our evaluations, though in theory normatively neutral, bespeaks an easy acceptance of its being just the way he finds it. For him utility is possessed by what our actual society finds beneficial, not what it ought to find beneficial.

Sympathy. The importance of the mechanism of sympathy in the genesis of evaluations is a widely recognised feature of Hume's ethics. It will not be necessary to stress again that sympathy is not the emotion of compassion, nor a moral principle of kindness to others, but a mechanism whereby we pass from a mere intellectual awareness of the feeling of others to an emotional involvement with the feelings they have. In the *Treatise* it is this mechanism which is supposed to explain our ability to go on to approve or disapprove of the persons who cause those states with which I sympathise. It seems that this psychological mechanism, and its attendant explanation of how moral evaluation takes place, is absent from the *Enquiry,* which proceeds throughout without drawing, as Book III of the *Treatise* repeatedly draws, on Hume's theory of the passions. In the *Enquiry* Hume is content to point out that 'Usefulness is agreeable, and engages our approbation' (*E.M.* 218), and to say that this is due to our 'fellow-feeling with others'. The work contains no direct account of how this fellow-feeling comes to be, and in consequence when the word 'sympathy' appears at all, it seems to be merely a name for it. Other names are 'humanity' and perhaps 'benevolence'. At one place Hume seems explicitly to disavow any interest in the possibility of a deeper explanation: 'It is needless to push our researches so far as to ask, why we have humanity or a fellow-feeling with others. It is sufficient, that this is experienced to be a principle in human nature. We must stop somewhere in our examination of causes; and there are, in every science, some general principles, beyond which we cannot hope to find any principle more general. . . . We may safely here consider these principles as original; happy, if we can render all the consequences sufficiently plain and perspicuous!' (*E.M.* 219– 220, footnote)

I do not think that this represents an explicit disavowal of the doctrine of sympathy as we have it in the *Treatise.* It rather reflects a willingness on Hume's part to settle for the readers' agreement that we do succeed in being concerned for the feelings of others, however we achieve this. The doctrine of impressions and ideas is as important in the *Enquiry Concerning Human Understanding* as it is in the epistemological sections of the *Treatise*; if we accordingly presuppose it in the second *Enquiry,* we can see that Hume would

147

have difficulty accounting for the fact of our concern for the feelings of others except by resort to some such mechanism as that of sympathy. I incline to think, therefore, that although Hume is prepared to settle for less in the *Enquiry,* his remarks there do not imply an abandonment of the doctrine of sympathy as we have it from the *Treatise,* but at most a lessening of interest in it, and a conviction that his account of evaluation, which is otherwise not changed, can stand in its other features without it. He would seem to be correct in this conviction, for the subtraction of the doctrine of synpathy merely leaves a gap between our recognition of the useful or harmful effects of the objects of our approval or disapproval, and the actual arousal of these two emotions: a gap which he proclaims himself willing to leave unfilled if the rest of his account can be accepted by his readers.[7]

Moral Judgements

I turn now to the question of the views, if any, which Hume held concerning the expression of evaluations, namely moral judgements. His primary objectives do not include that of giving an account of these at all. To evaluate a character or action morally is to experience a particular passion toward the person who has it or does it. This view is not identical with any contemporary 'ism' about the status of moral judgements. It is true that Hume does say the following: 'when you pronounce any action or character to be vicious, you mean nothing, but that from the constitution of your nature you have a feeling or sentiment of blame from the contemplation of it' (III 177/469). But I do not think that too much weight can be put on Hume's use of the word 'mean'.[8] While it is absurd to suggest that Hume was not of sufficient subtlety of mind to grasp the distinction between the content of an utterance and the circumstances of its use, it is not absurd to point out that this is not uppermost in his mind in the *Treatise*. It is certainly his view that what occasions the use of the terms 'virtuous' or 'vicious' is the prior occurrence of the feeling of approval or disapproval in the speaker. The problem is whether or not its occurrence is being reported in the statement that the speaker makes. If Hume thought that it is, then his view is open to the standard objection to Subjectivist analyses of moral judgements, namely that they make it impossible for there to be genuine disagreement about questions of value. If *A* reports that he has a feeling of approval, and *B* reports that he has a feeling of disapproval, these are entirely compatible with one another. The most familiar alternative analysis that attempts to maintain the emotional character of moral judgements and yet escape this Subjectivist difficulty is that which says that moral judgements are neither true nor false, but are simply ways in which we express or evince our moral feelings. This does nothing to preserve disagreement unless one adds on a separate sort of disagreement, namely disagreement in attitude. Such refinements are beyond the scope of Hume's analysis.

In spite of this I would hazard the following: that we should look seriously at the sentence which follows the above in Hume's text:[9] 'Vice and virtue, therefore, may be compared to sounds, colours, heat and cold, which, according to modern philosophy, are not qualities in objects, but perceptions in the mind: and this discovery in morals, like that other in physics, is to be regarded as a considerable advancement of the speculative sciences; though, like that too, it has little or no influence on practice' (III 177/469). It will be remembered that Hume offers strong objections in Book I to the very theory of primary and secondary qualities that he now refers to. But we must also remember that in Books II and III he takes for granted the common-sense belief in the reality of the external world that he examines in Book I; and in the present passage he treats the doctrine of secondary qualities as a scientific refinement of that common-sense belief. In comparing the moral characteristics of virtue and vice with the secondary qualities, therefore, he is offering us an analogy which he genuinely supposes to illuminate their nature. In this connection it is important to recall that the doctrine of primary and secondary qualities, as we find it in Locke, is not a mere denial of the physically real existence of colours or smells or sounds. It is also an assertion that our mental perceptions of these qualities are due to real physical or chemical configurations in objects, even though these configurations do not *resemble* the colour, smell, or taste sensations to which they give rise in us. Using this analogy which Hume offers, one can interpret him as believing the following: When I call some action or character virtuous or vicious, I am not merely expressing a feeling which it has aroused in me, but also stating something about those features in the object (the person) which have caused it to do so. More accurately, I am not merely expressing my approval or disapproval, but also claiming that the object has those characteristics, or causal properties, which produce in an objective observer the characteristic moral feeling which I myself am expressing.

149

Such a view would enable us, on Humean principles, to explain why we usually say a character is vicious, rather than that we disapprove of it: we are claiming that any objective observer would also disapprove of it. There is nothing in Hume's text to tell us, beyond this, whether he would think this latter to be part of the content of a sentence like 'This is vicious' or merely to be in some way conventionally implied by the utterance of it, though Hume's language suggests the former view. Such a theory would enable us to say that the sentence, or the utterance of it, conveyed the implication that any observer who felt a different feeling toward the character the speaker called virtuous or vicious was not an objective observer, and had had his view of the facts distorted by incomplete information or partiality. (A natural parallel exists here in the case of claims about secondary qualities: I can hold that oranges are not sour but sweet, and that the contrary view is due to the fact that other tasters consume too much sugar for the chemical components of oranges to affect them in the normal way.) This theory would preserve disagreement, since it would imply that each party to a moral dispute is of the view that the other has misconstrued the facts; though it would imply that this is the only sort of contrariety that is possible between them. In all these respects this view of moral judgements seems to fit what Hume says elsewhere. A final advantage such an interpretation has is that it makes more sense of Hume's view that it is people, rather than their characters or their actions, that are the real objects of approval and disapproval: for even if the agent himself is the sole real object of these feelings, these feelings toward him could still be aroused in us by his character or his actions, just as the sweetness we ascribe to the orange is ascribed to it by us because of the effects on us of the chemical constituents of it. And just as I can equally well say the fibres or juices of the orange are sweet, so this theory would provide a natural subsidiary explanation of why, when it is the man I approve or disapprove of, I can naturally lapse into saying I approve or disapprove of his character or his acts.

Obligation and the Artificial Virtues

Hume's account of moral evaluation is centred upon our approval and disapproval of persons who are the objects of these emotions because of their possession of states of character which we call virtues or vices when this approval or disapproval is expressed. Hume's readers notice that he seems primarily concerned to give us

150

an account of the virtues, and is only incidentally concerned with duty or obligation. There is certainly an oddity about this. Hume offers his theory of evaluation as an alternative to theories which he criticises, in part, for their failure to relate moral discriminations to action, a failure to which he himself draws our attention[10] by wondering how they can account for our sense of obligation. Yet it seems clear that an account of our recognition of the virtuous or vicious character of others only goes some way toward supplying this. For I can surely approve or disapprove of someone without thereby being moved to *do* anything to support or hinder the person towards whom I feel it. Hume says this himself: he tells us (III 281/586) that extensive sympathy may generate approval or disapproval, but generosity or benevolence is limited in human nature to those close to us; the very fact that enables us to approve or disapprove of people unconnected with us by anything more than common humanity, namely our capacity for sympathy, has to be contrasted with the motivating desire of benevolence, which leads us to action only in the case of those who have closer connections. Hume explicitly denies that we have a 'public benevolence' or a 'love of mankind, merely as such' (III 187–8/480) which is sufficient to move us to act. Even if he did not say this, it would follow from his assimilation of moral approval and disapproval to love and hatred. Love and hatred are not, of themselves, motives; they only lead to actions by generating the distinct emotions of benevolence or anger; and these, again, do not seem forthcoming in consequence of approval or disapproval.

Hume is quite clearly aware that men do act, from time to time, out of a sense of duty or obligation, and that he has to give some account of how this comes about. His ethical theory is one which entails that the sense of duty is not a necessary condition of moral action, but essentially secondary and derivative. If moral discriminations are not perceptions of moral fact, but emotional responses to the characters of persons, these characters must already be in existence, in the large part, for us to be able to respond to them. More simply, the motives that prompt men to act in ways that we value favourably or unfavourably must already be there before we make the value-judgements, so that the judgements cannot be themselves the source of those motives. This does not mean that in a world where moral judgements are made men cannot react to them and make their decisions in the light of them; but it does mean that actions so motivated will be necessarily a small minority of those

151

that are evaluated. Hume's understanding of the sense of duty or obligation is only intelligible against this background.

'No action', he tells us 'can be virtuous, or morally good, unless there be in human nature some motive to produce it distinct from the sense of its morality' (III 185/479). This follows from the sort of analysis that Hume has given of moral evaluation, though it would not of course be implied by any theory that allowed the possibility of intuition of moral facts. On Hume's understanding of evaluations, however, people already have to *have* their tendencies to act in certain ways before we can come along and approve or disapprove of them; and this entails that they have to have motives that prompt the actions they have a tendency to do. In addition it is only in so far as they flow from those entrenched motives that men's actions have moral interest for us, since the ultimate objects of our moral judgements are the agents themselves. So we judge actions to be morally good or bad by virtue of their manifesting benevolence, malice, and the like.

But how does this generate action from duty in those cases, however rare they are, where it does take place? In the first place Hume seems to think that the notion of obligation itself is derivative from that of vice, the word 'vice' being of course a term used to express disapproval of someone. At least he says this: 'when any action or quality of the mind pleases us after a certain manner, we say it is virtuous; and when the neglect or non-performance of it displeases us after a like manner, we say that we lie under an obligation to perform it' (III 220/517). In other contexts the same displeasure would be expressed, one supposes, by the use of the term 'vicious'. Hume's view appears to be that to say a certain action, or a certain sort of action, is one that we ought to perform, is to express disapproval at its non-performance, or at the character of those agents who tend not to do it. The trouble with this derivation is that it does not seem to get us any closer to the production of a distinctive motive for action, though Hume himself seems to think that the use of the word 'obligation' carries the suggestion of such a motive.

We find a somewhat deeper account when we turn back to Section I of Part II of Book III. Here Hume tells us that someone may be aware that he lacks the motive which causes us to approve of the performance of some action, and may then 'hate himself on that account', and may perform the action without the motive, 'from a certain sense of duty, in order to acquire, by practice, that virtuous

152

principle, or at least to disguise to himself, as much as possible, his want of it' (II 185–7/479). The use of the phrase 'a certain sense of duty' must warn us that this passage may not be intended as an account of *the* sense of duty, but I incline to think, in view of the context, that it is. For the paragraph begins with Hume's acknowledging that although, in general, moral approval requires the previous existence of some (non-moral) motive to be evaluated, there are still occasions when the sense of duty alone is enough to move us. In this context I take his use of 'a certain sense of duty' to indicate merely that this sense of duty (the only one he will admit) may not be acceptable as the genuine article to some philosophers. If this is correct then Hume regards the sense of duty as a motive to action in those cases where a person is trying to cultivate another motive, which is itself the proper object of moral approval. In detecting the absence of a virtuous motive in myself I disapprove of myself (that is I feel the emotion I would express by saying I ought not to be without it). I then try to escape from this disagreeable emotional state by performing the actions that flow, in others, from this motive, so that I can come to approve of myself (that is feel pride in myself) for having it in the future. The sense of duty is a substitute for the appropriate virtuous motive. Not only this: Hume seems to think it a *conscious* substitute, which we hope will give place to the original.[11]

Hume speaks of the virtuous motive of which we approve as itself a duty. This is puzzling, but only superficially. If calling something a duty is merely one form of expression of our disapproval of someone who does not have it, then since I disapprove of the absence in a father of the natural affection for his children, I can put this by saying that he ought to have this affection, or that it is his duty (II 185/478). The apparent paradox of Hume's saying that natural motives are themselves duties is a simple consequence of his saying that the language of duty is the language of moral disapproval of agents who do not have those motives. This explains also his very important insistence that unless these natural (and non-moral) motives to virtuous actions existed, we would have no obligations to those actions. For there would be no human tendencies to praise or blame unless there were common motives whose absence we could deplore. This is why benevolence, natural affections, and the rest, are all duties: their absence can be morally deplored. This is why they are also virtues: their presence can be approved of. But it is also why someone who has them is *not* someone who is motivated by a

153

sense of duty: such a sense could not even exist if they did not usually exist without it.

But even if this is accepted, it merely leads us to the problem to which Hume himself devotes all of Part II of Book III of the *Treatise*. There seem to be a large class of actions to which the sense of duty is attached (which some people do from duty, and which we blame one another for omitting), to which there does not seem to *be* a prior natural motive. Hume does not think men are all selfish: benevolence is a very common motive. But many actions that we regard as duties do not seem to have sources in human nature that correspond to our benevolent impulses, such as the repayment of debts to the wealthy. So although there are some cases where the natural motives of men remove the need for approval or disapproval to supply a motive of their own, there are many other cases where there seem no natural motives to fall back on. These are the cases where we act from *justice*. We do not seem to have any natural inclinations to such actions; nor are they even always to our own advantage, so that prudence could motivate them. Yet we do regard justice as a virtue, and in consequence regard just acts as our duty. How does the *practice* of justice, without which such approval and disapproval could not begin, become established? It is clear that it cannot be explained by reference to the sense of duty, since that presupposes the existence of the very practice that generates the moral evaluation of it that finds expression in the language of duty. So its existence must be due to other factors. What are these?

Hume is asking a question that is similar to the one Plato asks in the *Republic*. But it is only similar, not identical. Plato wishes to discover what needs in human nature and human society the practice of justice satisfies, in order to prove that justice is better for the man who practises it than injustice is, in spite of appearances to the contrary. He is trying to *justify* justice. Much of what Hume says about it could no doubt be enlisted for such a purpose, but his own objective is more modest, and more exclusively psychological. He is concerned to ask how it is that men come to act justly, and how they come to attach moral approval to just behaviour and disapproval to unjust behaviour. On his theory these have to be separate questions, since no such approval could be attached to any form of behaviour unless it were already independently motivated. But the puzzle about how justice comes to be practised baffles him more than the puzzle about how we come to approve it, since the latter, with minor qualifications, is not different in essence fom the parallel question about those virtues for which a natural motive does exist. Plato is concerned to see whether justice really is a virtue: whether our apparent obligation to act justly is a real one. That justice is a virtue Hume never questions, for it is obvious that men approve of it. His puzzle is how it has become sufficiently established in society to be available for such approbation.

He first brushes aside various easy answers (III 186/479). He asks why it is that I feel obliged to return money that I have borrowed. It is true that civilised man would answer by a simple appeal to a sense of justice or of obligation; but this does not help us to understand how this regard for justice came to be. We cannot explain this by reference to private interest, since this often causes us to act *un*justly; and our regard for the public good is a 'motive too remote and sublime to affect the generality of mankind'. Our natural benevolence is confined to those close to us, so although this might be a plausible source of just behaviour, such behaviour is often practised towards those far removed from the agent's own circle. So we seem unable to explain the fact that men act justly by reference to a sense of duty, yet equally fail to explain it by reference to other motives that naturally prompt us to the actions that justice requires. The only remaining possibility, says Hume, is that justice arises artificially, by human convention, and that some recognisable human motive is what prompts us to found the convention on which it depends.

Hume then proceeds to explain first how conventions establish the rules of justice, and second how those rules come to be regarded as precepts for *virtuous* behaviour. The former accounts for the institution of justice, the latter for its moral standing. He rather unhappily describes the first task as that of explaining our natural obligation to justice, and the second as that of explaining our moral obligation to it.

Men have needs which exceed their individual powers to satisfy them. They resolve this predicament by living together in society. To some extent the natural ties of sexual attraction and love of family act as a uniting force within society. But to a considerable degree they have a divisive effect also. While they stimulate generosity and concern for others, they also restrict the circle towards which these can be felt. In particular, they militate against the security of property that is one of the potential advantages of life in society. This defect in our natures we are able to overcome by intelligence. We are able to see the advantages that would follow from a

155

'convention entered into by all members of society to bestow stability on the possession of those external goods' (III 195/489). He calls this understanding a 'common sense of interest' and says we have a conventional agreement among us to refrain from violating one another's property. This view sounds very like the Social Contract theory in some of its forms. But Hume cannot make use of the notion of a contract in this account, since a contract involves a promise, and as he explicitly says, a promise seems necessarily to create a moral obligation, and his account must not make use of this notion. He claims instead that the convention on which justice depends is an implicit, not an explicit one, like the convention two oarsmen in a boat have to row in time with one another. It is, then, founded on mutual self-interest. Once this convention of justice is established the institution of the stable ownership of property becomes possible.

Hume rejects the claim that there has ever been a historical period during which men lived in a State of Nature as envisaged by Hobbes, or in a Golden Age where selfishness was unknown. In a wholly selfish state property would be impossible, and in a wholly benevolent state it would be unnecessary. These are both important truths, and myths about the past are fanciful ways of bringing these truths home to us. But they merely show us why we need the conventions that we have when human nature is mixed in the way it is. Hume consistently denies that we are wholly selfish; but the benevolence we show is not unrestricted; it is confined to those connected with ourselves. It is not in our interest that such confined benevolence be our only source of actions that are of benefit to others. The essence of justice is impartiality, and it is only convention that can introduce this into our conduct. It is because we depend on a convention to introduce it that we have to uphold the convention even when it has consequences that are not for the public good – as it has, for example, when justice requires us to uphold the legality of the bequest of a fortune to a miser who will make no use of it. The general rules of which this is an application are built into our conventions, and it is the convention, rather than the specific application of it, that we see to be in our mutual interests when all things are considered.

If this is how justice comes to exist, it is possible to see how the practice of it becomes a virtue. While interest establishes it, this does not give it moral status. This comes from sympathy. The way sympathy establishes justice as a virtue reinforces the hold that the

156

institution of justice has upon us even in those cases where we may lose sight of how it promotes our interests. For even if we cannot see that just actions are in our interests, we can very quickly experience how our interests are harmed when someone else is unjust to us. This alone (though Hume does not say this) might merely lead to hatred rather than that objectively founded form of it that constitutes moral disapproval. But we are not only capable of negative reactions when we are treated unjustly ourselves; we are also capable of participating through sympathy in the distress of others when they are treated unjustly, whether they are close to us or not. We are even able to recognise the actual or potential distresses that would be caused by unjust acts we might commit ourselves. So through sympathy moral disapproval of injustice becomes possible, and through this the status of justice as a virtue.

Hume shows considerable perception in basing this account on the disapproval of injustice rather than the approval of justice. To proceed in this way captures very neatly the essential unlovableness and unattractiveness of justice. It is displeasing to encounter its opposite, rather than pleasing to encounter it. It does not warm the heart but stills anxiety. It also connects neatly with Hume's own account of the nature of our sense of obligation: the obligatoriness of justice would, on this account, be a simple logical consequence of the disapproval of its violation. And while not all acts of justice lead to good results, and even some that do do not do so obviously, all acts of injustice are felt to lead to some distress.

So our sense of obligation to just action is an emotional reinforcement of a pattern of behaviour that men enter into originally through tacit recognition of the interest all have in the conventional institution of justice. It is not a reinforcement of a tendency to act in ways that are of themselves attractive to us. What distinguishes the artificial (or social) virtues of which justice is the generic name, is the fact that unless certain conventions were established out of mutual interest, men would not be disposed to perform such actions at all. Once they are so disposed, however, the emotional reinforcement of our evaluations helps to entrench them in essentially the same way that it helps to entrench the other, natural, virtues such as benevolence: by the pleasure of approval at the sight of their exercise and the discomfort of disapproval at the sight of their violation. These in turn, especially the latter, give us an additional motive to perform them, namely, the removal of discomfort at their omission and (at least in the case of the natural virtues) the cultivation of the normal motive to their performance. It is these motives that are the components of the motive of duty. Hume is not much impressed, it seems, by the power of the motive of duty to guide our conduct, though he does not deny it does it from time to time.

His account of the institution of promise-keeping (or the virtue of fidelity), in Section V of Part II of Book III of the *Treatise,* is an interesting application of his general position. Briefly summarised, his view amounts to saying that the moral obligation which attaches to promises, and which derives in their case from the utterance of a conventional form of words ('I promise . . . ') is also a derivative phenomenon, and is not the original motive for the existence of the institution of promise-keeping. In uttering the form of words a man is invoking an institution which we have entered into out of interest. Mutual services can be performed only if men have the assurance of future returns for present benefits, especially in those cases where the future returns are not independently attractive actions for the person who has to do them. The public announcement of the intention to perform future good offices puts the person who makes it in a position where he will be mistrusted if he does not deliver them. So to make commerce possible men expose themselves to this risk. So promise-making and promise-keeping are entered into from interest, or, as Hume insists on putting it, to the confusion of readers, 'interest is the *first* obligation to the performance of promises' (III 225/523). Once this institution exists, fidelity to one's promises becomes an object of moral approval in addition, and its opposite an object of disapproval, and the motive of duty is added to that of interest.

Government and Political Obligation

Given this analysis of justice, and Hume's tendency to accord derivative and second-class status to the sense of duty as a motive for moral action, it is not surprising that we find him impressed by the fact that men are very often tempted to violate the rules of justice. For they do not always feel the sense of their own interest that makes them seek just conventions to be strong enough to override contrary impulses; and on such occasions the sense of duty tends also to have little grip. So just as justice is artificially created, so it is artificially supported. It is supported by education and propaganda. More importantly, society seeks devices that will reinforce our natural obligation to (that is, our interest in) justice more effectively

158

than our sense of a moral obligation to it is usually able to do. What most hinders justice is not selfishness, but the characteristic in human nature which makes justice most necessary, namely 'narrowness of soul', or partiality. Men are capable of benevolence, but tend to limit it to those close to them. They are also liable to prefer closer goods to more remote ones even for themselves, and choose immediate benefits rather than long-term advantages. It is this preference for what is near that constantly tempts them to injustice, and even clouds their judgement of what acts are just and what are not, by biasing them too greatly in their own favour or in favour of those near to them. The solution that society takes is the introduction of a civil authority, a person or group of persons whose immediate interest it is to maintain just relationships among their subjects, and where necessary to impose sanctions that make it less in a man's apparent immediate interest to behave unjustly to others.

This is the origin of government. Once established, government can generate and enforce many co-operative enterprises that private individuals would find it difficult to carry through without it, and which are of great additional benefit to its subjects.

This account of the source of government assumes that men in society can perceive they have a common interest in strengthening an institution (justice) that their own weakness places in danger. So Hume does not hold that justice is in itself a consequence of government, merely that government exists to strengthen it afterward. He says, therefore, that institutions such as respect for property and fidelity to promises, can exist in societies that have no formal government at all. But a society to which men have added the authority of government is much better able to sustain them. He accepts, from the Social Contract theorists, the theory that in the first instance governments must come into existence through the subjects making an explicit promise to obey a magistrate. But, it will be recalled, he denies that justice itself is the outcome of any such explicit promise. He also denies that the citizen's duty of allegiance comes from any actual or implied promise to obey. The promise is merely needed to set up an authority in the first instance. Once set up, its benefits to the subjects are the source of its right to allegiance. Men set it up by promises, but they make these promises because of their perceived interest. Once it is established, this interest deepens because of the additional benefits government is found to confer. It is this interest that creates the natural obligation (that is the morally praiseworthy tendency) to obey the government; and this is in turn reinforced through approval and disapproval, which generate the moral obligation to obey.

Hume agrees with those Social Contract theorists who hold that once a government ceases to govern in the interests of the populace, the obligations which derive from that interest, cease also. There is no duty to obey government *per se*. Hume does not, however, accept their reason for saying this. For him an unjust government can be overturned because the obligation to obey it would only exist if obedience to it were in the public interest. He does not accept the argument that our obligation to obey comes merely from a promise and does not exist when no promise has been made. A citizen is bound to obey his government whether he has set it up by his own promises or has been born into it – provided it is a government whose actions are in the interest of its subjects. The obligation could only depend on the promise in the specific case of the founding citizens who made it, and even in their case it is the subsequent benefits of government that are the major source of their interest in it, and therefore their obligation to it.

'Is' and 'Ought'

Section I of Part I of Book III of the *Treatise* ends with the now famous 'is—ought' passage. I have deliberately omitted discussion of it until this point, even though the Section as a whole is of fundamental significance. The 'is—ought' passage itself seems to me to be of only modest importance in the development of Hume's theory of evaluation, however critical the matters raised in it might be for contemporary meta-ethics. The lively and protracted controversies surrounding it in recent years are mainly due to the fact that contemporary moral philosophers have been eager to enlist Hume on one or other side in the debate between Ethical Naturalists and Ethical Non-Naturalists.

Ethical Naturalists assert, and Ethical Non-Naturalists deny, that it is possible without logical infelicity to infer an evaluative conclusion, especially one which states an obligation, from non-evaluative premises. Non-Naturalists hold that such an inference is only possible if some open or concealed evaluative premiss is first added to the non-evaluative ones. In this paragraph Hume notes how 'every system of morality' he has met with is one in which the author seems to pass from sentences joined with an 'is' or an 'is not' to sentences joined with an 'ought' or an 'ought not', without explanation. Yet, he says, some explanation is surely required when

160

some new relation or affirmation like this makes its appearance, since it cannot be a 'deduction' from those mentioned previously. If we only observed the need for such an explanation, he says, this would 'subvert all the vulgar systems of morality, and let us see that the distinction of vice and virtue is not founded merely on the relations of objects, nor is perceived by reason' (III 178/470).

It seems to me that the context makes it clear enough that Hume's concern here is not with the logical question that today divides Ethical Naturalists and Ethical Non-Naturalists. For what is it that the 'vulgar systems of morality' fail to do? They fail to explain how moral distinctions can engage our feelings and dispose us to act. Hume's closing sentence says that no moral system that represents them as derived from reason can manage to show this. I take the whole passage to say that such moral systems *show* their inadequacy for this purpose by the way in which those who propound them slip unannounced from the 'is' language that Hume thinks reason is confined to, to the 'ought' language that he thinks needs explanation – an explanation he has previously insisted we cannot find in any theory that tells us there are discernible moral qualities in objects. What is needed to explain our moral evaluations, which we express in 'ought' language,[12] is some account that will make intelligible the way in which our evaluations actually arise, and the ways in which they relate to our choices. The theories he has attacked fail to do this, and show their failure by containing within themselves the very transition from factual to evaluative language that issues from the psychological processes they should help us to understand.

If this is correct, then Hume's position entails that the transition from factual knowledge to evaluation cannot be represented as a deductive inference; otherwise reason *could* perform evaluations. So the passage from 'is' to 'ought' is not due to an entailment-relationship between what is said by the use of the 'is' and what is subsequently said by the use of the 'ought'. Thus far Hume is in the Non-Naturalist's camp. In all other respects, however, those who see him as a Naturalist are more nearly right. Certainly he does not think that evaluative judgements must depend upon previous, higher-level evaluations, even unexpressed ones. They arise, for him, when emotions of approval or disapproval are aroused in us. This occurs when actions, or states of character, that please us, or are in our common interest, are objectively contemplated and generate approval; or when actions, or states of character, that displease us or are against our common interest, are objectively contemplated and

161

generate disapproval. Such an account does not coincide in the least with the Non-Naturalist aim of providing a deductive structure for our evaluations; for a deductive structure belongs to processes of reasoning, and for Hume the transition from understanding to evaluating is not a process of reasoning at all.[13] It also presupposes that 'ought' judgements play only a minor role in generating actions, since our approval and disapproval are directed toward actions men are already predisposed to do for other motives, such as pleasure, benevolence or interest.[14]

Once again Hume's major concern is psychological: that of explaining how our evaluations arise, and why we are disposed to act in ways that coincide with them. They arise because of our passions of approval and disapproval, and we act in ways that coincide with them because approval and disapproval reinforce motives to action that we have already. Hume's theory commits him to the denial of entailment relationships between 'factual' and 'evaluative' utterances; but it is not to such utterances, but to the evaluative processes of which they are the signs, that he directs our attention.

8 Religion

Hume's philosophy of religion has in recent years received some of the attention that its merits demand.[1] It is at least on the level of his epistemological work, and although it is not without its own ambiguities, these derive in part from the absence, or near-absence, of the positive pyschological considerations that cause some of the interpretative difficulties of Book I of the *Treatise*. Just as Hume's analysis of causal inferences changed the course of our philosophical understanding of the natural world, so Hume's analysis of 'natural religion' had the effect of destroying a whole tradition of theological reflection. This is not to say, of course, that no examples of this tradition survive; they do and always will. It is to say that Hume has discredited this tradition utterly.

The tradition Hume has discredited is the tradition of representing Christian religious beliefs as extensions of scientific knowledge; as beliefs which the informed man would naturally come to hold if he applied to theological matters the same unprejudiced habits of inductive reasoning that have given him the scientific knowledge that he has. Whatever ambiguities the *Dialogues Concerning Natural Religion* may contain they show unambiguously that this tradition has none of the credentials it claims to have.

But to recognise this is not to remove the difficulties that there are in determining what Hume believes about many related matters. Nor is it to remove the difficulties in relating the positions Hume holds in his philosophy of religion to the rest of his philosophy. I will comment briefly on some of these problems at the outset and return to them after detailed reflections on the *Dialogues* and other writings.

The claim that Christianity can be recommended to the reasonable man on the basis of arguments that utilise standard inductive canons was familiar in Hume's day in the Argument from Design. This argument was thought to show that the order and convenience of the natural world made it unreasonable for a dispassionate and informed observer not to recognise that the world was the result of the creative activity of a benevolent intelligence different in degree, but not in kind, from our own. This argument, even if successful, is patently unable to prove the truth of more than *some* Christian doctrines. It is obviously unable to prove that Jesus was the Son of God, that God is Three Persons, or that Christ rose from the dead. It is natural enough to argue, of course, that if the Design Argument does prove that the world is the result of the creative power of a benevolent intelligence, this makes it more reasonable than it would otherwise be to accept those Christian doctrines about that creative intelligence which the Argument in itself does *not* prove. The minimum outcome of the *Dialogues* is that this move is blocked. It is blocked because on close examination the Argument from Design shows at most that there is some degree of probability in the hypothesis of a creative intelligence, but goes no way to showing that this intelligence is of a sort that Christianity says that it is. It is not altogether clear whether Hume thinks that the Argument carries us even this far, and this is one of the major ambiguities of the *Dialogues*, especially in their closing sections; but I think it is quite clear that Hume is of the view that the most the Argument proves, whatever it is, is insufficient to recommend *Christianity* to the reasonable man.

If Hume is right about this, it is a point of central importance in the perennial debate about the reasonableness of religious belief. In the language of the title of the work, natural religion is not something that can be identified, even in part, with Christianity. In the context of Hume's own day the conclusion is especially devastating. A few historical comments are here in order. The eighteenth century was, in Great Britain, the era of the cult of reasonableness in religious life. This was slower taking hold in Scotland than in England, but its influence in both countries was considerable. The function of this movement was to entrench within the religious establishment itself the sort of compromise and tolerance that would put an end to religious strife and consolidate the political compromises that had emerged in spite of it, and which its renewal would always jeopardise. The result of this was a strengthening and a domestication of religious institutions which have not had to contend with the anti-clericalism which has been a hallmark of free thought on the European continent. In Scotland this movement was espoused by the Moderates in the Church, which numbered some of Hume's friends among its leading figures. The arch-enemy of theologians of this persuasion was *enthusiasm*, a word which was used to characterise intense concern over minor points of doctrine, and also all religious attitudes of an evangelical variety. The weakness of this movement was that it was religiously debilitating and encouraged spiritual and social complacency, but to many, including Hume, its tolerance was a welcome contrast to the 'bigotry' and gloom which they associated with the popular Calvinism they saw around them, and which he had rejected at an early age. The expression of it at the philosophical and theological level took the form of stressing only those elements of Christian doctrine that could most readily be recommended to the scientifically educated, and of relegating the remainder to the category of the non-essential. In its extreme form this could even involve denying the need for revelation altogether, and identifying Christianity with a rather platitudinous form of deism, which consisted in the belief of a creator and moral governor of the world who required moral rectitude and perhaps distributed rewards or punishments in a hereafter. Views of this sort were expressed in works like Toland's *Christianity Not Mysterious* (1696) and Tindal's *Christianity as Old as Creation* (1730). Of course views like this could also be held by those who regarded themselves as anti-Christian – the most famous example of this, much later, being Thomas Paine in *The Age of Reason.* The dangers of the simple identification of Christianity and natural religion were recognised by Joseph Butler, who argued in his *Analogy of Religion* (1736) that someone who is prepared to commit himself to the existence of a creator and moral governor has no sound reason to refuse to consider the claims of revealed religion also. It is important to recall that Hume had considerable respect for Butler, is thought to have removed the essay on Miracles from the *Treatise* partly in order to avoid giving Butler offence, and has plausibly been argued to have had Butler in mind as the model of Cleanthes in the *Dialogues.* [2] However ironic some of the deference accorded to Cleanthes in the *Dialogues* may be, there is no doubt that it is his arguments that are the constant object of attack and defence, and we can assume, therefore, that it is the views he represents which, above all other theological positions current in his day, Hume thinks worthy of extended consideration. He is therefore concerned to examine the thesis that the Argument from Design can establish the truth of those propositions of natural religion which would make a position like Butler's plausible. And there is no doubt that he considers himself to have destroyed this thesis. He may have had some sympathy with Butler in holding that if the propositions of moral deism were provable, the acceptance of revelation would have a greater rational basis than the deists admitted, but this does not mean he thinks the acceptance of revelation *does* have a rational basis. For he clearly holds that the Design Argument is unable to produce anything like the totality of the deistic position. In particular it is quite unable to show God's moral governance of the world. So both those deistic Christians who wished to dispense with revelation and those, like Butler, who wanted to preserve it as something that could commend itself to the reasonable man, are mistaken; for both assume more than the Argument from Design can establish — even though Hume perhaps agrees that it can establish *some* of what each requires.

So I think that Hume is attacking what was part of the conventional wisdom of his own day: the assumption that the propositions of deism can be inferred by any rational man from the observation of the natural order. Far less than this can be inferred. But again, Hume is far from crystal clear whether he thinks that *none* of it can. On balance I think that his position is not wholly negative, as Kemp Smith suggests, but that he does grudgingly come to accept *some* part of the deistic position, at least that much which is contained in the proposition, 'That the cause or causes of order in the universe probably bear some remote analogy to human intelligence'. How positive this is I am not at all sure. But we do know that Hume did not admit to being an atheist, although he was often called one. He did not even admit it in the company of atheists: there is a story that he visited Baron Holbach, the free-thinker, in Paris, and remarked that no one was a real atheist, only to be told that there were seventeen sitting with him at table.[3] One is not sure whether to interpret Hume's stance here as essentially prudential, or as a concession to the social harmony which the conventional wisdom served to sustain — and which he obviously valued highly — or as a genuine conviction that atheism was false. Certainly he did not hold to any form of theism which entailed a particular morality, and his analysis of morals is wholly secular. I will return to this in conclusion; for the present it is enough to say that the degree to which Hume himself espouses 'natural religion' is sufficiently tentative in its commitment and sufficiently attenuated in its content, that it can form no part of an argument to any 'system of religion', such as Calvinist Christianity. Its tentative character may be, on the most negative analysis, all that marks it off from the dogmatic atheism of Holbach and the French *philosophes*, who had none of Hume's temperamental and doctrinal hesitations about pronouncing what the universe did and did not contain. But whatever its nature and motives it results in his paying verbal service to the Design Argument in all those places where it is not the subject of discussion!

The choice of someone resembling Butler as the protagonist of the Design Argument in the *Dialogues* is significant in another way. Butler belongs to the empirical tradition in natural theology. He claims to base his arguments on experience. In this he contrasts with writers like Samuel Clarke, who is supposed to be the original of Demea.[4] Clarke argues confidently to theistic conclusions on the basis of *a priori* arguments, a method that Butler avoided. Hume can have no patience with this method either. He spends a mere five pages on the *a priori* proofs of God's existence in the *Dialogues*. The reason of course is that on his epistemology no matter of fact is capable of demonstration *a priori*, since its denial is never contradictory and never entails a contradiction. The Argument from Design is worthy of the most detailed examination, however, because it purports to show us that natural religion has the same sort of footing as natural science does.

PHILOSOPHICAL AND RELIGIOUS DOUBT

It is here that we run into the most difficult problem of interpretation. It is the problem of reconciling what Hume says about the differences between scientific and religious belief on the one hand with his insistence on the a-rationality of the foundations of scientific understanding on the other. He maintains that our natural beliefs are produced and sustained by forces in human nature that do not depend on reason and are too strong to be undermined by it, so that scepticism is incapable of producing conviction even though philosophical defences of our common beliefs are in all cases

167

based on bad arguments. It is clear, however, that he does not think that the immunity to philosophical criticism that he ascribes to our beliefs in the external world or the continuance of the self or the regularity of nature, extends to religious beliefs; except, perhaps, to the vague deism he seems willing to countenance at the end of the *Dialogues*. In this connection it is striking that it is in the sphere of religion that he makes his only clear statement of the distinction between questions of origin and questions of truth: 'As every enquiry, which regards religion, is of the utmost importance, there are two questions in particular, which challenge our attention, to wit, that concerning its foundation in reason, and that concerning its origin in human nature.' (*N.H.R.* 21)

Since the argument for theism that he takes most seriously is the one that attempts to ground it on scientific arguments, and since all scientific arguments are in turn founded on custom and not on reason, it is hard to see how Hume can consistently maintain the validity of the distinction he announces here. He is of course entitled to point out that the Argument from Design is *bad* scientific argumentation; and perhaps this is enough to show that the custom which sustains our belief in the regularity of nature is not enough to sustain our religious beliefs. But even if this is granted, one can still wonder why religious beliefs should be thought to be at a special disadvantage in consequence of this, when according to his analyses of our natural beliefs, scientific thought is in its turn devoid of any foundation in reason. In different terms, granted that non-religious scepticism has no hold on us in view of the character of the 'sensitive parts of our natures' why is it that religious scepticism should be offered us as a real possibility for our choice, even when disguised as an error? While I do not think Hume can be made altogether consistent on this point, I offer the following comments.

(1) Hume is not consistent throughout his philosophy in his use of the term 'reason'. In arguing against the view that moral distinctions are derived from reason, he clearly includes within reason the reflections on matters of fact which are founded, according to his own arguments, on custom. He would seem to follow the same practice in the *Natural History*, so that he can be read as contrasting scientific thinking with those forces in human nature to which he ascribes religion.

(2) It is not obvious that by showing that arguments of a scientific sort cannot establish any system of religion Hume considers himself to have shown that religious scepticism is an open

option for us in a way that scepticism of the senses is not. This would depend on the nature of those forces in our lives which are the real sources of religious beliefs. In the introduction to the *Natural History* he makes it plain that these forces differ in important ways from those which prevent us from being epistemological sceptics. They are not universal: 'Some nations have been discovered, who entertained no sentiments of religion'; and they seem to issue in a multitude of conflicting beliefs, so that no one religious doctrine can be grounded inescapably in human nature in the way our belief in the existence of body is. Consequently he says, 'The first religious principles must be secondary: such as may easily be perverted by various accidents and causes, and whose operation too, in some cases, may, by an extraordinary concurrence of circumstances, be altogether prevented.' (*N.H.R.* 21). If, therefore, it could be shown that religious beliefs can not be supported by arguments which are simple extensions of mental habits which are based on inescapable elements in human nature, it would follow that human nature without religion is a real possibility. The arguments of the *Natural History* are designed to show that the forces that actually generate religious beliefs have no relationship at all to scientific reflection, which suggests (though this is nowhere stated directly) that it would be surprising if the Argument from Design were cogent, since if theism were based in the way this would imply on those forces which produce our natural beliefs, these would surely have played a part in the generation of religious beliefs much earlier.

(3) It is not certain, because of the ambiguity of the *Dialogues,* that Hume does think that total scepticism about religious beliefs is an open option. It is perhaps the case that some attenuated form of deism is seen by him, at least occasionally, as inescapably grounded in human nature. If this is so, however, it is not because Hume has any doubts about the unscientific character of the Argument from Design; it is because he seems to think that this vague deism is inescapable in some other way. I defer further discussion of this.

I conclude these lengthy preliminaries with one assertion that seems to me unambiguously true. As far as revealed religion is concerned Hume's judgement is wholly negative. It is indeed veiled in irony, but the irony is thin, the animus is clear, and his contempt total. Hume clearly regards the influence of religious systems as he knew them to be wholly bad, and the explanation of their power to be a species of psychopathology. This is the source of his concern to show that even if natural religion has some rational foundation, it is not such as to support the claims of revealed religion, and to show that it is not underpinned by any universal forces in human nature. He is therefore quite frequently to be found saying that individual doctrines (such as the immortality of the soul) are only known to us through revelation. It is of course possible that by showing that such doctrines cannot be based on scientific reflection but only held on faith he is showing something that many religious believers would not resist but welcome. Not all Christians have ever believed in the reasonableness of Christianity.

THE MAJOR WRITINGS

Hume's major works in philosophy of religion, in order of composition, are as follows.

Of Miracles (*E.U.* Section X)
This is the best-known of Hume's writings on religion, and in some respects one of the weakest. It was originally intended (perhaps not in its present form) to be part of the *Treatise,* but Hume is believed to have taken it out to avoid offending Butler, and to try to ensure that the *Treatise* was not judged by any apparent religious or anti-religious implications in it. It was put into the *Enquiry* so as to gain some of the attention that the *Treatise* had not received, and because the *Enquiries* seek to relate Hume's philosophical discoveries to contemporary controversies. What Hume does in this essay is to argue that there are, and can be, no adequate *historical* grounds for accepting a miracle-story as the 'foundation of a system of religion'.

Of a Particular Providence and of a Future State (*E.U.* Section XI)
This was originally called 'Of the Practical Consequences of Natural Religion', which is a better title. The essence of the argument is that there are none. This essay gives us a simple preview of the much more complex arguments of the *Dialogues.* The key contention is that for moral guidance and future hopes to be based on one's belief in God, this belief has to involve far more than any inference from the observed character of the world can possibly justify.

The Natural History of Religion
This appeared in 1757 as part of *Four Dissertations,* which was in turn a revision of a volume of *Five Dissertations,* which was printed but suppressed by the publisher. The argument is moderately

complex, but is designed to show that historically religions have not been the result of the sorts of reflection on which natural religion as Hume's contemporaries knew it, is based; that they have been monotheistic only in relatively recent times; and that the growth of monotheism has been attended with moral and intellectual disadvantages from which polytheism has generally been free.

Dialogues Concerning Natural Religion

These were published posthumously in 1779 as a result of Hume's having required his nephew to arrange for their publication as part of the conditions of his will. He had been at work on them in manuscript over a period of about twenty-five years and had revised the text at least twice. He did not publish them in his lifetime because his friends advised against it, and he had been too much bruised by controversy about his religious opinions before to reject their advice. But at the time of his death he was determined that they should be published — he originally wished Adam Smith to arrange for its publication, but Smith was unwilling to commit himself to this, and hence Hume left it to his nephew instead. The *Dialogues* is in all respects Hume's maturest work and is beyond any question the greatest work on philosophy of religion in the English language. Kant saw a German translation of it, though we do not know exactly how far it influenced him. The *Dialogues* says virtually all that is worth saying about the Design Argument.

The combined effect of the arguments of these works is overwhelmingly negative. Such positive remarks as exist are either remarks which cannot, because of the use of dialogue form, be ascribed to Hume himself with certainty, or they are directed towards theses which are not the topic of discussion in the work in which they appear. There is one important exception to this, however. The final Part of the *Dialogues* contains positive sentiments which cannot be put aside as easily as this. I shall offer brief commentaries on all four works, and will offer a general interpretation of Hume's position in the course of a more detailed scrutiny of Part XII of the *Dialogues*. I begin with the *Natural History,* since its comparative method separates it markedly from the other writings.

The Natural History of Religion

This work is one of the earliest examples of the comparative study of world religions, though of course the data that Hume uses come

171

not from anthropological field-work but from the writings of world travellers and from his own reading in classical authors.

Hume begins, as we have noted, by saying that he intends to discuss the origin of religion in human nature, not its foundation in reason. For the purposes of this work he is content to say that the latter question is a very simple one, since no one can reasonably deny that the 'whole frame of nature bespeaks an intelligent author'. The obvious truth of the 'primary principles of genuine Theism and Religion' are asserted piously at intervals throughout the *Natural History*. The repeated assertions of the truth of these principles are used here to emphasise that, true or not, they do not form part of the original phenomena of religion, and are historically speaking, latter-day products of a much more sophisticated period. In the course of the work Hume also argues that they have come to be accepted for reasons other than the merits of those processes of reasoning which philosophers and theologians use to recommend them.

Originally, Hume says, religion is polytheistic. The earliest men who have left written records were polytheists. Once the obvious truth of monotheism is understood from the frame of nature, it could not (of course) ever give place to polytheism or idolatry, so there is no case for the view that monotheism existed *before* the polytheism that we find in the earliest records. Primitive men are in any case not excited by the familiar facts that form the basis for the Argument from Design; they are only excited by extraordinary or alarming phenomena. These on the other hand set primitive man 'trembling, sacrificing, and praying'. They do this by making men aware of the extent to which their lives depend on what are to them *unknown causes*. It is hope and fear, especially the latter, which cause men to think of 'invisible intelligent power': they think of it as like themselves, and in consequence come to embrace polytheistic religions in which each deity has the charge of some element in their environment that they depend upon. 'Men are much oftener thrown on their knees by the melancholy than by the agreeable passions.' (*N.H.R.* 31).

The many deities that men thus commit themselves to are not thought of as creators or formers of the world. Indeed, says Hume sarcastically, 'these pretended religionists are really a kind of superstitious atheists', to be ranked with those amongst our own society who believe in elves and fairies. We have, therefore, to ask how theism could have developed from polytheism, and here Hume gives an ingenious account which in its turn owes nothing whatever to that supposedly incontestable inference on which he says monotheism can be founded. Even in sophisticated monotheistic ages, the majority of men hold to the current monotheism for the same sorts of reasons that inspired the polytheism from which it grew. There is in fact a conflict between the ignorant, who believe in the particular interposition of the deity in daily life, and the refined theist, who is likely to assert that God created the world as a law-abiding place in which he does not interfere. So we cannot look to the existence of rational arguments for the source of the spread of monotheism. The real reason is the progressive refinements that attach to the practice of *worship.* It is natural enough for men who think there are many gods to consider that there is one god among the others who is especially theirs, or is the ruler over the other gods. They will then direct their religious energies to winning his favour, and this will lead them more and more to exaggerate his powers and to stress his supremacy. The fact that this is not based on rational reflection can be seen from the tendency men have to perform these exaggerated obeisances toward more than one being, or not to abandon the original belief in the human characteristics of the divinity, even though they are inconsistent with his exalted status. Christianity comes in for some sly digs for this.

Not only does the growth of monotheism out of polytheism not proceed on rational principles, but it is accompanied by some great moral evils, from which polytheism is free. The greatest of these, of course, is intolerance and persecution; but it is not the only one. Another is the growth of perverse forms of self-abasement: when the gods are only moderately superior to us, we do not abase ourselves before them, but when the one God is thought to be immeasurably greater than we are, this leads to the cultivation of 'the monkish virtues of mortification, penance, humility, and passive suffering, as the only qualities which are acceptable to him' (*N.H.R.* 52). A third attendant evil is the perversion of men's intellectual gifts to the service of religious authority: since monotheism is on the surface more 'conformable to sound reason' than polytheism is, philosophers cannot just shrug it off the way the Greek thinkers shrugged off their gods, and men of intellect put themselves at the service of religion, where they find themselves called upon to reconcile incoherencies, and help to satisfy the 'appetite for absurdity and contradiction'. This in turn leads to a general hypocrisy and self-deception, where men are afraid to acknowledge their doubts

173

either to themselves or to others, and oscillate all through their lives between conviction and disbelief. Hume argues, in other words, that the unsystematic and non-explanatory nature of polytheism renders it harmless in ways in which the monotheism that grows from it is not harmless. Monotheism requires a kind of intellectual prostration from its adherents, who have come to hold to it for non-intellectual reasons but have to defend it against their own better judgement. This is an odd view to hold alongside any genuine conviction that the tenets of monotheism can be established from the contemplation of the order of nature. But the oddity is deliberate, since Hume does not think that most of them (or perhaps even any of them) can be.

Hume drives home the inner conflicts which he sees in sophisticated monotheism in a chapter entitled 'Impious Conceptions of the Divine Nature in Popular Religions of Both Kinds'. He points out that although fear is the basis of religious worship, worship requires respect and adulation to the very being that one fears. In polytheism this can be dealt with by addressing praise in the temple to the god whom one complains about outside the temple. But the monotheist dare not indulge in this expedient, and has to internalise his inconsistency. 'The heart secretly detests such measures of cruel and implacable vengeance; but the judgement dares not but pronounce them perfect and adorable. And the additional misery of this inward struggle aggravates all the other terrors, by which these unhappy victims to superstition are for ever haunted' (*N.H.R.* 67). In an elaborate footnote which purports to express the views of the Chevalier Ramsay, Hume makes it abundantly clear that he has in mind the Protestant supporters of the doctrine of predestination.

Hume's conclusion is an ironic lament on the contrast between the belief in a sovereign author of nature which a contemplation of the works of nature should bring us to, and the disfigurement of the image of God as we find it in popular religions. His last paragraph is impossible not to quote:

The whole is a riddle, an enigma, an inexplicable mystery. Doubt, uncertainty, suspense of judgment appear the only result of our most accurate scrutiny, concerning this subject. But such is the frailty of human reason, and such the irresistible contagion of opinion, that even this deliberate doubt could scarcely be upheld; did we not enlarge our view, and opposing one species of superstition to another, set them a quarrelling; while we ourselves, during their fury and contention, happily make our escape into the calm, though obscure, regions of philosophy. (*N.H.R.* 76)

Of Miracles

The conclusion that Hume reaches in this essay is more carefully expressed than some of the arguments by which he reaches it. The conclusion is 'that no human testimony can have such force as to prove a miracle, and make it a just foundation for any such (i.e. popular) system of religion' (*E.U.* 127). This clearly confines Hume's result to a negative verdict on the power of *testimony* to establish that a miracle has occurred, and thereby to establish a popular system of religion. Hume is arguing against those who appeal to the alleged historical occurrence of miracles in order to establish the authority of a religious system. He is attacking the attempt to base the credentials of revelation upon historical evidence. He says nothing, at least directly, about how one should respond if one seems to be a witness to something miraculous oneself. Nor does he say anything about how one should respond to the testimony of others to some miraculous occurrence if one already has independently strong reason to believe that there is a God whose character is such that he might very well intervene in nature in the way the purported witnesses tell us that he has. For the latter sort of question is one that can only require an answer for someone who already accepts a system of religion. Hume is concerned with those who try to establish one *from* miracle stories. For someone who wishes to do this, the historical authenticity of the story has to be established independently, by purely historical criteria. Judged by these criteria, testimony to the miraculous must always be far too suspect to serve an apologist's purpose.

For this reason it does not matter that Hume defines a miracle in two different ways. The first, in the text (*E.U.* 114), is: 'A miracle is a violation of the laws of nature.' The second, in a footnote (*E.U.*115): 'A miracle may be accurately defined, a transgression of a law of nature by a particular volition of the deity, or by the interposition of some invisible agent.' For Hume is attacking the claim that because some events that are contrary to the laws of nature have been proved to have taken place, we must ascribe them to the interposition of God. The briefer definition mentions only that aspect of the miraculous which can be assessed by historical standards; the longer one includes that aspect of it which we ascribe by inference to the event thus established, once we have agreed that

175

the evidence for its occurrence is overwhelming. The longer definition includes the earlier one, and is not inconsistent with it.

Hume's argument in bare outline, is this. A wise man proportions his belief to the evidence. To do this requires him to take a certain attitude to the content of any story that is recounted to him, and also requires him to take a certain attitude to the testimony on which it is based. With regard to the content of the story, the wise man will take account of the likelihood of the occurrence of events of the kind reported. This will be a function of the number of times events like it have been observed to occur in the past, and how frequently events of a contrary kind have been observed. Our estimate, if based on experience, can vary all the way from 'the highest certainty to the lowest species of moral evidence' (*E.U.* 110). The same is true with respect to testimony. Only experience can teach us how we should respond to testimony, for only experience can teach us how far individuals of a certain degree of intelligence, education, disinterestedness, and the rest, are likely to be reliable witnesses to phenomena of certain kinds. Only experience, that is, can enable us to distinguish good testimony from bad.

But even when we have learned the lessons that experience has to teach us, we can run into difficulties. For we may be confronted with an inherently likely story, attested to by dubious witnesses; or with an inherently unlikely story, attested to by very good witnesses — 'from which contradiction there necessarily arises a counterpoise, and mutual destruction of belief and authority'. Testimony to miracles is an extreme case of this. For a miracle is a violation of a law of nature, and in such a case there is a uniform past experience against it, 'otherwise the event would not merit that appellation'. In such circumstances even the most impeccable testimony cannot make it reasonable to believe that the event has occurred. The most it can do is to outweigh our determination to deny it, so that our judgement is suspended. It cannot even do this much unless the falsehood of the testimony would be more miraculous than the event it supports.

Hume then proceeds to show how far short of impeccability our actual testimony has always fallen. The quality of the witnesses has always been questionable. The very outrageousness of miracle-stories has always made it easier for some men to accept them and pass them on, for men are not 'wise' all the time. Miracles are further undermined by being reported primarily among 'ignorant and barbarous nations'. And the systems of religion that miracle stories are used to support are incompatible with one another, so that the testimony that favours the stories of one tends to undermine the credibility of the stories of the other.

Hume's arguments do destroy their primary target: but they are certainly not free of difficulties. One notorious problem is that they do not allow him to admit the rationality of paying heed to *repeated* testimony in favour of events which happen not to have been noticed in the past, or to be admitted into the current formulations of natural law.[5] We have to be able to allow high-quality testimony, as well as our own observations, to lead us to change our understanding of what natural laws there are. This objection, though serious for Hume's argument as it stands, is one that can be accommodated: for it does not require us to admit the possibility of miracles. Miracles are *contrary* to natural law, and no elasticity of outlook that merely caused us to reformulate our statements of natural law would force us to admit the existence of events that violated it. Every time a new sort of event was admitted, it would be admitted as an example of the operation of natural law better understood, not as an exception to natural law.

Ninian Smart has pointed out, very importantly, that those who believe in miracles do not believe that the occurrence of one undermines a natural law.[6] They believe that natural law holds, except on those occasions, in themselves rare, when God has chosen to intervene and suspend them. (This view of miracle allows one to reject the assumption, common to Hume and many of his critics, that a miracle is thought to be unique. There can be several miracles of the same sort: there are two resurrection miracles reported in the New Testament – that of Lazarus as well as that of Jesus.) The recognition of this feature of the believer's understanding of miracle, however, does not affect Hume's argument. If anything it strengthens it. For to view miracles this way, and to accept that there may have been some, is to add a theological dimension to one's conception of what a natural law is. It is to view a natural law as a regular sequence which God has arranged and may, at his choice, suspend. On almost all occasions this conception of natural law can happily co-exist with one which makes it a matter of logic that natural laws have no exceptions whatever. But they cannot co-exist happily when the question at issue is whether some event which is contrary to a stated law has taken place. For then the theological understanding of what a natural law is will make it rational to think of the miracle-story as possessing a degree of intrinsic likelihood that it cannot possess for someone who has not *already* determined that natural law is a divinely determined sequence that God can lift. For someone who does not so regard it, only repeated testimony that is sufficient to make him doubt the status of the stated law itself can be sufficient to undermine the superior reasonableness of scepticism. Without this even the highest quality testimony to the alleged event has to contend with the scientific standing of the law it is alleged to violate, and can do no more than lead to suspended judgement. But Hume's thesis is just this: that if we are trying to establish the miracle in order *subsequently* to establish the system of religion it supports, we must disregard any likelihood which the miracle story might derive from the truth of the propositions of that system of religion. We must judge the miracle story by the same criteria that are used by the man who does not assume the truth of these propositions, and by these criteria the story will not merit acceptance. Even if it is rational for a believer to expect some miracles to have occurred, it is not rational to *become* a believer on the basis of reports of them.

There is no doubt that Hume is far less temperate than this, and his intemperance has weakened the appearance of his argument. In particular his insistence that the existence of natural laws makes it unreasonable to countenance miracle stories leads him to talk of 'a direct and full *proof*, from the nature of the fact, against the existence of any miracle'. All his argument requires is the more modest claim that the nature of the story makes it more rational to refrain from accepting it, if testimony alone is what supports it. As Wollheim puts the matter, 'the credibility of testimony can never be assessed independently of the plausibility of what it asserts'. Hume's own essay, however, shows us why the implausibility of the story may only neutralise, and not wholly demolish, the testimony.

Of a Particular Providence and of a Future State

The argument of this Section is a preview of the major arguments of the *Dialogues*, and can be summarised briefly. It is presented as an imaginary defence by Epicurus against religious critics. Epicurus, while 'denying a divine existence, and consequently a providence and a future state', alleges that the moral consequences of his views are the same as the moral consequences of the view of his critics, when these are properly understood. His critics are said to base their beliefs in the divine government of the world upon observation of the order of nature, which they think manifests the clearest signs of

178

an intelligence and design as its cause. If one accepts this, says Epicurus, we must recognise that the argument, being from effect to cause, can only establish the existence of an intelligence or design adequate to produce the natural order as it is found to be in experience. But if one assumes that 'Jupiter' has attributes greater than those sufficient to produce the world that we have, one indulges in 'mere hypothesis'. Yet such speculation is essential if we are to infer any degree of reward for virtue or punishment for vice, here or hereafter, beyond that precise degree which we now find in the world as it is. So the practical effect of believing in a divine ordering of the world is exactly the same as that of denying it, if one bases one's understanding of the divine character and purposes on experience of the world God is said to order. Those who argue that society requires a loftier view of how God deals with virtue and vice, have to find the view that they need in some source other than the evidence. So it is not possible to base practically relevant doctrines about God's governance upon experience.

Hume then considers an important counter-argument. Surely, the argument goes, we do sometimes infer causes that are capable of producing effects greater than those from which we infer them? Do we not do this when we come across a half-finished building, and decide it has been produced by a builder who would go on to add to it? Would we not do this when we found the imprint of one foot in the sand, and decided it had been made by a being with two feet, the imprint of the second foot having been effaced? Is a similar inference not equally reasonable in the case of the order and design we find in the universe as a whole? The answer, obvious and devastating once Hume has given it for us, is that the cogency of such inferences depends upon our having independent knowledge which we bring to bear upon the case before us. Experience has taught us that buildings are made by builders. Experience has taught us that most beings who have one foot also have another. If it has not taught us these things, our inferences would not be justified. In the case of God the cause is known only through the observed effects, and we are therefore only justified in inferring him to have powers and intentions sufficient to produce that degree of perfection that the world is found to contain.

He concludes, under the transparent disguise of offering a difficulty to the defender of Epicurus, by questioning the very possibility of inferring a cause at all in circumstances where the alleged effect is 'entirely singular'. We are only entitled to infer from

179

an effect to a cause when we have observed two *species* of objects to be constantly conjoined. Only then will experience support the claim that there *is* a cause, or a claim about what it is. But the antagonists of Epicurus offer us an inference from a unique 'effect' (the whole universe) to a unique 'cause' (the Deity). Since Epicurus has only been supposed to accept this inference for the sake of argument about the significance of its practical consequences, the import of this final consideration is obvious. Natural theology, even if based on experience, is of no practical interest. But the claim to base it on experience at all is due to a misunderstanding of the conditions of causal demonstrations.

Dialogues Concerning Natural Religion

An adequate treatment of this great work is impossible here. I shall attempt a more modest objective: I shall try to indicate something of the structure of the argument, and offer a possible resolution of some of its ambiguities. Of all Hume's writings, the *Dialogues* most obviously defy summary. The very care Hume lavished upon them, the very polish and refinement of the prose, indicate that any difficulties of interpretation that they present are difficulties that come from the considered hesitations of Hume's maturest reflection, not (as in the case of some of the difficulties in the *Treatise*) from the hastiness of a youthful intellect.

The very fact that the work is presented in dialogue form has itself to be taken with maximum seriousness. Unless the protagonists are obviously unevenly matched, as they are in many of Plato's Dialogues, or in Berkeley's, the philosophical lessons have to be learned from the conversations as a whole, rather than from the contributions of one of the speakers taken singly. In this respect it is quite clear that Demea, who combines unbending orthodoxy with a belief in the cogency of *a priori* proofs of God's existence and attributes, and who shows no capacity for dialectic whatsoever, is present to represent views that Hume wishes to dismiss. It is in the interplay between Cleanthes, the empirical theologian, and Philo, the careless sceptic, that the lessons are primarily to be found. Cleanthes is stated, in the concluding sentence, to be the victor. But this verdict is supposed to be passed by Pamphilus, the pupil of Cleanthes who reports the conversations; and it cannot be assumed to represent Hume's own verdict upon the argument, even though many informed readers have so regarded it. If one does not regard it in this way, one is forced to read Pamphilus's verdict as a not-very-transparent attempt on Hume's part to mislead careless readers, or hint at his real views for the benefit of perceptive readers, or head off attacks on the work from the orthodox. Since the work was one which he knew would not be published until after his death, the last possibility is probably less likely than it would have been in the case of many of his earlier writings. In addition the irony that undoubtedly exists in the work is far less barbed and edged with sarcasm than that which we find in his other works on religion, so that it becomes far more reasonable in the *Dialogues* to wonder whether particular passages are instances of it. These considerations weigh in favour of taking the accolade to Cleanthes at its face value, as an indication that on the whole it is he who represents Hume's own views. Against this, however, we have to face the fact that such an interpretation puts the *Dialogues* considerably at variance with Hume's other writings.[7] We also have to consider the greater quantity, forcefulness, and subtlety of the arguments that Hume gives to Philo, and the extent to which the stature of Cleanthes has to be sustained by devices such as sudden changes of subject, or unexplained embarrassment in his opponent.[8] And Hume's conventional deference to religious opinions with which he did not in the least agree should not be taken as a sign of fear: even if he felt this (and there is no evidence to suggest it) it was outweighed, notoriously, by an interest in being discussed; and there is every reason to think that Hume set considerable store by the conventional prerequisites of calm disputation, which would certainly be worth purchasing at the price of a modest dose of dissimulation, in a climate where the penalty for its absence was a bigoted hostility which could only impede philosophical reflection.

Taking these considerations together, I think we must follow Kemp Smith in the view that for most purposes Hume holds to the arguments presented by Philo, not to the arguments presented by Cleanthes – except, of course, where the two agree, as in some critical areas they do. This has generally been taken to imply that Hume embraces the 'careless scepticism' that Philo is said to hold to, and that the overall import of the *Dialogues* is wholly negative. That it is wholly negative toward Cleanthes's version of the Argument from Design and its empirical theism seems to me quite true. But it is not quite so obvious that it is wholly negative toward theism in all its possible versions. This is not obvious simply because the position of Philo himself appears to undergo a strange transformation in the final Part, and to conclude on a far less unorthodox note than that on which it begins. Nelson Pike has recently argued for a far more positive reading of this Part, and therefore of the *Dialogues* as a whole, than the one offered by Kemp Smith. I incline to think that the truth lies somewhere between them. I shall not consider the reasons for this rather tame conclusion, however, until I have outlined some of the main features of the argument of Parts I to XI.

Before turning to this it is important to emphasise the benefits, as well as the ambiguities, that the reader gets from the dialogue form of Hume's work. This form enables him, in the simplest and gentlest way, to make several points of major importance, all of them points favouring religious scepticism. Firstly, Cleanthes and Philo agree at the outset that the theist need not concern himself with the criticisms of the radical or Pyrrhonian sceptic who questions our common-sense convictions or our scientific knowledge. It is common ground between them that the question to be discussed is whether or not the standards of conviction that satisfy us in these ordinary realms are satisfied by the claims of natural theology. This agreement is obviously intended by Hume to make clear that the negative arguments of Philo do not presuppose a radical scepticism, but should be taken to apply with any force they have even if this is rejected. This agreement also has the consequence of putting aside the *a priori* arguments of speculative metaphysicians; and to this Demea naturally objects, since he sees at once that theological arguments based on this common ground can only lead to doctrines which make God's nature penetrable by human intelligence: 'surely, by this affected candour, you give advantage to atheists, which they never could obtain, by the mere hint of argument and reasoning' (*D.R.* 143–4). This opens, at the outset, a theological gulf between anyone who wishes to woo the religious sceptic by using arguments following canons that he can accept, and those who wish to stress the infinite greatness of God. The sophistications of natural theology are bought at the price of potential anthropomorphism. This becomes clear much later, when Cleanthes professes himself unable to find much sense or value in doctrines which proclaim the infinity of God's attributes.

Secondly, Hume does not use Philo, but Cleanthes, to refute the *a priori* arguments for God's existence that Demea expounds in Part IX. There is no question here but that Cleanthes speaks for Hume himself; and with very crisp effect. But in choosing Cleanthes for the purpose Hume is drawing attention not only to the actual divisions that exist among apologists, but to the extent to which the natural theologians of his day had seen fit to abandon metaphysical traditions on which they had hitherto been able to rely for support.

Thirdly, and most important of all, Hume is able to emphasise a critical defect in the natural theology of his contemporaries by making Demea side with Philo against Cleanthes during the discussion of evil. For Cleanthes to maintain that the moral qualities of the creator can be discerned solely by viewing his handiwork around us, it is essential that he minimise the evils at large in creation. His disagreement with Philo over this is a mere empirical disagreement. But his clash with Demea is much more. For when Demea emphasises the prevalence of evil he is merely emphasising those factors in our lives against which theism is supposed to arm us. Religion cannot be the sort of moral force its adherents proclaim it to be if it makes us believe that there are fewer evils in the world than we thought. On the contrary it has to make us see the evils as greater than we thought, so that we turn to God for support in contending with them and do not rely on our own resources. The very structure of Cleanthes's argument leads him into a wholly un-Christian complacency, and it is Demea, the champion of orthodoxy, who makes us see this.

I shall now attempt a bald summary of the argument of the *Dialogues* up to the end of Part XI.

Parts I–IV. The function of Part I is to make explicit that the grounds for theism that will be considered are grounds in which the standards of ordinary life and natural science are appealed to. Cleanthes insists that theism can be established on these grounds alone; Philo doubts this, but is careful to insist that his doubts are not based upon any appeal to radical scepticism. He also makes it clear that his doubts can quite properly be shared by someone like Demea, who is apt to insist, at least on appropriate occasions, that the mysteries of the divine nature are beyond the normal capacities of the human intellect to uncover. With the stage thus set for a chronic shifting of alliances, Cleanthes proceeds to state his argument:

Look round the world: Contemplate the whole and every part of it: You will find it to be nothing but one great machine, subdivided into an infinite number of lesser machines, which again admit of subdivisions, to a degree beyond what human senses and faculties can trace and explain. All these various machines, and even their most minute parts, are adjusted to each other with an accuracy, which ravishes into admiration all men, who have ever contemplated them. The curious adapting of means to ends, throughout all nature, resembles exactly, though it much exceeds, the production of human contrivance; of human design, thought, wisdom, and intelligence. Since therefore the effects resemble each other, we are led to infer, by all the rules of analogy, that the causes also resemble; and that the Author of nature is somewhat similar to the mind of man; though possessed of much larger faculties, proportioned to the grandeur of the work, which he has executed. By this argument *a posteriori*, and by this argument alone, we do prove at once the existence of a Deity, and his similarity to human mind and intelligence. (*D.R.* 143)

This argument tells us that the world is a vast machine, consisting of an infinite number of lesser machines. The machines, and their parts, are 'adjusted to each other', and show a constant 'adaptation of means to ends'. Such adaptation is manifested (though less well, it would seem) by objects that men have produced. Since the effects are similar, we are justified in inferring a similarity in their causes. Hence the 'Author of nature' can be concluded to be an intelligence like ourselves.

Philo's first round of criticisms includes four main attacks. (i) The argument openly depends upon an analogy. Arguments that depend upon analogy are as strong or weak as the analogy on which they depend. In this case the analogy is weak because of the extravagant vagueness with which the comparison is drawn. The likeness required is between the whole universe on the one hand and human artefacts, such as houses, on the other. While some vague analogy may perhaps be said to exist, it is surely not exact enough for such a conclusion. (ii) Not only is the alleged likeness very imprecise, the comparison is of the oddest kind. It is not the comparison of one object, or set of objects, with another, but of the *whole* of the universe with certain selected *parts* of it. Such a comparison has no more force than one between the growth of a hair or a leaf and the generation of a man or a tree. (iii) Even if such comparisons are permissible, it is arbitrary to pick out intelligence as the causal force within the universe, and say that it, rather than other observed causal forces, is the creative source of the universe as a whole. In fact, as Philo repeats elsewhere, if one compares the whole universe with *all* the 'machines' in the universe, and does not confine oneself to human artefacts (and on the terms of the argument one should do this), then one has to face the fact that in our experience it is only in the case of the human artefacts that the order and adaptation we find is observed to be the effect of intelligence. In other cases it is apparently the effect of non-intelligent causes, such as animal or vegetable reproduction. To deny that these are the *real* causes is to depart from experience and assume the argument's conclusion in stating the evidence. (iv) Our knowledge of causes and effects comes from our observing phenomena of one kind being succeeded regularly by phenomena of another kind. So no causal inference can have any weight unless the causes and the effects under consideration belong to *classes* of phenomena with which we are familiar. But the universe is clearly unique, and belongs to no class. When astronomers have seemed to compare worlds, the worlds they compare are not universes, but individual planets within the one and only universe. So Cleanthes's argument, however refined, cannot do more than masquerade as an example of causal reasoning of a scientific kind.

In Part III Cleanthes offers a strange reply. He asks Philo to imagine two cases. The first is the case of a loud and melodious voice coming from the clouds, heard by all nations, conveying a wise message. No one could reasonably hesitate before deciding that this was the voice of a benevolent and powerful being, yet Philo's objections would apply to that conclusion, since it would not be supported by experience in the ways he has required. The second example is a world in which books are propagated naturally, like vegetables or animals. No one could refrain from inferring that the first volume proceeded from an intelligent source, however natural the intermediate causes might be known to be. Yet such an inference would also violate Philo's principles. These principles work upon your minds after they have been smitten with the force of the argument for design, and cannot remove that force altogether. We need only consider the composition of the eye to be struck immediately by the 'idea of a contriver'. This appeal to a direct apprehension of design is not directly answered by Philo — a point Pike has emphasised, and to which we must return. Instead, Demea intrudes upon Philo's discomfiture by objecting to the anthropomorphism that Cleanthes seems to accept; Cleanthes, however, retorts that those theologians who deny the similarity of the divine mind to the human mind are 'atheists without knowing it', since a God with a mind that is wholly unlike ours would have no mind at all. This provides Philo with an opportunity to attack Cleanthes from a new perspective. He now

185

begins to draw out the awkward consequences of the anthropomorphic understanding of God, beginning with the fact that human minds appear to be dependent upon human bodies. The argument Cleanthes has presented is one that urges the need to trace the order in matter to the planning of a mind; but the order found within the mind is found in experience to be dependent on matter in its turn. Once one looks for the cause of the world outside it, there seems no reason to stop with an ordering mind: once can raise a question about the origins of that mind and its reasoning powers in turn. To this Cleanthes reiterates the claims of Part III: that the order of nature bespeaks 'in the clearest language and intelligent cause or Author' — and that he does not feel the same compulsion to trace this cause to a prior cause . . . 'and here I stop my enquiry'.

Part V. Philo now draws out some inconvenient consequences of Cleanthes' argument, and of the anthropomorphism it entails. (1) An argument from an effect to a cause will only establish the existence of a cause adequate to produce that effect. If the world has to have a mind to cause it, then that mind will not need to be an infinite mind, but will have all limitations consistent with its product. (2) If the world contains flaws, then there is no reason to ascribe perfection to its author any more than infinity. Even if it did not contain them, its perfections might be acquired in the way those of human artefacts often are — as the result of a long process of cosmic trial and error. (3) There is no reason to assume the unity of God. The world may be the handiwork of a large number, as experience teaches us that human productions often are. (4) If God's mind is like ours, why do we assume that he is not mortal as we are, and there is no family of deities? Why do we assume God has no body?

Parts VI–VIII. Having shown the doctrinal inconveniences of Cleanthes' argument, Philo now shows that similar arguments can be used in support of even more heterodox cosmogonies. (1) There is as good reason to compare the universe with an animal organism as with a machine: it appears self-sustaining, and its parts work together as the parts of an organism do. Such an analogy would suggest the conclusion that there is a God who is not distinct from the created order but is a world-soul, animating it. Cleanthes obtusely says that the world is not much like an animal, in that it has no organs, and a vegetable would be a better analogue! He adds the more interesting point that Philo's suggestion would entail the eternity of the world, and that there are good reasons to think the world has only existed for a finite time. Many familiar phenomena

186

are recent, for example the planting of vines in France, or the discovery of America. If they had had an eternity in the past to come about, they would have come about long before they did. To this Philo replies that there are evidences of enough recurrent 'convulsions' in history to explain why development has proceeded in cycles. The world may well be governed by innate principles of order which explain the development within each cycle, and the convulsions which require new beginnings. This, he says, is the cosmic theory he would feel least unhappy in adopting if he had to adopt any.[9] (2) If the universe can be likened to an animal or vegetable organism, we could reasonably suggest yet another account of its origin: that it came to be through biological generation, as organisms do. When Demea complains that such a suggestion is fanciful, and has no data to support it, Philo is easily able to reply that the design hypothesis is in no better case, and that the anatomy of cosmic generation is no more obscure than that of the divine mind. (3) The final possibility that Philo explores is that the world as we know it has come to exist, as the Epicureans maintained, by blind chance; through the fortuitous assemblage of atoms. The obvious difficulty about this is the *persistence* of order and predictability in our world. But this can be accounted for by the suggestion that once chance had thrown up an orderly assemblage of particles, the very order it had fortuitously introduced served to sustain itself against destructive forces. Order, in other words, may be a preserving force, but not itself be the result of anything other than accident. This is a preview of the doctrine of Natural Selection, and it has the same explanatory force as that doctrine does: the reason we see order around us is simply that those conglomerations of particles that do not exhibit it have not survived. Cleanthes objects to this hypothesis that it would not explain why we find forms of adaptation that seem to be better than is required for sheer survival – a point to which no direct answer is given, but which is indirectly dealt with in the later discussions of evil. Throughout all these passages, Philo's position has remained consistent: that one cosmic hypothesis is likely to be as strong or as weak as another, through the very vagueness of the analogies on which it depends. This does not destroy Cleanthes' hypothesis, but renders it in no way superior to an indefinite variety of other possibilities.

Part IX. We now have a short interlude in which Demea introduces, and Cleanthes dismisses, 'that simple and sublime argument *a priori*' which 'cuts off at once all doubt and difficulty'.

What he offers us is a version of the Cosmological Argument which openly depends on the Principle of Sufficient Reason which Hume has attacked in Section III of Part III of Book I of the *Treatise*. Since everything has to have a cause, and is caused by what precedes it, there must be an end to the potentially infinite regression of causes into the past; at least in the sense that there has to be a reason for the existence of the whole series, rather than none. So we are forced to invoke a necessarily existent being, who 'carries the reason of his existence in himself, and cannot be supposed not to exist without an express contradiction'. Cleanthes's refutation cannot be expressed more briefly or more eloquently than it is as it stands: 'I shall begin with observing, that there is an evident absurdity in pretending to demonstrate a matter of fact, or to prove it by any arguments *a priori*. Nothing is demonstrable, unless the contrary implies a contradiction. Nothing, that is distinctly conceivable, implies a contradiction. Whatever we conceive as existent, we can also conceive as non-existent. There is no being, therefore, whose non-existence implies a contradiction. Consequently, there is no being, whose existence is demonstrable.' (*D.R.* 189)

Parts X and XI. The subtle and intricate treatment of the problem of evil begins with Demea and Philo declaiming responsively for several pages about the evils and sufferings in the world. They agree that a proper awareness of the depth of this evil is necessary for a 'due sense of religion'. Philo, however, is then able to pounce upon Cleanthes's belief in the moral attributes of God, which seem at odds with the unproductive pains of this world, which exist alongside the pleasures in great profusion. Cleanthes agrees that it is useless to show that God is powerful and wise if one cannot also show he is good. He further agrees that this would be shown if mankind could be proved to be 'unhappy or corrupted', He proceeds to assert, doggedly, that the world is not as bad as his friends have agreed that it is: 'The only method of supporting divine benevolence (and it is what I willingly embrace) is to deny absolutely the misery and wickedness of man. Your representations are exaggerated: Your melancholy views most fictitious: Your inferences contrary to fact and experience. Health is more common than sickness: Pleasure than pain: Happiness than misery. And for one vexation that we meet with, we attain, upon computation, a hundred enjoyments' (*D.R.* 200). Philo is easily able to expose the weakness of this argument, which does not lie so much in the questionable statements about how much evil there is, as in the tacit admission that there is still a good deal. For although the existence of some evil, even a moderate amount, is perhaps *compatible* with the existence of an all-good Deity, what Cleanthes has to do is to infer God's total goodness *from* the facts as we find them, and they cannot establish his conclusion if there is any evil at all. Cleanthes tries to evade the force of this by cheerfully disowning any ascription of infinite goodness to God on the grounds (which no doubt Hume would accept) that such adjectives are uninformative, but Philo replies by detailing some of the evils that the world contains — evils which show how *ill*-adapted creatures are to survive and prosper. Pain is of great biological importance, when it surely need not be. Many evils, which come, no doubt, from the fact that we live in an environment governed by natural law, could be avoided by an all-powerful and benevolent God in ways that did not detract from the *appearance* of law. Nature is often niggardly in her endowments, thus making it unnecessarily hard for creatures to survive. Nature is equally often too prodigal with her benefits, and destroys her creatures with tempests and floods. The world is therefore one in which the good is mixed with evil, and in such a world it is implausible to suggest that any mind which causes the universe is wholly good or wholly bad. It will either, as far as the evidence tells us, be partly good and partly bad, or, more likely, 'have neither goodness nor malice'.

HUME'S FINAL POSITION

We can now turn to the position of Philo in Part XII. Even if it is Philo and not Cleanthes who is the real (as opposed to the nominal) hero, we have to contend with some strange ambiguities and apparent reversals that emerge when he recapitulates the arguments, and says where they have led them. Demea has left, and Philo, who does by far the greatest amount of the talking, is speaking at ease with Cleanthes, with whom he lives 'in unreserved intimacy'. The first thing he says, astonishingly, is that in spite of his freedom in argument, 'no one has a deeper sense of religion impressed on his mind, or pays more profound adoration to the divine being, as he discovers himself to reason, in the inexplicable contrivance and artifice of nature. A purpose, an intention, or design strikes everywhere the most careless, the most stupid thinker; and no man can be so hardened in absurd systems, as at all times to reject it' (*D.R.* 214). He then recalls 'with pleasure' Galen's descriptions of the intricate adjustments in human anatomy,[10] and declaims that a philosopher would be obstinate to doubt a supreme intelligence in the face of such evidence. He continues: 'Now according to all rules of just reasoning, every fact must pass for undisputed, when it is supported by all the arguments which its nature admits of, even though these arguments be not, in themselves, very numerous or forceful: How much more, in the present case, where no human imagination can compute their number, and no understanding estimate their cogency?'

Cleanthes repeats his comparison of the world to a man-made machine, and says that in the face of such an 'obvious and natural' opinion, a doubter cannot offer one that is better established, but can at best 'start doubts and difficulties' that lead to suspense of judgement. But this is a state of mind that it is hard to sustain: 'A false, absurd system, human nature, from the force of prejudice, is capable of adhering to with obstinancy and perseverance: But no system at all, in opposition to a theory, supported by strong and obvious reason, by natural propensity, and by early education, I think it absolutely impossible to maintain or defend.' Philo agrees, but expresses his agreement oddly. So much does he agree, he says, that he fancies that the apparent disputes that there are about this matter to be unreal, verbal ones. He twice says that the theist and the atheist do not have any genuine conflict! Both times his description is this: it is evident that natural phenomena have a 'great analogy' to human artefacts, even though there are also 'considerable differences';[11] if we ask about their causes, we should infer that these causes resemble the causes of human artefacts in the same manner; both the theist and the atheist will follow us thus far, but at this point it is a matter of wholly unreasoned preference whether the original intelligence which both have arrived at is one that should be said to be greatly different from ours, though resembling us, or said to be very like us, though immensely different. The decision what to *call* this originating cause will depend on whether one is by temperament sceptical, in which case one will be reluctant to use the language of human personality, or temperamentally dogmatist, in which case one will be struck by the practical value of doing so.

At this point there ensues a lengthy attack by Philo on the moral disadvantages of popular religion. Both he and Cleanthes are agreed in venerating *true* religion, but Cleanthes thinks that the moral needs of man are better met by false religion than by none, whereas Philo denies this. Philo's attack is reminiscent of the gloomy psycho-pathology of the *Natural History of Religion*, and its details need not concern us here. He follows it by this:

If the whole of natural theology, as some people seem to maintain, resolves itself into one simple, though somewhat ambiguous, at least undefined proposition, *that the cause or causes of order in the universe probably bear some remote analogy to human intelligence:* If this proposition be not capable of extension, variation, or more particular explication: If it afford no inference that affects human life, or can be the source of any action or forbearance: And if the analogy, imperfect as it is, can be carried no further than to the human intelligence; and cannot be transferred, with any appearance of probability, to the other qualities of the mind: If this really be the case, what can the most inquisitive, contemplative, and religious man do more than give a plain, philosophical assent to the proposition, as often as it occurs; and believe that the arguments, on which it is established, exceed the objections which lie against it. Some astonishment indeed will naturally arise from the greatness of the object: Some melancholy from its obscurity: Some contempt of human reason, that it can give no solution more satisfactory with regard to so extraordinary and magnificent a question. But believe me, Cleanthes, the most natural sentiment, which a well-disposed mind will feel on this occasion, is a longing desire and expectation, that Heaven will be pleased to dissipate, at least alleviate, this profound ignorance, by affording some more particular revelation to mankind, and making discoveries of the nature, attributes, and operations of the divine object of our Faith. A person, seasoned with a just sense of the imperfections of natural reason, will fly to revealed truth with the greatest avidity: While the haughty dogmatist, persuaded that he can erect a complete system of theology by the mere help of philosophy, disdains any further aid, and rejects this adventitious instructor. To be a philosophical sceptic is, in a man of letters, the first and most essential step towards being a sound, believing Christian, a proposition which I would most willingly recommend to the attention of Pamphilus.

Pamphilus, however, awards the victory to Cleanthes, and the *Dialogues* end.

It is undeniable that the tone and content of Philo's speeches comes as a surprise to the reader, whether he has identified Philo with Hume or whether he has not. It is not that Philo has never uttered pious sentiments in favour of true religion before. He has done this frequently. But they have been drowned out by the insistent negativities of his attacks on the Argument from Design. Now they seem to dominate; and, more to the point, they are accompanied by an apparent acceptance of that argument, and an implication that the earlier negative thrusts were merely the sorts of cavils that might cause a philosopher to hesitate, but not in the end to reject it. If one accepts this reading of Part XII, then Philo has reversed his position without warning, and there is reason to take his final expression of longing for a revelation at its face value as well.

Kemp Smith holds that Philo's change of heart is entirely feigned, and that Hume's position is consistently negative. According to him, Philo does admit that nature does produce in the mind an overwhelming impression of design, but that it is indefinite and ambiguous; and that it should not lead us into any form of theism, in view of the negative arguments Philo has offered us in Parts I–XI. Hume, then, is the agnostic he seems from the concluding peroration of the *Natural History of Religion*. There are several features of Part XII which support this view.

(1) There are many suspicious covering phrases in Philo's speeches in support of the Design hypothesis. No one, he says, pays more profound adoration to the divine Being, 'as he discovers himself to reason'. The arguments for a divine intelligence must be undisputed since the inferences to the alleged design are so numerous and 'no understanding (can) estimate their cogency'. The analogy between the works of nature and the productions of art should lead us to infer a likeness in their causes 'if we argue at all concerning them'. (2) There is a certain oddity about saying that the design hypothesis is so obviously cogent that disputes between theists and atheists (disputes which the argument was supposed, after all, to settle in the theist's favour) are shown by it to be merely verbal ones. (3) The italicised proposition in Philo's final speech is vague, only nominally theistic (if even this) and explicitly devoid of any ethical implications. (4) The 'longing desire and expectation' of a revelation that Philo expresses in his final speech is certainly bogus, if Philo is a mouth-piece for Hume. It is one more example of Hume's habit of professing respect, in one of his writings on religion, for the specific religious claims with which that work does not deal, and which he attacks in one of the others. For Hume has attacked the credentials of Christian revelation in his assault on the historicity of miracles. Furthermore it is hard to see how there could be any rational *expectation* of a revelation from a being about whose moral attributes Philo has himself insisted, in this very paragraph, we have no reason to form any opinion.

In spite of these facts, I do not think it can be denied that Philo does seem to espouse one fundamental part of Cleanthes's position in a manner which is surprising. This is the proposition that it is more probable than not that the orderliness which the world exhibits does have a cause which bears some analogy to human intelligence. He admittedly refuses to say that this cause has moral qualities like ours, and Cleanthes of course argued for this also. But to accept even as much as he does is to accept something which he certainly seems to attack in Part II and raises further puzzles about in Part III. Pike is surely correct in saying that this is not as negative a view as Kemp Smith says it is.[12] It is certainly not the same as the apparent agnosticism of the close of the *Natural History*. Devoid of religious import though it is, it is still part of what Cleanthes has argued for. Pike suggests, plausibly, that Philo can be rendered consistent if we recall that he does not reply directly (indeed he is said to be embarrassed and unable to do so) when Cleanthes, in Part III, uses the analogies of the voices in the clouds and the self-propagating library to say that the impression of intelligent design is immediately compelling. He says that this claim of Cleanthes is distinct from the original argument in Part II, which depends upon an appeal to the observed sources of order in the world; that Philo's negative arguments apply only to this mediated argument, not to the one Cleanthes proffers in Part III.[13] If this is so, then by accepting that purpose, intention, or design strike all of us everywhere he is agreeing with Cleanthes that his own sceptical doubts and difficulties do not undermine the force of this unmediated recognition of design. If this is so, then Hume would be admitting that a belief in rational design is something to which human nature is universally prone, and which cannot be dislodged by sceptical argument.

I am not sure whether this is correct or not, though at the time of writing I am inclined to think it may be. It is not unlikely that the ambiguity of Part XII is due to some chronic indecision on Hume's part. He may be unsure whether or not this belief in an ultimate source of order is or is not itself a product of religious indoctrination or convention: of the 'early education' which Cleanthes lists among the barriers to suspended judgement. However this may be, it is clear that Philo does not ascribe the same assurance to any particular view of the moral qualities (if any) that the cause of order has. Nor does he even consent to decide whether the order in the universe has one cause or many. The language seems to eliminate pantheism,[14] but easily allows polytheism, indeed any principles that are intelligent but otherwise impersonal. 'Intelligent' is itself too strong a word: all

193

he will consent to is a cause or causes that are probably *somewhat like* our intelligence. There is also no doubt at all that the world-view Philo espouses is one which gives us no ground to plan our lives or to form our moral opinions by reference to anything outside the order of nature. It is at most a practically irrelevant deism.

This means that the apparent agreement between Philo and Cleanthes has to be interpreted with the greatest care. Professor Hendel has suggested that the concluding statement of Pamphilus that Cleanthes is nearer the truth than Philo represents Hume's own final judgement that a temperate 'dogmatism' (the theistic preference, as it were, in Philo's 'verbal' dispute) is the only practically possible course for a human nature which cannot tolerate suspended judgement.[15] Although this is perceptive, I cannot quite agree with it. I think Hume does accept that the wise man will agree with Cleanthes on the surface, but that this agreement is more social than intellectual.

One of the points at issue between Pike and Kemp Smith is the extent to which it is safe exegesis to take the positive proclamations of Philo at face value, and the extent to which they are ironic. In support of the latter view, Kemp Smith says that Hume's policy is that of 'stating his sceptical positions with the least possible emphasis compatible with definiteness' (*D.R.* 73). Pike finds this an odd estimate, when one thinks of the hostile tone of Hume's other writings on religion, and of the sustained attack on institutionalised religion in Part XII. I incline to think that there is a better interpretation than either of theirs, which takes into account the frequent hints that Philo cannot mean *quite* what he says, but also does justice to the fact that such ironies as are present in the *Dialogues* are far blander, and far less laced with sarcasm, than those of the Miracles essay, or of the *Natural History*.

What I consider to be the most fundamental and delicate irony is the appearance of agreement between Philo and Cleanthes as to what 'true religion' is. Cleanthes continues throughout to think, ingenuously, that true religion is a socially domesticated Christianity. The recurrent unholy alliance that one finds from time to time in the *Dialogues* between Philo and Demea is in part designed to make it clear that Hume does not think this at all. Just as Philo agrees with Demea about this, so does Hume agree on this, though on nothing else, with Kierkegaard and his modern followers. They merely say here what he says, in a different tone of voice. To Philo true religion is a conviction of the omnipresence of natural order, a vague deistic

194

belief in the probable existence of an individual intelligence (or perhaps several intelligences) at the back of it all, plus a sober recognition that any knowledge relevant to our moral decisions must come from reflection upon the natural order, not from supposed insight into the character of that intelligence. He is conscious that the belief in a causal intelligence represents some departure from his own principles, but concedes that the application of these principles does not eradicate this belief. In addition to this Hume (that is Philo *in the reflective mood of Part XII*) also sees that a sceptic who will allow this much can co-exist, and even co-operate, with Cleanthes' sort of Christian. For Cleanthes's sort of Christian also abhors 'bigotry'; and he is also committed, in practice, only to those elements in Christianity which coincide with polite morality and can be founded upon observation of human nature and scientific fact. There is no good philosophical reason for the free-thinker to refuse to allow the slight likelihood of a vague theism being true, or to refuse to pay lip service to it, provided he is not also asked to subscribe to institutionalised and revealed Christianity. To the end Philo and Cleanthes agree to differ about how beneficial or harmful the latter is. But the critical point of their consensus is that neither of them engages in it himself. Hume clearly thinks that Cleanthes and the Moderates he represents at this point, achieve their tolerance and moral wisdom at the price of ignoring the real character of the revealed tradition out of which they have come, and also at the price of removing from their stated convictions any doctrines which are in genuine conflict with those which the cautious sceptic will concede. Two hundred years before its appointed time, and in the idiom of his own day, Hume has made clear to us the doctrinal emptiness of secularised Christianity. He does not claim enough metaphysical knowledge to *deny* the concrete propositions they still occasionally assert, and as long as they keep quiet about the hell and damnation, he will live with it.[16] Philo in the last Part, then, is Hume's considered public *persona*, in which the claims of scepticism are restrained by the recognition of the value of moral consensus.

The above interpretation still implies that Hume is torn between sheer negativity towards the claims of theism, and the attraction of the unmediated argument which Cleanthes presents in its simplest form in Part III. (Either way he has rejected, indeed destroyed, the mediated argument of Part II.) In so far as he remains unsure between these two options, he remains unsure what constitutes the lowest common denominator of belief which human nature requires of us. This very lack of assurance itself is a reason for nominal accommodation.[17] This assessment of Hume's stance seems confirmed by an important letter of 1751 to Gilbert Elliott. In it Hume asks Elliott for help in strengthening the case of Cleanthes; and adds in the postscript the following:

> If you'll be pleased to assist me in supporting Cleanthes, I fancy you need not take matters any higher than Part 3. He allows, indeed, in Part 2, that all our inference is founded on the similitude of the works of nature to the usual effects of mind. Otherwise they must appear a mere chaos. The only difficulty is, why the other dissimilitudes do not weaken the argument. And indeed it would seem from experience and feeling, that they do not weaken it so much as we might naturally expect. A theory to solve this would be very acceptable.[18]

Adequate help was not forthcoming, but the form of the request is significant. Hume is anxious for a theory that will account for the fact that we do not seem to be wholly disillusioned with the Design argument, even though it is so readily undermined formally by the objections he puts into the mouth of Philo in Part II. I incline to think that Philo's closing speeches have the form they do because Hume still has no theory to account for this, and takes this fact seriously. Kant also took this fact seriously, partly, no doubt, because he read the *Dialogues*.[19] For Hume, taking it seriously would mean recognising the limits which human nature places on the agnosticism which is the logical outcome of Philo's arguments.

Notes and References*

1. HUME'S LIFE AND PHILOSOPHICAL OBJECTIVES

1. The letter is printed on pp. 12–18 of the first volume of Greig's edition of Hume's letters. For Mossner's identification, see chapter 7 of his *Life of David Hume.*
2. See Chapter 8.
3. A convenient introduction to Hume's historical work is *David Hume: Philosophical Historian,* ed. David Fate Norton and Richard H. Popkin (Bobbs-Merrill, New York, 1966). It contains valuable interpretative essays, extracts from the *History of England* and T. E. Jessop's list of the posthumous editions.
4. For example, Selby-Bigge, in the introduction to his edition of the two *Enquiries:* 'The *Treatise,* as was noticed at the time of its publication, is full of egoisms. Even in this severe work, together with a genuine ardour and enthusiasm, there is an occasional note of insincerity, arrogance or wantonness which strikes the serious student painfully. The following pages will perhaps show that Hume, in re-casting the *Treatise* into its new form, displayed the less admirable sides of his temper rather freely.'
5. See the famous footnote to Section XII of the first *Enquiry* (*E.U.* 155) in which Hume points out that Berkeley is a sceptic *malgré lui* and tells us that this is revealed by the fact that his arguments 'admit of no answer and produce no conviction'.
6. This essay appears on pp. 213–31 of vol. 3 of the Green and Grose edition of Hume.

*When not quoted in the Notes and References, full bibliographical details are given in the Bibliographical Notes, pp. 211–17.

7. I omit discussion here of the unappetising arguments of Section I of Part IV of Book I of the *Treatise*, 'of Scepticism with Regard to Reason'. They certainly represent more than a flirtation with the extreme view that no demonstrative knowledge is possible at all; but this negativity seems to be abandoned in the *Enquiry*.

8. A consequence of this would be that a combination of outward conformity and inner rejection is a possibility for them also. Again, see Chapter 8. A key passage here is at the beginning of Section IV of Part IV of Book I of the *Treatise* (I 215–16/225) where he distinguishes 'in the imagination between the principles which are permanent, irresistible, and universal ... and the principles which are changeable, weak and irregular'.

9. Compare, for example, competing interpretations of his treatment of personal identity; see notes to chapter 4.

10. For an excellent short treatment of this, see Price's essay 'The Permanent Significance of Hume's Philosophy' .

11. An indispensable reference here is G. E. Moore's classic essay, 'Hume's Philosophy'.

12. See Chapters 6 and 7 for more detailed discussions. The most well-known place where Hume contends that evaluative conclusions do not follow from evaluative premisses is the 'is–ought' passage, and I do not wish to overrate its importance by singling out Hume's 'deductivism' here, even though the parallel between Books I and III is in this respect exact. It is important to stress that many of Hume's anti-rationalist arguments in Books II and III are designed to show that reason in its subordinate, empirical employment in common life does not make evaluations or generate conduct.

13. See Locke, *Essay Concerning Human Understanding*, book IV, chapter III, p. 190 in the Campbell Fraser edition (Oxford University Press, 1894; reprinted by Dover Publications, New York, 1959) vol. II.

14. Hume is sometimes accused of making the same assumption himself. See Chapter 4.

15. Hume's discussion of causal inference proceeds without any explicit recognition that it depends upon our right to distinguish between inner and outer phenomena. It is the better for this. But the integration of the piecemeal treatments of the three main themes of his epistemology is a matter of speculation.

16. The *Enquiry* really gives it all away! 'But, except the mind be disordered by disease or madness, they (i.e. ideas) never can arrive at such a pitch of vivacity, as to render these perceptions altogether undistinguishable.' (*E.U.* 17)
17. McNabb, *David Hume,* p. 26.
18. On Hume's treatment of Abstract Ideas, see MacNabb, Flew and Bennett.
19. Chapter XXXIII of Book II of Locke's *Essay* is entitled 'Of the Association of Ideas'.
20. See Chapter 2.

2. CAUSATION AND INDUCTION

1. On Hume's views about volitions, see Chapter 6.
2. These contentions are of some importance in Hume's strategy. His major target is the view that we have to ascribe unobservable powers to natural objects in order to account for their causal properties. But he is also seeking to refute the Occasionalists, who argued that connections between mental and physical phenomena could only be understood as miraculous interventions of God; and, I think, Berkeley, who held that physical causation could only be understood on the model of mental causation, so that the perceptions that constitute natural sequences in the physical world are controlled by the divine mind in the way in which the ideas of our imagination are controlled by human minds. Hume tries to undermine all these theories together by arguing that both physical and mental causation are wholly familiar, and that any mystery attached to one should be attached equally to the other.
3. See Part Two of *Probability and Hume's Inductive Scepticism.* I am much indebted to this remarkable book, which no serious student of this topic can afford not to read.
4. Ibid., p. 91.
5. Ibid., p. 97.
6. This is the burden of arguments like those of Norman Malcolm in 'The Verification Argument' in *Philosophical Analysis*, ed. Max Black (Cornell University Press, Ithaca, New York, 1950).
7. See P. F. Strawson, *Introduction to Logical Theory,* chapter 9 (Methuen, 1952).

8. See e.g. F. L. Will, 'Will the Future be like the Past?' in *Logic and Language*, ed. Antony Flew, Second Series (Blackwell, Oxford, 1953).

9. This is the point at which to mention that in both accounts Hume proceeds on the assumption of the existence of external objects – and also on that of a continuing self which observes them. The sceptical doubts about these topics play a wholly trivial part in the *Enquiry*, where it is striking that the apparatus of impressions and ideas is only brought into play when Hume turns to the idea of necessary connection. In the *Treatise* the perplexing discussions of these topics come *after* the discussions of causation. Price has pointed out that if it is true that our ideas of cause and effect are the product of our observation of constant conjunctions, it is far from clear that such conjunctions are to be met with among our impressions, whatever we may say about physical objects. ('It is very doubtful whether there *are* any constant conjunctions of sense-impressions. If we try to formulate any one drowsy nod or blink will refute us.' (H. H. Price, *Hume's Theory of the External World*, Clarendon Press, Oxford, 1940, p. 7). There seem to be three possible alternatives open to us if we attempt to supply the connections that Hume does not make. (1) We could say that the conjunctions are indeed between impressions, and are thought to be constant when they are not. (2) We could say that the conjunctions are between physical objects, so that the imaginative construction of the external world that Hume describes in Part IV, Section II, is completed before the mechanisms of causal thought can begin. (3) We could say that the development of one set of habits proceeds alongside the development of the other, so that we cannot really separate the belief in constant conjunction from the belief in the distinct and continued existence of objects. Hume avoids this issue by his piecemeal treatment; but it remains. Although it is speculative as well as difficult, I would suggest that only (3) is even moderately plausible, and that it could be worked out without formal inconsistency. Had Hume himself attempted it, his epistemological psychology would have been even closer to that of Kant than it is.

10. This is why causal judgements can be contested. If Hume thought the idea of causation were wholly derived from an

internal impression, he would be committed to the incorrigibility of causal statements (see Price, 'The Permanent Significance of Hume's Philosophy'). The reason that the subjectivity of our idea of power or necessity does not prevent genuine empirical disagreement about causal judgements is that they commit those who make them to the objective characteristics of contiguity, succession, and constant conjunction. There is a close and deliberate analogy here with Hume's analysis of moral evaluations. Although he adopts an 'emotive' interpretation of them, he also holds them to be occasioned by a supposedly objective survey of the actions to which we apply them, so that the judgements in which we express them can be genuinely contradicted. See Chapter 7.

11. See Flew, *Hume's Philosophy of Belief,* p. 127.

12. This seems especially evident in considering historical causes. See William Dray, *Laws and Explanations in History* (Oxford University Press, 1957).

13. There is a short passage in the Section 'Of the Probability of Causes' in the *Treatise,* reproduced in Section VIII of the *Enquiry,* 'Of Liberty and Necessity', in which Hume discusses the phenomenon of 'contrariety' in our observations. He is concerned with cases where a cause is apparently not followed by its usual effect, and wishes to explain them in a manner that preserves our commitment to the universality of the connection between causes and effects. He says that in such cases the expert will detect an additional 'contrary' cause which the layman overlooks — such as a speck of dust which prevents the force of the spring from moving the hands of a clock. Such discoveries preserve the principle that causes are regularly followed by their effects by showing that there are other causes present when they seem not to do so. MacNabb suggests (*David Hume,* pp. 56–7) that this passage is Hume's account of why we believe in the Causal Principle. If it is, it is a failure, for reasons additional to those MacNabb offers. An explanation of why we believe that if a cause appears to fail there is another cause interfering is not an explanation of why we believe that every event has some cause or other. The former principle entails that every cause, left to itself, will always have the same effect. The Causal Principle does not entail this, nor is it entailed by it.

3. PERCEPTION

1. H. H. Price shows that Hume never manages to clarify this
   distinction. See *Hume's Theory of the External World*,
   pp. 18–19. No student of Hume, or of the problem of
   perception, can afford to neglect this splendid book.
2. This is a fundamental difference from the doctrines of Berkeley,
   to whom Hume's theories of perception are otherwise much
   indebted.
3. This argument is inconsistent with Hume's view in Book II of
   the *Treatise* that some impressions, namely those of the calm
   passions, can be present but not noticed, and with his view in
   Book III that some impressions, such as those of moral
   disapproval and hatred, can be confused with one another.
4. Had Hume not blinded himself to the logical truth that
   numerical identity does not entail invariance, he would still have
   had to deal with the problem of the gaps in our perceptions. But
   it would then have appeared in the same light whether the
   perceptions on each side of the gaps in a series showed
   constancy or whether they showed coherence. Since he defines
   identity in terms of invariance, he has to regard constancy as the
   more fundamental.
5. There is a noteworthy unclarity in Hume's views about the
   representative theory. In Section IV, 'Of the Modern Philosophy', he treats it as a misguided but intelligible attempt to
   rescue our perceptual beliefs from scepticism and to refine
   them. He does not dismiss it as meaningless in the way he holds
   theories of substance to be meaningless. Yet his arguments in
   Section VI of Part II, referred to above, suggest strongly that he
   believes there is no clear sense to the view that existence can be
   ascribed to anything other than perceptions. It is the former
   view of representationism as intelligible but unverifiable that is
   dominant in Section II of Part IV, though the latter, more
   radical, view seems needed for Hume's attack on the vulgar
   system to begin.

   Even allowing for this ambiguity, however, it does not seem
   possible to follow Price's suggestion (*Hume's Theory of the
   External World*, p. 13) that when Hume tells us doubt about the
   existence of body is 'idle' he means it is meaningless. For even if
   he denies that distinct and continued existence can meaningfully be ascribed to anything other than perceptions, he

certainly insists that it is intelligible to ascribe it to them. If it can meaningfully be ascribed to them, it can meaningfully be denied of them also. And on his analysis, this is what a denial of the existence of body would amount to.

4. THE SELF

1. The account of Hume's doctrine that is presented here is a briefer version of the one I originally put forward in an essay 'Hume on Personal Identity' in 1955. It has recently been challenged by James Noxon and by Lawrence Ashley and Michael Stack. See the Bibliography for detailed references.

2. I express no view here on whether the relationship between successive stages of a person's mental history can constitute sufficient criteria of personal identity, or whether they cannot. I insist merely that Hume has not shown that no adequate criteria of personal identity through time are possible and that, here as elsewhere, the relationships between an entity's successive stages are bound to be the grounds for ascribing unity to it. In the case of persons there is the special problem that arises when we try to assess, as Hume does not, the importance of their psycho-physical character.

3. This criticism is involved in Strawson's comments on Hume in the closing sections of his essay, 'Persons' (see pp. 145–6 in V. C. Chappell's *The Philosophy of Mind,* Prentice-Hall, 1962). I made it myself in the article 'Personal Identity' in vol. 6 of *The Encyclopedia of Philosophy,* ed. P. Edwards, especially p. 100.

4. It might be objected here that one cannot decide, with or without philosophical shock, that all the perceptions one has are one's own alone, until one has already generated the idea of others as well as the idea of oneself. But it is not at all clear that Hume is unable to accept this. He can happily agree that human nature has to generate a belief before philosophers can raise questions about it. He is only involved in vicious circularity if it can be demonstrated that the unity each of us ascribes to the series of perceptions he has is one which must be construed, *ab initio,* as the unity of my mind as distinct from someone else's. His second thoughts on personal identity in the Appendix make it clear that what has concerned him throughout is that we ascribe unity to the series in the face of the clear fact (as he sees the matter) that a perception can very well exist apart – apart

from any mind, not in yours as opposed to mine. Hence the ascription he accounts for is one that could be made without any prior thought of the existence of other selves.

5. See MacNabb, *David Hume*, p. 251; and Passmore, *Hume's Intentions*, pp. 82–3.

6. See Nelson Pike, 'Hume's Bundle Theory of the Self: a Limited Defense', pp. 159–65. Although I disagree with Pike's interpretation of Hume's analysis of our belief in self-identity, my arguments in this chapter are much indebted to his. I have attempted a more detailed response in 'Hume's Theory of the Self Revisited'.

7. I have attempted to explore the distinction in 'Self-Identity and Self-Regard' in *The Identities of Persons,* ed. Amélie Rorty (University of California Press, 1975).

8. See Kemp Smith, *The Philosophy of David Hume*, pp. v, 179–83.

5. THE PASSIONS

1. See P. L. Gardiner in *David Hume: A Symposium,* ed. D. F. Pears; also chapter one of Anthony Kenny's *Action, Emotion, and Will.*

2. See, for example, II 85/367 and II 127/415.

3. On this topic, and indeed throughout this chapter, I am much indebted to Páll S. Árdal's *Passion and Value in Hume's Treatise.* See p. 95ff.

4. I here follow Árdal.

5. Compare *D.P.* Section I, pp. 139–43.

6. Not surprisingly Hume oscillates between talking of causes and objects as though they are things or their qualities and talking of them as though they are the ideas of these; but it is the latter view that appears in his most careful theoretical statements, such as his summary of the associative mechanism that generates the indirect passions. (III/289).

7. One solution might be to say that the separate pleasure or uneasiness produced by the cause of pride, and so on, will be some direct passion which is in each case possessed of pleasantness or unpleasantness as tonal quality. So a beautiful house leads to the direct passion of aesthetic appreciation, moral virtue in someone leads to moral approval, each in turn

leading to pride or love if the person himself engages my attention. This does not square readily with Hume's inclination to think of these objective passions as alternatives to the interested ones; but I see no reason to regard them as exclusive. Disinterested approval can lead to love, and aesthetic appreciation to pride.

8. This difficulty does not seem to arise with love and hate in quite the same way it does with pride and humility. In the cases of love and hate it seems reasonable to regard the loving or hostile interest in the person as a consequence of the esteem or aversion caused by the causes connected with them. The difficulty is rather that the causes alone produce (and Hume's language is significant) esteem and disapproval, not love and hate, which again seem to be a result of the interest in the person himself. So in these cases the emotion is not in fact mentioned in Hume's account, only a precedent one.

9. In addition to Árdal's work, I have found much helpful guidance in Philip Mercer's *Sympathy and Ethics*, chapters II–IV.

10. His use of it, and related terms, in *E.M.* is *not* the technical use described here.

11. In fact his text is ambiguous: 'However instantaneous this change of the idea into an impression may be, it proceeds from certain views and reflections, which will not escape the strict scrutiny of a philosopher, though they may the person himself who makes them.' (II 41/317.)

12. This example is enough to prove that sympathy is not, in Hume's usage, a principle that only gives rise to unpleasant passions, since pride is a pleasant one.

13. It is significant that this appears as an example of comparison and not of sympathy.

14. If it is not, but is another name for love, as it is elsewhere, we still have a complex emotional response involving two simultaneous passions, one of which requires us to overlook the very fact which the existence of the other requires us to notice.

15. Bernard Williams, 'Pleasure and Belief', *Proceedings of the Aristotelian Society* (1959).

16. H. A. Prichard, *Moral Obligation* (Clarendon Press, Oxford, 1949) p. 53.

1. I have suggested that Hume makes the distinction between the primary passions and the direct ones very hard to explain coherently by failing to distinguish between the pleasure or pain that may cause me to feel some emotion and the pleasure or pain I expect to experience if something I want or fear comes to pass. See above pp. 93–6 and 104–10.

2. It is clear that these desires and aversions are not to be interpreted as wholly selfish or hedonistic. That they are not wholly selfish is sufficiently proved by the inclusion of benevolence and pity. That they are not wholly hedonistic is obscured by Hume's predilection to say that the direct passions are all caused by pleasure and pain, and by his unfortunate phrase 'good and evil, or, in other words, pain and pleasure' (II 148/439). But it is striking that when he introduces the primary passions, he says that they 'produce good and evil, and proceed not from them' (II 149/439); this would seem not only to mean that the pleasure or pain connected with them is anticipated and not felt previously, but also to embody a recognition that it is the named objects of the desires and not the pleasure they are expected to give, that the desires are *for*. In spite of the lack of sophistication that Hume shows over the notions of pleasure and pain, the charge of psychological hedonism is unfair. Even if we are inclined to accuse him of it, however, we have to accuse him of it in a form that allows the pleasures we seek to include pleasure in the well-being of others, and the pains we avoid to include the pain we feel at the distress of others; and we have to recognise that he includes among the springs of action a general appetite to good and aversion to evil 'considered merely as such' which allows for long-term enlightenment about pleasures and pains, or prudence.

3. His arguments are to be found in Section II of Part III of Book II of the *Treatise,* and in Section VIII of the first *Enquiry*. The major difference between the two accounts is the presence of a positive definition of liberty of spontaneity in the *Enquiry*.

4. There is a particular irony in Hume's combining this view of freedom with the thesis, central in his moral philosophy, that it is men and their character, not individual actions, that are the objects of moral approval or disapproval. For this means that we

approve or disapprove of something to which the concept of freedom, as he analyses it, has no application.

5. It is also, of course, a direct consequence of his analysis of causation: 'The distinction, *which we often make* betwixt power and the exercise of it, is equally without foundation' (I 169/171; my italics).

6. Hume's example, anger, is obfuscatory, because anger is not a desire. But we must recall that in his classification it is — that is the desire to injure another.

7. Hume partially sees this himself. At III 168—9/459—60 he states that a man who bases his choices on an error of fact is 'more to be lamented than blamed'. But he persists in admitting that his action can 'in a figurative and improper way of speaking' be called unreasonable. Of course it cannot, and this is just what makes it more to be lamented than blamed.

8. The same applies to reactive passions like anger or distress.

9. On this point see Chapter V of Rachael M. Kydd's *Reason and Conduct in Hume's Treatise.* In spite of detailed errors in her account of Hume's theory of the passions, her book is still the most philosophically stimulating critique of the anti-rationalist arguments I have discussed here.

7. MORALITY AND SOCIETY

1. For helpful accounts of Hume's predecessors, and his relationship to them, see chapter I of Kydd's *Reason and Conduct in Hume's Treatise,* and chapters I and II of Raphael, *The Moral Sense.*

2. For comments on the concept of a moral sense, especially in Hutcheson, see Raphael, *The Moral Sense.*

3. Árdal, *Passion and Value in Hume's Treatise*, chapter 6.

4. There is some temptation, in spite of the natural reading of the texts, to treat approval and disapproval as the independent pleasure and pain that actions or character-qualities give rise to, and to think of them as leading on to love and hate as these have been understood from Book II. In its favour this reading would have the fact that Hume never succeeds in distinguishing love from esteem or admiration, or in distinguishing hatred from contempt. He even says (in the footnote to III 301/608) that 'love and esteem are at bottom the same passions, and arise

from like causes'. But this interpretation, though tempting, does not only seem blocked by the natural understanding of most of the texts, but also by the fact that Hume's views on the way sympathy helps to generate moral approval and disapproval enable him to offer another candidate for the necessary role of the independent pleasure or uneasiness that the schema of the indirect passion includes.

5. His theory of obligation could not be stated without this.

6. J. Kemp, *Ethical Naturalism* (Macmillan, 1970) p. 44.

7. There is an excellent discussion of the relation between the *Treatise* and the *Enquiries,* with detailed comments on the treatment of sympathy, in the Appendix to Stewart, *The Moral and Political Philosophy of David Hume.*

8. In the *Enquiry* we find the following: 'The hypothesis which we embrace is plain. It maintains that morality is determined by sentiment. It defines virtue to be whatever mental action or quality gives to a spectator the pleasing sentiment of approbation; and vice the contrary. We then proceed to a plain matter of fact, to wit, what actions have this consequence.' (*E.M.* 289)

9. What follows is speculative. I would merely suggest that it is consistent with what Hume says, and avoids some of the difficulties attaching to theories he could reasonably be said to commit himself to if this passage is dismissed.

10. Especially in the 'is—ought' passage, discussed below.

11. It is not merely that duty is second-best to other motives, such as natural affection. Hume seems to be suggesting here that to do something from duty *is* to do it in order to acquire natural affection. If it were merely second best, it could still be allowed to be an independently intelligible motive in its own right, and Hume's point seems to be that it is not. If this is indeed Hume's view, then he has wholly failed to understand the sense of duty. For I can do something from duty not only when I do not want to do it, but also when I do not want to want to do it either: as when I kill someone, from duty, in war.

12. Not only in 'ought' language, as his closing sentence indicates: there is, in addition, at least the language of 'vice' and 'virtue'.

13. This shows, of course, that a Naturalist reading of Hume is at best *more nearly* right. If it were wholly right, Hume would be committed to saying that the transition is a piece of legitimate non-deductive reasoning, and he does not say this either. He does not think it is a piece of reasoning at all.

14. Alasdair MacIntyre says that 'the notion of "ought" is for Hume only explicable in terms of a consensus of interest' ('Hume on Is and Ought', *Hume*, ed. Chappell, p. 249). This is a mistake. It suggests that Hume only considers the concept of obligation to apply in the sphere of the artificial virtues. In fact Hume thinks it fits all areas of conduct where we can disapprove of the absence of an action or of a feeling or of a character-trait.

8. RELIGION

1. I am greatly indebted in this chapter to the critical editions of Hume's *Dialogues* by Norman Kemp Smith and Nelson Pike, and to the relevant sections in the volumes by Hendel and Flew.
2. See E. C. Mossner, 'The Enigma of Hume'.
3. See Kemp Smith, *Dialogues*, pp. 37–8.
4. See Mossner, 'The Enigma of Hume'.
5. See C. D. Broad, 'Hume's Theory of the Credibility of Miracles'.
6. See chapter II of his *Philosophers and Religious Truth*.
7. In particular the *Natural History*, the most consistently sarcastic of Hume's works. A major drawback in Nelson Pike's reading of the *Dialogues* is that unless we are prepared to accept that the two works are inconsistent, we have to take the verbally positive statements in the *Natural History* at their face value, which I am unable to do.
8. See Kemp Smith, *Dialogues*, pp. 55–75.
9. This preference for an immanent, rather than a transcendent, priniciple of design is one that Philo at least seems to abandon in Part XII — see p. 193.
10. Kemp Smith detects mockery in the astronomical number of purposes and adjustments Philo's account implies, and he is surely correct in this, though perhaps not in what he infers from it.
11. The second time we get the delightful comparison of 'the rotting of a turnip, the generation of an animal, and the structure of human thought'.
12. N. Pike, *Dialogues*, pp. 204–38.
13. To accept the unmediated argument is not necessarily to accept at face value the two imagined cases Cleanthes associates with it. An adequate discussion of what *they* would show is beyond my scope here.
14. See note 9.

15. See chapter twelve of Hendel, *Studies in the Philosophy of David Hume.*

16. What most concerned Hume was the suggestion, frequently made by his enemies, sometimes to his permanent disadvantage, that his scepticism about revealed religion, was morally dangerous. 'Of a Particular Providence' (*E.U.*, Section XI) is a partial answer to this. So is the anonymous *A Letter from a Gentleman to his Friend in Edinburgh,* written to counter such attacks when he was a candidate for the Chair of Philosophy at Edinburgh.

17. This accommodation could still be made, and for the same moral reasons, if Hume were more firmly negative about the design hypothesis and Philo were merely meant to express a conviction of an orderliness in nature rather than a conviction that this has a transcendent cause. While this would fit Hume's other writings more readily, it would entail a more substantial practical accommodation and is a less natural reading of Part XII.

   I think my interpretation is supported by a further, minor consideration. Pike points out that in Philo's last speech the italicised proposition is offered as a view of natural theology that 'some people' maintain, and suggests that these will be the atheists Philo has referred to earlier, rather than Philo himself. I suggest that it does refer to them, but also expresses Philo's own opinions. For he has been at pains to insist that a cautious atheist only differs verbally from a cautious theist. The message of the chastened Philo of Part XII to such atheists is that they should not disturb the harmony that can reign between them and cautious theists by pressing these irresoluble and practically empty disagreements.

18. Greig (ed.), *The Letters of David Hume,* vol. I, p. 157.

19. See Section 3 of chapter III of the Transcendental Dialectic of the *Critique of Pure Reason,* 'The Impossibility of the Physico-Theological Proof'; pp. 518–24 of Kemp Smith's translation. See especially p. 520.

Bibliographical Notes

HUME'S PHILOSOPHICAL WRITINGS

DAVID HUME, *Philosophical Works,* ed. T. H. Green and T. H. Grose. In four volumes, originally published by Longmans Green, London, in 1878. Currently available in reprint published by Scientia Verlag Aalen, 1964. The most complete collection of Hume's philosophical writings, containing also Greens's lengthy and very hostile introduction.

A Treatise of Human Nature, ed. L. A. Selby-Bigge (Clarendon Press, Oxford, 1888). Numerous reprintings. Widely used as the standard text, though there are rumours of its being superseded.

A Treatise of Human Nature, with introduction by A. D. Lindsay (J. M. Dent, Everyman's Library, 1911). Many reprintings. A convenient and readily accessible edition.

Enquiries Concerning the Human Understanding and Concerning the Principles, of Morals, ed. L. A. Selby-Bigge (Clarendon Press, Oxford, 1894; 2nd ed. 1902). The most widely-used edition of the *Enquiries* containing valuable tables comparing each with the corresponding portions of the *Treatise.*

Enquiry Concerning the Human Understanding, ed. C. W. Hendel (Bobbs-Merrill, New York, 1955).

Enquiry Concerning the Principles of Morals, ed. C. W. Hendel (Bobbs-Merrill, New York, 1957).

An Abstract of a Treatise of Human Nature, ed. J. M. Keynes and P. Sraffa (Cambridge University Press, 1938). This very important document has been reprinted, somewhat more accessibly, in several collections, among them *Hume: Theory of Knowledge,* ed. D. C. Yalden-Thomson (Nelson, Edinburgh, 1951).

A Letter from a Gentleman to his Friend in Edinburgh, ed. E. C. Mossner and J. V. Price (Edinburgh University Press, 1967).

The Natural History of Religion, ed. H. E. Root (Adam & Charles Black, London, and Stanford University Press, Stanford, Cal., 1956).

Dialogues Concerning Natural Religion, ed. Norman Kemp Smith (Nelson, Edinburgh, 1947; reprinted by Bobbs-Merrill, New York, no date). Indispensable introduction.

Dialogues Concerning Natural Religion, ed. Nelson Pike (Bobbs-Merrill, New York, 1970). Excellent commentary, essential for anyone concerned to assess the importance of the *Dialogues* in the development of the philosophy of religion.

The Letters of David Hume, ed. J. Y. T. Greig, 2 vols (Oxford University Press, 1932).

New Letters of David Hume, ed. R. Klibansky and E. C. Mossner; Clarendon Press, Oxford, 1954.

GENERAL WORKS ON HUME

ERNEST CAMPBELL MOSSNER, *The Life of David Hume* (Nelson, Edinburgh, 1954; reprinted Clarendon Press, Oxford, 1970). A full, very readable, and philosophically sensitive biography; essential for an understanding of how Hume the man and Hume the thinker are related.

D. G. C. MACNABB, *David Hume: His Theory of Knowledge and Morality* (Hutchinson, 1951; 2nd ed. 1966). Combines easy readability with expertise; an excellent companion as one embarks on a consecutive reading of the *Treatise* for the first time. The same author's article 'Hume' in *The Encyclopedia of Philosophy* ed. Paul Edwards (Crowell Collier & Macmillan, New York, 1967) vol. 4, is warmly recommended.

C. W. HENDEL, *Studies in the Philosophy of David Hume,* new edition (Bobbs-Merrill, New York, 1963). A scholarly and wise exposition of Hume's major doctrines, with a valuable survey of recent Hume scholarship.

NORMAN KEMP SMITH, *The Philosophy of David Hume* (Macmillan, 1941; reprinted 1964). The major work of Hume interpretation in our century. The multi-layered presentation is daunting, and a student is well advised to begin with Kemp Smith's two articles on 'The Naturalism of Hume' in *Mind* (1905).

J. A. PASSMORE, *Hume's Intentions* (Cambridge University Press, 1952). Lively and learned analysis; the perfect corrective to any simplistic picture of the major themes in Hume's philosophy.

A. H. BASSON, *David Hume* (Penguin, 1958) reprinted as *David Hume,* by A. P. Cavendish (Constable, London, and Dover, New York, no date). Uneven, but interesting on Hume's general aims and methods and on his scepticism.

ANTONY FLEW, *Hume's Philosophy of Belief* (Routledge & Kegan Paul, 1961). Excellent detailed study of the first *Enquiry,* relating Hume's arguments to the concerns of his contemporaries and those of ours.

JONATHAN BENNETT, *Locke, Berkeley, Hume: Central Themes* (Clarendon Press, Oxford, 1973). Rigorous and stimulating commentary on Hume's doctrines on causation and objectivity.

JAMES NOXON, *Hume's Philosophical Development* (Clarendon Press, Oxford, 1973). A study of Hume's methods and of the nature of his indebtedness to Newton. Suggests a more radical change in Hume's attitudes from the *Treatise* to the *Enquiries* than I assume in this book.

COLLECTIONS

V. C. CHAPPELL (ed.), *Hume* (Doubleday, New York, 1966).

A. SESONSKE AND N. FLEMING, *Human Understanding* (Wadsworth, Belmont, Cal., 1965).

D. F. PEARS (ed.), *David Hume: A Symposium* (Macmillan, 1963).

BOOKS AND ARTICLES ON THEMES IN INDIVIDUAL CHAPTERS

These are, of course, additional to the relevant portions of works referred to above.

Chapter 1

My Own Life is reprinted in many places, among them pp. 611–15 of Mossner, and pp. 1–8 of vol. 3 of Green and Grose, where it is followed by Adam Smith's letter to William Strachan concerning Hume's last days.

H. H. Price's 'The Permanent Significance of Hume's Philosophy' appeared in *Philosophy,* vol. XV (1940), and is reprinted in Sesonske and Fleming.

G. E. Moore's 'Hume's Philosophy' appeared in his *Philosophical Studies* (Kegan Paul, 1922) and is reprinted in H. Feigl and W. Sellars, *Readings in Philosophical Analysis* (Appleton-Century-Crofts, New York, 1949).

On Hume's scepticism, see Richard H. Popkin, 'David Hume: His Pyrrhonism and His Critique of Pyrrhonism', *Philosophical Quarterly*, vol. I (1951); reprinted in Chappell. There is also valuable background in Popkin's *The History of Scepticism from Erasmus to Descartes* (Van Gorcum, Assen, Netherlands, 1960) and his essay 'Skepticism' in vol. 7 of Edward's *Encyclopedia of Philosophy*. See also W. Robison, 'Hume's Scepticism', *Dialogue*, vol. XIII (1973).

On some of the defects in the doctrine of impressions and ideas, see R. P. Wolff, 'Hume's Theory of Mental Activity', *Philosophical Review*, vol. LXIX (1960), reprinted in Chappell.

For critiques of Hume's theory of belief, see H. H. Price, *Belief* (Allen & Unwin, London, 1969) pp. 157–88, and chapter V of Flew.

For detailed treatment of the differences between the *Treatise* and the *Enquiries*, one must go to the introductory analysis in Selby-Bigge's edition of the latter, and to the Appendix to John B. Stewart's *The Moral and Philosophical of David Hume* (see bibliographical notes for chapter 7).

Chapter 2

D. C. Stove, *Probability and Hume's Inductive Scepticism* (Clarendon Press, Oxford, 1973). A novel and wholly first-class treatment.

The literature on induction and causation is enormous, and all of it owes something to Hume. Recent works that include worthwhile comment about him are: Bertrand Russell, *Problems of Philosophy* (Home University Library, Oxford, 1912) chapter VI; William Kneale, *Probability and Induction* (Clarendon Press, Oxford, 1949); A. J. Ayer, *Probability and Evidence* (Macmillan, 1972); G. H. von Wright, *The Logical Problem of Induction* (Blackwell, Oxford, 1957); L. J. Cohen, *The Implications of Induction* (Methuen, 1970). See also the extracts from Popper, Gasking, and Strawson in Sesonske and Fleming.

A recent analysis of the argument in Section III of Part III is G. E. M. Anscombe, ' "Whatever Has a Beginning of Existence must Have a Cause": Hume's Argument Exposed', *Analysis*, vol. 34 (1974).

Chapter 3

The essential reference here is H. H. Price, *Hume's Theory of the External World* (Clarendon Press, Oxford, 1940). No student of Hume, or of the problem of perception, can afford to ignore this excellent work.

See also John W. Cook, 'Hume's Scepticism With Regard to the Senses', *American Philosophical Quarterly,* vol. 5 (1968), and the relevant sections of MacNabb, Basson and Bennett.

Chapter 4

For a fuller statement of this interpretation see my 'Hume on Personal Identity', *Philosophical Review,* vol. LXIV (1955); reprinted in Chappell and in Sesonske and Fleming. For criticisms of it, see James Noxon, 'Senses of Identity in Hume's *Treatise*', *Dialogue*, vol. VIII (1969), and Lawrence Ashley and Michael Stack, 'Hume's Theory of the Self and its Identity', *Dialogue,* vol. XIII (1974). I have attempted to defend my interpretation in 'Hume's Theory of the Self Revisited', which is due to appear in a volume of Oberlin Colloquium proceedings on Hume, edited by Norman S. Care.

Nelson Pike's partial defence of Hume is in 'Hume's Bundle Theory of the Self: a Limited Defense', *American Philosophical Quarterly,* vol. 4 (1967).

Other discussions of Hume are to be found in P. Butcharov, 'The Self and Perceptions: A Study in Humean Philosophy', *Philosophical Quarterly,* vol. 9 (1959); Nathan Brett, 'Substance and Mental Identity in Hume's *Treatise*', *Philosophical Quarterly,* vol. 22 (1972); and D. F. Pears, 'Hume on Personal Identity', in *David Hume: A Symposium.*

Godfrey Vesey's little book, *Personal Identity* (Macmillan, 1974) is an exploration of the problem that begins from 'Hume's "Labyrinth" ' and skilfully explores contemporary discussions related to it. It has an excellent bibliography.

Chapter 5

Apart from the relevant discussions in Kemp Smith, there was, until quite recently, very little of importance available on Hume's analysis of the passions. This has now been corrected, and the indispensable work is Páll S. Árdal, *Passion and Value in Hume's Treatise* (Edinburgh University Press, 1966). This not only leads the reader through some of the key parts of Book II, but also establishes beyond serious question the importance of Book II for the understanding of Hume's ethics. It is therefore relevant to the concerns of chapters 6 and 7 also.

Philip Mercer, *Sympathy and Ethics* (Clarendon Press, Oxford, 1972), is an extended critical study of a topic which usually receives superficial treatment in discussions of Hume's moral psychology.

Hume's method of analysis of the passions is criticised in P. L. Gardiner's contribution to *David Hume: A Symposium,* and in chapter one of Anthony Kenny's *Action, Emotion and Will* (Routledge & Kegan Paul, 1963).

Chapter 6

The fullest treatment of Hume's arguments for the impotence of reason in human choice is in Rachael M. Kydd, *Reason and Conduct in Hume's Treatise* (Clarendon Press, Oxford, 1964). Occasional misinterpretations (e.g. of the doctrine of calm passions) are more than compensated for by the close engagement with Hume's arguments.

On free will, the *Enquiry* version is well handled in Chapter VII of Flew. The vast literature on freedom is much indebted to Hume; to assess his interpretation of our common understanding of freedom one should at least ponder the similar reading found in Chapter VI of G. E. Moore's *Ethics* (Williams & Norgate, London, 1912) and the critique of Moore in J. L. Austin's lecture 'Ifs and Cans', in *Philosophical Papers*, ed. Urmson and Warnock (Oxford, 1961). The clearest statement I know of a view of freedom opposed to that of Hume is Harry G. Frankfurt, 'Freedom of the Will and the Concept of a Person', *Journal of Philosophy,* vol. LXVIII (1971).

For a sustained attack on Hume's opinions on power and free choice see M. R. Ayers, *The Refutation of Determinism* (Methuen, 1968).

Chapter 7

In addition to works already cited for Chapters 5 and 6, the following are of importance for the study of Hume's ethical work:

John B. Stewart, *The Moral and Political Philosophy of David Hume* (Columbia University Press, New York, 1963), which contains an important Appendix on the relation between the *Treatise* and the *Enquiries*; D. D. Raphael, *The Moral Sense* (Oxford University Press, 1947), John Kemp, *Ethical Naturalism* (Macmillan, 1970), John Kemp, *Reason, Action and Morality* (Routledge & Kegan Paul, 1964) chapter V; T. A. Roberts, *The Concept of Benevolence* (Macmillan, 1973) chapter 3; Bernard Wand, 'Hume's Account of Obligation', *Philosophical Quarterly*, vol. VI (1956); reprinted in Chappell.

There are essays on the 'Is—ought' passage by Alasdair MacIntyre, R. F. Atkinson, Antony Flew, Geoffrey Hunter, and W. H. Hudson, in Chappell. Those who want more can find it in W. H. Hudson (ed.), *The Is—Ought Question* (Macmillan, 1969).

Chapter 8

In addition to the critical material in the editions of the *Dialogues* by Kemp Smith and Pike, and chapters VIII and IX of Flew, the following relate directly to Hume's philosophy of religion:

E. C. Mossner, 'The Enigma of Hume', *Mind*, vol. 45 (1936); C. D. Broad, 'Hume's Theory of the Credibility of Miracles', *Proceedings of the Aristotelian Society* (London, 1916—17), reprinted in Chappell; Anders Jeffner, *Butler and Hume on Religion* (Diakonistyrelsens Bokforlag, Stockholm, 1966), a scholarly and perceptive comparison; Ninian Smart, *Philosophers and Religious Truth* (S.C.M. Press, 1964) chapter II; Richard Swinburne, *The Concept of Miracle* (Macmillan, 1970); Richard Swinburne, 'The Argument from Design', *Philosophy*, vol. 43 (1968); Terence Penelhum, *Religion and Rationality* (Random House, New York, 1971) chapter 19; Richard Wollheim, Introduction to *Hume on Religion* (Collins, 1963).

Name Index

219

Subject Index

221